GRUNDTVIG

N. F. S. GRUNDTVIG
from a portrait by C. A. Jensen, painted in 1831
(courtesy Ny Carlsberg Glyptotek, Copenhagen)

by HAL KOCH

Professor of Church History
University of Copenhagen

GRUNDTVIG

Translated from the Danish
with Introduction and Notes
by LLEWELLYN JONES

THE  ANTIOCH   PRESS

Printed in The United States of America
by The Antioch Press, Yellow Springs, Ohio

Contents

Translator's Introduction

Outside of Denmark, Grundtvig is perhaps chiefly known to three groups of people today: to travellers, for the new Grundtvig church in Copenhagen, to exponents of adult education as originator of the folk high school movement, and to students of democratic trends as the reverser for modern Denmark of the expectations of history. In the mid-nineteenth century, after three wars, Denmark stood as landless as Turkey after 1918, and under circumstances which would have led a Marx or a Toynbee to predict her assimilation into the German cultural system. Instead, thanks to Grundtvig, she emerged a distinct nation, a laboratory of practical democracy. In his own day, of course, Grundtvig's fame abroad rested almost exclusively on his poetry, and it was as one of Denmark's grand old men of letters that Edmund Gosse sought him out, along with Hans Christian Andersen and two others, and wrote of him in *Studies in the Literature of Northern Europe*.

Of his celebrated contemporary, Soren Kierkegaard, Grundtvig is almost the exact antithesis, the man who, in a bad situation, finds something to do about it, as opposed to the man who makes it the object of reflection. In view of his country's losses, Kierkegaard is on record as having said to King Christian VIII: "Your Majesty's sole misfortune is that your wisdom and sagacity are too great and the country too small; it is a misfortune to be a genius in a market town." And Kierkegaard's mood of "anguish" as expressed in his philosophical writings not only found a ready ear in the Europe of that day but has become the keynote of much of the thought of ours.

Grundtvig, likewise in the counsels of the royal family, took a different attitude. The slogan of the moment in Denmark was: "Restore from within that which has been taken from us from without," and while economists were busy with plans for turning sheep pastures into rye fields, Grundtvig talked schools, schools of a special type that should educate the Danish peasantry, less than a century removed from serfdom, for life as a free people. His message to a small country in its hour of defeat has continued to be borrowed piecemeal by the larger world ever since, often without knowledge of its source. Discussed as a whole, this message might prove to have further values for large countries that have as yet attempted to use only a few small patterns of limited application such as the folk high school.

In Denmark, Grundtvig is, quite naturally, regarded as the father of his country, revered as originator of everything that is good in Denmark today, from the hymns best loved and most sung in the churches, to the spirit which enabled the nation to weather a German occupation. Even in 1921, when persons were still living who could remember him, Mrs. Olive D. Campbell, seeking material for her chapters on Grundtvig in *The Danish Folk High School* (New York, 1922) found him already almost a legendary figure.

As a book about Grundtvig for the present age, Hal Koch's could hardly be surpassed. In the first place, being co-editor of the edition of Grundtvig's works now in process of publication in Copenhagen, Mr. Koch has an almost unprecedented knowledge of his voluminous writings and has thus been able to produce a critical biography that has something the quality of an autobiography as well. Secondly, as professor of church history, he has a command of the development of modern European thought that equips him both to sketch the background of Grundtvig's contribution to education and to evaluate that contribution. And if he goes into the problem of Grundtvig's poetry somewhat less fully, he nonetheless scatters sufficient excerpts through the text to provide a representative selection, something that has hitherto not existed in English.

For the very important and absorbing things that it does, Professor Koch's book naturally speaks for itself. And from the viewpoint of translation, some advantage attaches to the fact that it was originally written for translation into Swedish rather than for the Danish public and hence had the needs of at least a semi-foreign audience in mind. Any Scandinavian reader would however bring to it a certain general knowledge not only of the legendary Grundtvig but of the gist of countless earlier studies, of

Grundtvig's hymns, now the greatest single contribution to the Danish hymnal, and of his vast output of prose and verse—all of which items are as yet inaccessible to Americans who do not read Danish. The following paragraphs have therefore been written to give the reader a brief but sufficient sampling of this material and thus permit him to get the most from Professor Koch's pages.

First of all, a possible misapprehension should be removed. The reader who first hears of Grundtvig in terms of his accomplishments in education and in the hammering out of Danish democratic institutions is quite likely to envisage him as one of the world's great liberals or political progressives—which he was not. Religiously, after a brief spell of Rationalism, but a Rationalism within the framework of the Lutheran state church, he became a champion of the old-time Lutheran orthodox piety, but with a new slant. He began his conscious political life as an upholder of absolute monarchy, but insisted that it be accompanied by a genuinely free press. Only after visiting England and seeing that democracy was an inevitable development did he counsel his monarch to accept it, but to make of it a blessing, not a curse, by means of a new approach to the education of the peasants.

The empiricism of Grundtvig's thought processes thus suggests a possible wholesome alternative to the prevalent overly rigid adherence to blueprints. For, while upholders of such blueprints as Socialism, Communism, Single Tax, Social Credit, or Eugenics remain locked in mutual debate, "burly scoundrels rule the world"—as John Dewey once plaintively remarked.

Grundtvig, as we shall see, discarded blueprint after blueprint. His accomplishment was the result of another sort of consistency, his consistent cleaving to two insights which he never lost after they had once come to him.

The first of these insights was that the life of the church depended for perpetuation not on the written record of revelation but on the continuity of certain spoken words, namely those of the creed, of the communion, and of baptism—words which had been used from the beginning of the Christian community and which therefore formed the almost physical linkage of its generations one to another. Baldly stated, this may sound merely fanciful. But Professor Koch shows us what an immense role the idea played in Grundtvig's fight for the spiritual reform of a state church which under rationalism had become formalistic and dormant.

Grundtvig's second insight was dependent upon his first. In his boyhood he had revolted against the Latin curriculum of the preparatory school, and later he revolted against the whole tendency of upper-class Denmark to despise the native language, which was largely left to the peasants, or used for issuing orders to them. Consequently when Grundtvig developed the folk school idea it was again in terms of the spoken word that he did so.

That neither narrowness nor backwardness of outlook is implied in his arrival at either of these two insights becomes obvious from a glance at Grundtvig's own education. The culture and the colloquial speech of rural Denmark, he had absorbed at his mother's knee and among the peasants, but at school he became a competent Latinist, competent enough to undertake the translation of Saxo Grammaticus later on, and when he proceeded to Copenhagen to study theology he moved in an atmosphere that seems almost as modern as today. Although the word "semantics" had not yet been coined, his instructor in logic began the course with a definition of "what a definition is." All his teachers were practitioners of the Higher Criticism, but with some of them intellectual daring went even farther. One of them, a Professor Gamborg, was "known both for his attacks on the Pentateuch narrative" and for his proposal to improve the singing quality of the forest birds: "have sparrows hatched out by canaries and when the canaries have taught them to sing turn them loose in the woods to teach the other birds." C. F. Hornemann, another Biblical teacher, apparently cultivated the humorous approach. When discussing God's setting a mark on Cain's brow after the murder of Abel so that nobody should kill him, Hornemann remarked: "I do not know whether the mark was a blue band (the Order of the Elephant) or a white band (the Order of Dannebrog) but it is certain that from that time on nobody ever dared do a thing to him." On another occasion, when a candidate was attempting an exegesis of a passage of St. Paul and making a poor job of it, Hornemann burst out: "What the apostle says is nonsense, but you have made it ten times worse." On yet another occasion Grundtvig heard Hornemann lecture on the Epistle to the Romans. He spoke under two heads: 1) what Paul thought; 2) what he ought to have thought. Another teacher, D. G. Moldenhawer, who "always talked graceful Latin and never joked," made no impression on Grundtvig. "We called him the Jesuit," said Grundtvig, "because he never denied but always eluded the Christian truths."

Grundtvig's own early comment on the doctrine of the Trinity, as quoted by Professor Koch, recalls a passage in a comparatively recent American work, *I, Yahweh,* by Robert M. Gray. After the council of Nicea, Mr. Gray's theologians tell Yahweh, "The formal description of Thy being is settled for all time. Thou, Yahweh, being one, art also three." And Mr. Gray's Yahweh asks, "How am I three? By division or addition?"

So long as Grundtvig remained in this sceptical and rationalistic mood, he was in the best ecclesiastical company of the day. But his "modern" religion failed him when he faced the first great crisis of his life: his love for a woman whom he could never possess on honorable terms. In this emergency, two other systems were likewise tried and found wanting: the hero-cult of early Northern mythology, which was later to play a decisive part in his religio-patriotic regeneration of his country, and the German idealistic-romanticism which had seemed to promise so much when he was first introduced to it.

The story of Grundtvig's return to "old-time" religion will have very special connotations for the reader who is familiar with the development of Pragmatism in America. Grundtvig will appear as a precursor of William James in his utilization of "the will to believe"—as, indeed, later in the story he will appear to be a precursor of John Dewey in pedagogical theory. That he was not a thorough precursor of either man will, however, become evident upon closer scrutiny. Grundtvig had a feeling for history, and an extraordinary knowledge of it, but for science he had no feeling, and it would seem to have remained entirely outside his purview, in spite of a rather close personal acquaintance with the Oersted brothers.

The controversy with H. C. Oersted, discoverer of the relationship between magnetism and electricity, to which Mr. Koch refers, bears curious witness to Grundtvig's attitude. The beginnings of this controversy were somewhat quaint and complicated. Grundtvig had published a paper by a predecessor of his father's that he had found in the Udby rectory after his father's death, which paper collated all the Biblical prophecies of the Anti-Christ and then summed them up as pointing to Frederick the Second of Prussia, a conclusion which Grundtvig's father had altered in favor of Napoleon. Oersted, who, a year or so before, had been offended by a published statement of Grundtvig's to the effect that the thriving of certain sciences showed that the spiritual life was on its deathbed, then seized upon this "Prophecy" and took up the cudgels for science. "His thoughtless declamations against the sciences, of which he has no idea, . . . have emptied his works of all love and humility," is one of the mildest things Oersted says about Grundtvig, and in Grundtvig's reply one of the least vehement counter-accusations against Oersted hinges on the "idea-less distinctness of mathematics." They kept it up for one more round, but in spite of mutual acrimony, the whole thing ended in a sportsmanly manner—unlike some of Grundtvig's other controversies. A few years later when Grundtvig visited England he asked Oersted for letters of introduction to certain English scholars and obtained them.

On the other hand, although Grundvig's stand against science prevents his being regarded as a complete precursor either of Pragmatism or its successor Instrumentalism, it still remains an example of productive thinking as opposed to the patterned and static thought of rationalism, Marxism, or any other *a priori* system. As was pointed out by Professor Karl Popper of the University of London, himself not an instrumentalist but a critical rationalist, in the 1950 William James Foundation lectures at Harvard, a "probable" hypothesis may not be fruitful at all, while a bold hypothesis may be exceedingly productive, if only through the process of proving it wrong. Thus while scientists and "liberal" Christians may condemn Grundtvig for unrealism, and more orthodox Lutherans condemn him on other grounds, Grundtvig's justification lies in the fact that no matter how bizarre some of his ideas may have been, he always used them operationally, i.e., his end result was not the affirmation of the idea but the establishment of a new situation.

Whether even his own disciples understood at the time that the manner in which Grundtvig's thought moved was one of its basic values is very doubtful. Take, for example, the efforts to start a new sect in his name that Grundtvig made a business of discouraging. To be sure, there was a time when it looked as though Grundtvig's hymns could never be sung unless such a sect were formed. But the course that Mr. Koch describes as having actually been taken resulted in the hymns ultimately becoming the treasured possession of all Danish church-goers, not of a single group. Another long-fought battle was over the words of the sacrament of baptism. Because he laid so much stress on the oral continuity of the sacraments, Grundtvig protested violently against changes resulting from a revision of the prayer book of the state church. Slight as the divergence may be between "the holy universal church" and "one holy, Christian church, "or between "the resurrection of the flesh" and "the resurrection of the body," the mere fact of any change in the ritual as past generations had heard it offended Grundtvig and his followers very deeply. How serious a matter it was to them may be seen from an incident that occurred as late as 1866: a parishioner had requested a pastor to use the revised form of the baptismal service, and a country school teacher who was supposed to say "Amen" at a certain point was constrained by the dean to do so as usual. But afterwards the wrongness of the whole proceeding smote both pastor and teacher, and the pastor resigned his pulpit, with a pension, and the school teacher retired, without one. It came to Grundtvig, however, that secession by his followers would only constitute a schism and solve nothing, whereas the mere loosening of the parish bond would solve all. That is, if an old-style believer were not bound to his parish church, he could simply avail himself of the offices of some old-style pastor. And in the end the authorities were brought around to Grundtvig's view.

As to Grundtvig's political contribution, Mr. Koch tells us of his election first to the lower, then to the upper house of the Danish parliament, and of what he did, and what he did not, accomplish as a legislator. By other biographers his campaign for election to the upper house from the district of Præsto, where he had once served a church, is described in some detail, and it is perhaps worth transcribing for its typical features. At first, Grundtvig had refused the proffered nomination: a bishop with whom he was not on good terms was seeking the office, and Grundtvig did not wish to carry ecclesiastical opposition into the wider field. The bishop was defeated, but his successful opponent was later discovered to have had a shady past and he resigned. This meant a new election with the bishop eliminated, and Grundtvig ran as an independent candidate. When he left Copenhagen for Præsto to make his appeal to the voters, his friends warned him that if he stayed with his old friend Baron Stampes it would cost him a great many votes. Grundtvig not only did stop with the baron, but rode to the hustings in his carriage. His opponent, running on the "Friends of the Peasants" ticket, was a parish constable, Jens Jensen, from Grundtvig's native parish, and Jensen's friends were using the slogan, "No officials and no squires." Grundtvig made his speech and was followed by Jens Jensen, who, as one Grundtvig biographer reports it:

". . . spoke forthrightly and fluently of the ability of the farmers to be their own spokesmen, and explained what he would work toward if elected to parliament. Otherwise, he continued, it was not a pleasure for him to stand against Grundtvig, who had confirmed him 36 years before, and to whom he must give the highest testimonial as a broad-minded man and a real friend of the farmers. With the recall of these memories, Jens Jensen became moved, and declared that he himself would vote for Grundtvig, and advised the others to do so as well."

They all did vote for him with the exception of eleven diehards, and Grundtvig afterwards wrote: "Thus I became elected as member of the Rigsdag in a wonderful and yet fundamentally a uniquely simple and natural way, so that the brilliant was eclipsed by the kindly."

As has previously been indicated, Grundtvig's political career, like his polemic writing and speaking upon education, exhibits what is now called the operational approach. Beginning as a believer in the absolute monarchy—on the general ground that the fewer the cooks the better the broth—Grundtvig nonetheless saw democracy coming, and saw its dangers as well as its possibilities. He was foremost among those who advised Denmark's last absolute monarch, Kristian VIII to cede power to the people, and he represented just as insistently that a new form of education must be developed if democracy was not to end in class conflict.

One of the most attractive sides of Grundtvig's personality—which had many sides, some of them not so attractive—comes out in his relationships with his royal "rulers." When, after being for many years in the bad books of the ecclesiastical authorities and unable to get a church, Grundtvig was again given a license to preach and to administer the sacraments in Copenhagen, Frederik the Sixth, in the course of an audience confirming the appointment, remarked, "Now don't let me see you persecuting the other ministers"—a warning for which there was abundant justification. Grundtvig replied, "It is rather they who have been persecuting me, Your Majesty." Since this reply was likewise justified, the King admitted the fact: "Ah yes, there is something in that."

Frederik died and was succeeded by Kristian VIII in December, 1839. Kristian and his consort, Caroline Amalie, had long been admirers of Grundtvig. Shortly before their accession the royal influence had been used to end the long-standing censorship on Grundtvig's writings to which Mr. Koch refers in the text. When Grundtvig visited Caroline Amalie to express his thanks the visit developed into the first of a long series of conversations on the necessity of folk education. On King Frederik's death the new Queen asked Grundtvig to compose a poem to be read at the funeral, and was delighted with the result, except for the third line of the first stanza:

> King Frederik the Sixth died in peace
> And journeyed to his fathers.
> He never harmed so much as a cat.
> Never a better king's son was born.

The Queen's acknowledgement is a model of tact and sagaciousness: "We wish more than words can tell to have a number of copies of your song about the King printed for distribution among the peasants who will carry and accompany the body. Will you permit us to do that? However I have one very special request to make of you: Will you not alter the third line in the first stanza? I know that you have never denied the heart of a woman and the lips of a woman any reasonable request, and therefore you will surely not deny this prayer of my written word which nevertheless springs from a living heart."

Grundtvig then made the stanza read:

> King Frederik the Sixth died in peace
> And is resting now with his fathers,
> And all the little birds therewith sang:
> Never a better king's son was born.

However, when a pastor who was a mutual friend of the Queen and Grundtvig asked the latter to send him a number of copies of the song he specified that he wanted "those with the cat."

Queen Caroline had herself been quite critical of the schools provided for poor children in Copenhagen, and Grundtvig found her a ready auditor for his ideas. She, in turn, pleaded with the King, who issued a decree that one elementary school in the capital be removed from the jurisdiction of the school authorities and run along the "progressive" lines laid down by Grundtvig. Corporal punishment was abolished, for example, and unattractive and unsuitable courses were eliminated, while things like singing were stressed. When the King visited the school, the pupils sang a song of gratitude that had been composed by Grundtvig.

And it was Queen Caroline who provided the money for Grundtvig's 1843 visit to England, a record of which exists in a series of letters to her. From these letters we learn that Grundtvig visited the House of Lords when it was debating a statement by 600 leading Scottish clergymen to the effect that if they were not granted more democracy they would leave the Establishment—which gives Grundtvig a chance to grind his favorite axe, namely, the loosening of the parish bond, by saying how much better the state church is run in Denmark, that, in fact, the set-up would be perfect if only the law binding the parishioner to his own parish (for such purposes as confirmation, marriage and baptism) could be eliminated.

Again, he visited an academic ceremony at Oxford where the students in the galleries made such a noise during the reading of a Latin address by the professor of poetry that no one could hear a word of it. At the dinner following, Grundtvig was asked to speak, and took occasion to say that he had never before so much enjoyed listening to a Latin oration, a remark which went rather well as coming from a man known to be both an expert Latinist and a foe of Latin as a vehicle of education.

While at Oxford he made a study of the spiritual state of the Established Church, and wrote that he had had talks with Newman and Pusey, and that he thought both of them were in danger of becoming Papists. He then visited Scotland and met Dr. Chalmers, head of the protesting Scottish clergymen, whose petition had been denied by the House of Lords, and who ultimately seceded to form the Free Church of Scotland.

Grundtvig also reported at some length on the extraordinary industrial activity he had seen in England, remarking both upon the pathos of men working as mere anonymous cogs in a great machine and upon the near-sublimity of universal activity and production. His over-all impression of England was that on those paths where she followed the possibilities of freedom she was creative and joyous, but that where she lived by tradition she was anemic and torpid.

A curious interest for our mid-twentieth century attaches to one of the last letters in this 1843 series to Queen Caroline, where Grundtvig remarks that he has heard talk of the possibility of Denmark's one day seeing a Russian queen upon the throne, which he regards as ominous, since the Russians' dearest wish is "to incorporate us into the great Slav federation," but that he entertains the hope that "Our Lord regards little, despised Denmark in too fatherly a way to make it a Russian dependency with a Hessian viceroy. Should that be the end of it, I feel certain that God has for me a hut among Norway's or Northumberland's mountains, where my children freeborn as myself could breathe

in free air and think and speak in the free spirit of the northlands;
... if I were ninety years old I would ask to be carried away from
a land where either German or Russian ruled."

Few people would contend that the value for us of Grundtvig's ideas lies in building folk schools, though fine examples of
the folk school exist in America. For us the value of Grundtvig's
work consists in its demonstration that political democracy is
best implemented, perhaps can only be implemented, in personal-
istic terms and by means of instrumentalist or opportunistic tech-
niques. In these respects, of course, American traditionalists meet
Grundtvig half way. And the scant success of American radicals
has been due precisely to the fact that they have been un-Grundt-
vigian in their approaches. They have gone to foreign sources for
their socialism, when native pioneers in social reconstruction
would have better served their turn. For the inspiration of idealistic patriotism they have substituted an all too premature reliance
on the prestige of "international" movements—whether labor
movements or "congresses." Indeed they have left the very concept of patriotism to be used by imperialists.

True, what is now called "nationalism" is an almost unmiti-
gated evil, and Grundtvig has been called a nationalist. But at its
best Grundtvig's nationalism was not Jingoism or pan-Danish-
ness in a sense similar to pan-Germanism. In international relations it was essentially a recognition of instrumentalism or a sort
of nominalism. The idea of the universal is a dangerous one,
whether in the hands of imperialists who think of the universal
as an extension of their own system, or in the hands of church-
men who see their own ecclesiastical organization in that light.
And Grundtvig's nationalism was a protest against such univer-
salism rather than an embodiment of it. Just as the old nominalist
monk vowed never to eat fruit but only apples, pears, oranges,
plums, so Grundtvig averred that in this world there were Danes,
English, Russians, Germans, but no universal men. A Dane could
be no more than a Dane—if he tried hard enough to be more
than a Dane he would probably end up by becoming less
than one.

A Dane was primarily the product of his history and of his
language. Even his commerce with his God was limited to what

revelation was expressible in Danish history and the Danish mother tongue. In one of the poems quoted by Mr. Koch, Grundtvig does what probably no other believing Christian has ever done: he tells God in plain terms that he has made certain sacrifices for Him—and gladly, and ends by saying that if God asked him to give up his Danishness he would obey, but that then he would be through: there would be nothing for it but to sit and fold his hands and wait for heaven to receive him.

The point of all this is, consequently, not that Danishness is all or is over all, but simply that it is all for the Dane. It would be equally true that Englishness is all for the Englishman and Frenchness all for the Frenchman. Which of course does not exclude the idea of free trade in ideas and feelings as well as in goods. Not only was Grundtvig a believer in all the economic freedoms, but his own culture had been enriched by the cultures of Germany, England and France. The point that here enters in, however, is that everything the Dane, or Englishman, or Frenchman appropriates from another source suffers a sea-change. This applies even to the religious values: we have only to compare Martin Niemoeller with any representative Scandinavian Lutheran to see that German Lutheranism and Danish or Swedish Lutheranism are not identical religions, even though the formulae may be almost identical.

What Grundtvig teaches us, therefore, or will teach us when we know him, is not how to build folk schools or how to derive spiritual vigor from the Norse sagas, but how to utilize for our own specific good every drop of living sap now running in the deepest roots of the tree of our own more complicated national culture.

Note on the Translation of Poems

Excerpts from Grundtvig poems quoted in the text have, as far as possible, been translated word for word and line for line. Usually some rhythm comes over along with the meaning, due to the similarity between Danish and English, and rhymes now and then reappear either as full or as half rhymes. But because the important point is to give with a certain exactitude the content, upon which Mr. Koch's argument depends, no effort has been made to reconstruct Grundtvig's rhyme-schemes and other metrical effects as such.

So far, the present translator has been able to discover only two previous attempts to represent Grundtvig in English as poet or hymnologist. *A Book of Danish Verse* (American-Scandinavian Foundation) gives three of his poems, "Denmark's Consolation," The Harrowing of Hell," and "Day Song," using the meters and the rhyme and assonance schemes of the originals. *Hymns and Hymnwriters of Denmark,* by J. C. Aaberg (Committee on Publication of the Danish Evangelical Lutheran Church in America: Des Moines, Iowa), gives 20 or more of Grundtvig's hymns in corresponding English hymn forms as translated by Pastor Aaberg and other Danish-American Lutheran clergymen. It is to be noted that Edmund Gosse's essay on Grundtvig and three other poets in *Northern Studies* gives no examples of Grundtvig's verse.

To the above should be added *Hymns of the North, World of Song,* and *A Sheaf of Songs* by Rev. Sören Damsgaard Rodholm (1877 to 1951) a former president of Grand View College (Des Moines, Iowa) and for many years a pastor in the Danish Lutheran church in America. In those books and also in the Danish Lutheran hymnal are a number of understanding translations of Grundtvig's hymns and poetry.

GRUNDTVIG

I
Childhood and Youth

Nikolaj Frederik Severin Grundtvig was born September 8, 1783, at Udby parsonage near Vordingborg in a sunny and smiling district of South Seeland. His childhood and earliest youth belong therefore to the period of Denmark's history that has justly been called the happy era of the Bernstorffs and the Reventlows, when progress and prosperity set their seal upon society and when an optimistic faith in enlightenment and reason prevailed within the church.

The first years of Grundtvig's childhood were, however, very little touched by these new influences. His father, Johan Grundtvig, who came of an old clerical family, was one of the comparatively few pastors who remained more or less untouched by the rationalism of the Enlightenment, and who consistently held to the old-time Lutheran Christianity. Although not a particularly significant figure, he was an upright and dutiful servant of the Lord.

Grundtvig's mother, Catherine Bang, seems to have been of stronger fibre. She came of a gifted and able family which took pride in the belief that it could trace its origins back to the Hvide line of the time of Waldemar. One of her sisters had married Steffens, the physician, and was the mother of Henrik Steffens. A brother was the famous physician and professor, F. L. Bang of Copenhagen, stepfather to Jacob Peter Mynster, who was later to become bishop of Seeland and Grundtvig's chief adversary. In spite of delicate health, the pastor's wife at Udby was a firm and capable housewife, and it was she who left her impress on the children's education. There were in all four sons and one daughter, and Frederik, as they called him, was the youngest. The mother herself taught them to read and carried them considerably beyond the initial difficulties of the ABC-book, notably

3

so in the case of the youngest, who had great trouble learning
his letters, but who afterwards developed an almost insatiable
appetite for reading.

> You taught your boy his letters
> In weeping and in woe,
> That he had no mind for books
> Appeared quite plain to you;
> But you prayed and said: Amen!
> God so bade, and straight your boy
> From letters went to words,
> Read his book as if in play.
>
> O, that was an evening custom
> We shall never on earth forget,
> There your young one sat with joy
> At his pretty little table,
> Read about the olden days,
> In a voice distinct and strong,
> Followed, through the church's story,
> His Savior, with a will.
>
> Then from out his study,
> Old father to us came,
> Had the reading told to him,
> And explained its Christian bearing,
> Answered sensibly and gently
> Questions kept until he came—
> O, how could we forget
> Such a holy hour of mirth!

Thus did Grundtvig many years later sing of the reading
sessions in his childhood home. Denmark's saga and church history were the solid fare that gave sustenance to his childish mind,
and powerfully was his imagination stirred by reading about
Northern antiquity and about Luther at Worms.

But modernity forces its way through even the tightest parsonage fence. And so here. In the lectures *Mands Minde* (1838)
Grundtvig tells of his first meeting with the Zeitgeist:

During the severe winter of 1788 a new schoolmaster came to our town who caused a complete revolution not only in my own little brain but even more so in the old folks', for hitherto the parish clerk himself had been called "M'sieu," and the schoolmaster had been utterly disregarded unless he possessed special talents as calculator or crier or auctioneer and the like. But the new schoolmaster was an old divinity graduate who had for many years been a French teacher in the capital, and so at once became "Herre." ...

He was as thorough a Jacobin as could possibly have been born on Funen, and so wrapped up in his own freedom that he never had time to think about other people's. It was his pride that he had reprimanded counts and barons and had once said to a professor—who was vice-chancellor into the bargain—"You whited sepulchre!" Naturally, then, he rejoiced when the French revolution broke out, a fact of which I myself was hardly aware until he and the beadle began to quarrel over how the war was likely to end. Only then did I discover that the whole world was in ferment, and, thinking that I ought to take sides like the rest, I immediately started reading the Berlings-Avisen, ranging myself for the time being on the beadle's side, partly because the revolutionary schoolmaster seemed to me half-crazy, and partly because I had read that the French in former times had dealt very hardly with the West Goths, who belonged, even if very far back, to my own family.

Thus was the five-year-old boy first confronted by the problems of the time.

But apart from that the schooling at Udby was bad enough. In the Jacobin schoolmaster the parish had not drawn a prize. Any knowledge that Grundtvig acquired during the next few years he owed far more to home instruction and to his own reading than to his school. It soon became necessary, therefore, to think of making some provision for more regular instruction, and Johan Grundtvig decided to send his youngest son to Laurits Feld, the teacher of his older brothers, who was now parish priest at Tyregod, in Vejle. When only nine, then, Frederik had to leave his childhood home for the Jutland heath. Thus, although an islander by birth, he early acquired a living familiarity with Jutland nature and the character of its people. The next six years, 1792-98, were spent at the Tyregod parsonage.

Feld, a bachelor, conducted a sort of miniature boarding school where he prepared boys for the upper classes of the Latin school. He was a competent teacher who gave solid instruction, especially in Latin, but being of a notably arid disposition was unable to awaken the boys' interest or in any very deep sense influence their spiritual development. Personally, he was the sort of man to whom you would expect Johan Grundtvig to confide the care of his sons, old-fashioned in his thinking, exceptionally orthodox. Yet tolerance was one of his leading traits, and he permitted his pupils free access to the newer literature, which reached the parsonage in packages of books sent out by a reading club.

For Grundtvig, his stay at Tyregod meant a tremendous broadening of his horizon in all directions. He did not enjoy the lessons much, but he did eagerly absorb almost everything he could find to read. He continued his historical studies with the aid of Huitfeldt and Suhm, and meanwhile became a warm admirer of the works of P. A. Heiberg, Rahbek, and Malthe Conrad Bruun. He also acquainted himself with the newest theology. In the spring of 1796, the book package contained the first number of Otto Horrebow's famous periodical *Jesus and Reason,* and this was soon followed by Bishop Balle's answer, *The Bible Defends Itself.*

As yet, however, there was no question of Grundtvig losing his childhood faith. On the contrary he dreamed of someday joining the old bishop in the defense of Christianity. But he did acquaint himself with contemporary thought, did become familiar with the spiritual content of the Enlightenment and with its view of life: before many years this would bear fruit. Nor should it be forgotten that at Tyregod, both in the parsonage and at church, he was in contact with the old-time piety, something that had found its most beautiful expression in Kingo's hymns, always used at household devotions. At the time, the impression made may not have appeared very strong, but later it proved of lasting significance.

In September 1798 Grundtvig had reached the point where he could report himself to the Aarhus Latin school for admission to the next to the highest class. Of the two years that he spent at this school Grundtvig was ever afterward to speak with the greatest contempt: poverty of spirit, cramming, boredom, card-playing, smoking, and idling are the most prominent accents in the picture. But this judgment is surely too severe. For one thing, Grundtvig undoubtedly worked diligently, since after two years he was able to matriculate with a fine record, for another, Rector Krarup and Associate-rector Stougaard were both competent men. The former was a proficient Latinist, and certainly deserves credit for Grundtvig's having really mastered the language, which was to be of great use to him, especially when he later translated Saxo Grammaticus, not a task for the dabbler in Latin. The associate rector was a man of wide pedagogical interests, particularly as appertaining to the mother tongue and to history, and such a man's instruction and his direct personality can hardly have failed to exert a positive influence—indeed Grundtvig himself admits such an influence in his earliest memoranda. With Stougaard's help he went deep into history, finding through Suhm and Huitfeldt the way back to Saxo.

True, none of the teachers had anything to offer their pupils in the field of religion, and with Grundtvig this meant the development to a finish of the process so handsomely started at Tyregod: he became a thorough-going child of his time.

What does that imply? What sort of time was it?

It was, as we have already said, the happy time of the Bernstorffs and the Reventlows. There had not been a war for almost a hundred years, and everybody thought that the folly of war was definitely over and done with, that reason and humanity had replaced the barbarism of the past. There might be unrest elsewhere in Europe, but, under the wise guidance of A. P. Bernstoff, Denmark had been able to keep out of the political conflicts of the great states. Meanwhile commerce flourished as never before, the Danish flag was to be seen in distant ports, great mercantile companies were founded, and war in no wise diminished the profits. Lines of communication both mercantile and cultural united Denmark with the great world. Style and dash stamped the life of Copenhagen, which had become one of the principal staple goods centers of northern Europe. People began to think of themselves as Europeans and citizens of the world. So it was in the 1780's. In the 1790's, war brought difficulties, but business continued and wealth streamed into the country as never before. People were only too willing to believe that Denmark's peaceful existence was real, and would last, until one day a great military power—that time it was the British fleet—taught the country otherwise.

Meanwhile it was not alone commerce and industry that had profited by the "prosperous" period. The new age energetically asserted itself in the reform movements then initiated, whose finest fruit was the abolition of serfage in 1788. And the peasant reforms with their accompanying land allotments actually succeeded, economically favored as they were by high grain prices and rising prosperity. Coincidently, a strong freedom movement made itself felt: the negro slave trade was abolished, the Jews were in most localities given civic rights, and freedom of the press was secured and extended. All of which was consummated by a thoroughgoing reform of the educational system from common school to university, and of social welfare. Meanwhile this whole activity was not alone, or even mainly, borne on the wave of economic expansion, but had its basis in a bright and joyous faith in humanity, enlightenment, and progress.

It is commonly said that the Renaissance "discovered" man. And the statement is undoubtedly justified. But the Renaissance liberation of man was first and foremost an emancipation of the individual, of the "genius," and therefore had a marked aesthetic emphasis. The Enlightenment, on the other hand, legitimate child of the Renaissance, discovered "mankind," and desired to release all men from bondage. About the Renaissance belief in man there is something of the rebel's bravado, of the defiance of hell and high water, whereas the Enlightenment is identified with a calm, ethically toned belief in humanity and its works. Self-assertion had become a right. Thus, though a bright and harmonious period, the Enlightenment is also a great period.

It has become the fashion nowadays, notably among the many who make mock of our elders' and their elders' times, to look with contempt upon the naïve officiousness of the Enlightenment. For this attitude there is no justification. The Enlightenment's best men are identified with a steadfast faith in an all-wise Providence, which had created the world and which continued to direct everything in this best of all worlds. This faith in Providence meant to them approximately what the belief in evolution meant to the generation before ours. One approached the earthly life with a joyous and thankful confidence and dared to have dealings with it. Faith in Providence gave them faith in life. Man was called to collaborate with Providence, and his work was not in vain, of that they were convinced. It conduced to ever brighter and happier states. Who could possibly doubt this? Did they not see, literally before their eyes, how humanity was forging ahead, how freedom grew, how welfare spread, how reason and morality triumphed over savagery and barbarism? And man was happy in his vocation, for within himself he possessed the sure compass that pointed forward, namely the voice of conscience and the light of reason, or, reduced to a single term, the moral reason. Life's yardstick was no longer to come from without, from the church as during the Middle Ages, or from scripture as in the era of orthodoxy. No, man had himself become the measure of all things. Existence was not dark and mysterious, it was not delimited and allocated by higher mystical powers but grew according to its own inner law, autonomously. Thus there was something of clarity about it, something manageable and perspicuous. This was a world in which immense abysses did not open before one, and where one did not encounter insurmountable obstacles. It was not a world of paradoxes but one of work, where man had his obligations.

It was by this faith that the Enlightenment succeeded in laying the foundations of modern knowledge, of both the natural and the mental sciences. These are indebted to the Enlightenment's clear vision, determined industry, and steadfast faith for their mighty upsurge. The Enlightenment likewise laid the foundations for the political and democratic developments of the 19th century. Here in Denmark probably nobody as yet thought seriously of an emancipation of the lower classes, but at all events the discovery had been made that peasants were also human, and this initiated peasant emancipation and elevation, to which Grundtvig was destined to make a larger contribution than most.

The religiosity of the period has commonly come in for the harshest condemnation, nor is it to be denied that the fall from old-style Christianity was great. Empty churches and religious indifference were frequently bewailed—when have they not been? But the fact must be properly understood. It in no sense meant that religion was dying out. From of old, one of religion's pillars had been the demand for personal integrity—one of mankind's most precious treasures, well worth guarding. This demand was held in high honor. People refused to take orders from churchly or dogmatic authorities, but roamed at will over religion's common pasture, appropriating only what they really had a use for. In consequence, what religion they had was real, in the sense of being an everyday religion that determined their actions and filled men with an insatiable desire to act for the popular good and the common welfare. Take those pastors with their enthusiasm for schools and philanthropy, for potato planting and vaccination. They were veritably fathers to their parishes not only spiritually but temporally. Faith was close to reality in the way it gave them all the work their hands could do. And for another thing, the Enlightenment ought never to be painted as an arid age of reason when the feelings did not receive their due. Never have more emotional or nobler persons lived in this country, never have tears flowed more freely, never have hearts been more moved to compassion than in the case of the warm-hearted citizens and citizenesses of that day.

But, granted all this, the fact remains that the Enlightenment had created a world which must end by becoming deadly sad and boring in the midst of all its gladsome desire for action, a humanity which had been born old, inasmuch as all possibilities were staked out in advance, and one knew the way. There was plenty of feeling, but a lack of passion. Discernment and resourcefulness existed, but fantasy and wings for flight did not. Of understanding and light upon existence there was an abundance, but life itself was at ebb. In *Mands Minde,* Grundtvig uses words which might well stand as the epitaph of that world in which he spent his youth:

We are enormously rich in ideas, but beggars in reality, rich in knowledge and experience, but poor in vitality, warmth and fulness.

Had the men of that time been told that they were on the verge of losing touch with reality, they would surely have laughed: no one could be more realistic than they were—they were like the pre-world-war generation. But their reality had become a closed, finished, curled and powdered world, where all was mapped and calculated, where life could be counted and measured, and where man with his moral reason had become sovereign lord. This was why an event like the Lisbon earthquake could make such a powerful impression upon Voltaire and upon the young Kant—as the sinking of the Titanic did shortly before the great war. Here were powers from a primeval abyss, powers which properly should no longer have existed, which made existence alien and unruly.

It was of this Enlightenment that Grundtvig had become a child by 1800 when he was sent up from the Aarhus Latin School to the University of Copenhagen to begin his theological studies. That he was its child shows on nearly every page of his school-day and early undergraduate diaries. He congratulates himself upon having begun his studies free from prejudice—thanks to reading Bruun and other radically minded writers. In many ways he has adopted the radical critics' frivolous style. We find in the diary:

All too serious though it may sound, those pious children of God who mourned the devil's triumph over Grundtvig may now console themselves with the thought that he has since taken his revenge upon the prince of hell and simply denied him all authority, yes, all but denied him existence. I doubt not that all the orthodox, who hate the devil like original sin, will at this point raise a Te Deum, etc., for they should certainly rejoice to see somebody take the offensive against the devil when all the defensive war waged against him for these thousand odd years has rather increased than diminished his jurisdiction.

And he expresses profound contempt for ecclesiastical dogma, particularly as regarding the Trinity, "that product of stupidity and rigorism, the caricature of arithmetic and the antipodes of all sound reason."

This frivolity is, however, but a sacrifice upon the altar of metropolitan taste. Behind it, Grundtvig is a true Christian in the spirit of the time, replete with morality and the desire to do good. During a visit to his brother on Falster he made every effort to get a teacher for a neglected school in the neighborhood, and while reading Scholtz's depiction of peasant life, *Geschichte des Dorfleins Traubenheim,* in a Danish translation, his eyes filled with tears and he dreamed of a future ministry when he would be able to "give his all for peasant enlightenment," fight against superstition, vices, and poverty. The few sermons he preached as a student are likewise quite in the spirit of the time, treat of compassion, and of the thought of death as a safeguard against vice and a motive to virtue.

In reading the records of Grundtvig's student years one gets the impression of an angular and awkward country student who in a marked degree felt himself the victim of circumstances. Of soaring above existence, of air under one's wings, not much is to be found there. His economic situation alone was repressive. At home they were poor, and even with the aid of elder brothers and well-to-do relatives he had difficulty scraping together enough money for the bare necessities. Like so many other students, Grundtvig was forced to subsist on the hospitality of others. His dinners he ate at the house of his maternal uncle, Professor Bang, but his visits there were not happy occasions. His shabby clothes and awkward bearing made him impossible in Copenhagen society. In truth, reality was not living up to the dreams of happy student life he had dreamed as a Latin-school boy at Aarhus. While defects as to apparel could gradually be remedied in a measure, getting rid of his confirmed awkwardness was a longer process. It was slowed up by the fact that at least for the first two years he lived pretty much isolated in the midst of his comrades.

Only with the Bornholmer, P. N. Skovgaard, had he struck up a close friendship. Presumably the two had met in the student corps that was organized in the spring of 1801 to share in the country's defence. This corps, in the end, played no part; it had been formed too late. The actual battle of Maundy Thursday

Grundtvig witnessed from Langelinje, but it does not appear to have made any very deep impression on him. Peace was soon concluded, and the war forgotten.

His acquaintance with Skovgaard, on the other hand, had a lasting influence. Though a mathematician by training, Skovgaard had eagerly studied Northern history, was familiar with Saxo, the Eddas and the Icelandic sagas, and thanks to him Grundtvig's old love of history was reawakened and a fresher breeze lightened his student years. In *Mands Minde* Grundtvig makes grateful mention of how Skovgaard introduced him to Northern history and showed him that beyond the sphere of examinations there lay a world of knowledge well worth exploring. Thus was he rescued, he says, from the abyss of boredom and apathy.

"If my life," he continues, "has, or is to have, any scholarly significance, that [the friendship with Skovgaard] was the manifest cause, but it was neither the source of power nor the lifespring, for *that* is only *spirit,* and of spirit my Bornholm friend had as minimal a concept as I myself. That is, if spirit is anything else than, on the one hand, our good reason and on the other a sparkling wit."

These words are to the point. Grundtvig's interest in history sprouted new shoots, and from a purely technical and linguistic angle he acquired the prerequisites for finding his way back to the Northern past, but that was all. Skovgaard himself had not been possessed by the spirit of the past, and his point of view on human life and on history was entirely that of the Enlightenment.

As to the actual examination subjects, they were kept up just sufficiently to avoid failure, without enthusiasm or interest. The "First Examination" Grundtvig took in 1801, as was normal. Then he began his theological studies, which terminated with the qualifying examination (where he got a "first") in 1803. In his old age, Grundtvig loved to characterize his student years as pure sloth. Undoubtedly he did waste a great deal of time, but, in return, he knew how to buckle down when time ran low. Spiritual profit was another matter. This was certainly meager, though not to the point of justifying the judgment that he later passed upon his teachers. The faculty consisted of competent men, among

them F. C. Münter, afterwards bishop of Seeland, a man of European fame as archæologist and historian, whose lectures it must
have been a real benefit to hear. It was, on the contrary, a fact
that during these years Grundtvig himself appears not to have
been very susceptible to spiritual influence.

That this was the case is most clearly shown by the manner
in which Grundtvig reacted to the great literary event of the day,
namely Henrik Steffens's famous lectures at Elers College in the
winter of 1802-03. Steeped in German nature philosophy and
romanticism, Steffens had returned to Copenhagen in the hope
of awakening a new spiritual life here. His lectures did make a
great sensation, the hall was packed, but the immediate results
were extremely meager. Oehlenschlaeger was inspired by a personal conversation with Steffens to become a poet, but to all outward appearances nothing much happened besides that, and soon
afterwards the enthusiastic evangelist returned to the south.
Grundtvig, Steffens's ten years younger cousin, attended the lectures, and later in life repeatedly referred to Steffens as the man
"of whose words all my own later development was the fruit";
as the man whose influence was recognizable in most of the men
"who were famous for genius in Denmark"; and with reason
gave special emphasis to the fact that from Steffens he had derived
the inspiration for his "historico-poetic" view of human life. This
nonetheless does not alter the fact—to which the diaries are sure
witness—that these lectures were not at the moment capable of
arousing Grundtvig at all. With a certain sceptical wonder he
listened to his "foreign cousin," at much he "laughed outright,"
some he appropriated, but more simply sank into his uncon-
sciousness where it lay ready to germinate when the time came.
Most important at the moment was the fact that these lectures
opened his eyes to German poetry, especially to Goethe and
Schiller. Any description of the romantic evangel which Steffens
preached we shall postpone until a later chapter.

Further testimony to Grundtvig's imperviousness to spiritual
impressions exists in a diary entry of 1803 evoked by a reading
of Oehlenschlaeger's first poem collection. A queer customer
truly, to be able to read one of the world's finest poem collections
and permit it to elicit only certain pseudo-wise remarks on lack

of "the correctness one ought to demand," even while admitting that "a portion of it pleased him." Oehlenschlaeger made no more impression upon him than that; he was far more engrossed in his own poetical activity in its many varied forms.

Verse he had been writing since his schooldays, bad verse and a great deal of it, nor did his efforts improve at the university. Sometimes it would be historic doggerel totally lacking in truth to the time, sometimes comic rhymed-tales modelled upon Wessel and marked by the somewhat frivolous style of the day. He was always beginning something new, but most of his efforts luckily remained unfinished. "I am well aware that it is no use, and yet I still see no prospect of the craze leaving me," he wrote in his diary.

From a purely formal viewpoint one may note some advance after the young poet has made the acquaintance of Baden's Danish prosody, but his ambitions rose in proportion, he threw himself into greater and more exacting projects. He began both a drama and a tragedy, neither of which was ever completed. He had better luck with his comedy *The Schoolmasters;* no sooner was it completed than he blithely sent it to the Royal Theatre, whence he promptly got it back. Though this was a disappointment, it by no means sufficed to stop him. For a new comedy, *The Letter,* he succeeded in getting an amateur performance—in the midst of reading for examinations—he himself playing the male lead. Simultaneously he flung himself with ardor, but not with much more talent, into historical narratives from Northern antiquity— truly astonishing productivity in a young theological student reading for examinations. The same productivity that marks his life as a whole thus goes all the way back to his youth, when as yet he had really nothing to write about, and was very far from having mastered form.

It is curious to see how even the faculty of poetic formulation first gradually manifests itself as his poetry gains content. During his student years, Grundtvig's existence lacked depth and seriousness, was, to use a modern term, without dimensions. It was a world which was an outgrowth of the age, clear and perspicuous, with no dark shadows, no tremendous leaps, no insurmountable obstacles, no intense passions. Here everything is subject to scrutiny and control, and as to the yardstick no doubt exists, man bears it within himself, the moral reason. In this existence there was, meanwhile, nothing for poetry to draw on. Grundtvig made verses, being driven both by the rhyme-devil and by ambition, but he certainly had nothing to poetize about, and as yet there was nothing that pointed ahead to the man whose road was to lead "between abysses."

The happiest and brightest side of Grundtvig's student years still remains to be mentioned, namely his holidays at home in Udby or with his brother Otto, the pastor of Torkildstrup on Falster. In his parents' house, life flowed calmly and quietly—too quietly to suit the son, and he therefore had a predilection for visiting his brother's parsonage where they lived a cheerful social life, and where the beautiful daughters of the neighboring clergyman, Dean Blicher, exercised a strong attraction. The young rationalist, who had believed himself superior to feminine charms, quickly succumbed to tender feelings for the eldest of the dean's daughters, and in his diary, like a typical rationalist, he discusses with himself the condition of his heart. When he returned after passing his examinations, however, he found the young lady engaged to another. The diary contains a "heart-rending" description of his despair, but before long he had discovered that there were other girls besides Marie Blicher in the world, and was soon just as much in love with her younger sister, Lise.

The pattern of Grundtvig's falling in love is typical of the world in which he lived, if, indeed, he can be said to have fallen in love at all. For there is here no question of passion, of strong and ardent emotion, causing him to forget himself and all else. Quite the contrary. It was the sort of thing that evolves out of mildly erotic moods which fantasy ties to the first object that offers, and it gathers warmth in terms of the stock sentimentality of the age, but at the same time—and this is exceptionally typical —it was governed by the most utterly prosaic and pseudo-rationalistic considerations. Thus the moods themselves exerted no deeper influence and remained highly transitory. A young lady arriving from another parsonage on a visit bade fair to drive Lise Blicher altogether out of Grundtvig's mind—and the whole matter is again discussed in the diary with a disarming directness.

In all this, however, there are traits which point ahead, which suggest that Grundtvig was not destined to remain forever in this commonplace dimensionless world. Firstly, in spite of all his activities, at bottom he felt bored—which a legitimate child of the age would not have. Time after time he lets his diary reveal that he has long since lost interest in the whole business. And secondly, observations now and then occur which seem to favor the supposition that the world may conceivably have abysses still unspanned, perspectives leading out into infinite space. Suddenly death stands before him not as "a gentle liberator from the bond of mortality" but as "a mill of annihilation." He is dismayed by the thought that man's existence may be like that of the flame which shines briefly, then disappears. He seeks consolation through firm trust in a providence friendly to man, but even so it looks as though his confidence in existence were about to forsake him, as though he suspected that the powers of existence were far mightier and more unpredictable than he had hitherto realized. Mere hints though these may be, they are nonetheless presages of a new existence.

II

Love and Romanticism

Grundtvig took his degree in 1803, and then spent his first year as divinity graduate partly at his brother's rectory, where his emotions and his joy in life had free scope to develop, and partly at home in Udby, where he further applied himself to reading, particularly in the earliest history of the North. He now selected the historical tale as the true field for his literary ambitions and in that genre completed several small works having no great value but showing a considerable advance over his earlier efforts. No publisher could he find, however, and meanwhile it became necessary to think seriously about making a living. In those days a pastorate was not to be expected for several years after taking a degree, and divinity graduates must be satisfied if they could obtain fairly good positions as private tutor. Such was Grundtvig's lot. Having no choice but to bury himself in a distant corner, he became tutor in the family of the country gentleman, Steensen de Leth, at his estate of Egelykke on Langeland, but it meant a living. In March, 1805, he left his idyllic Falster-South Seeland parsonage existence for the Langeland estate, but in so doing, without realizing it himself, he was leaving the old and the charted for a wholly new world.

So far as nature itself went, the idyllic existence of Langeland did not intrinsically differ much from that of fertile Seeland. The new thing was life on a manorial estate. Though Grundtvig had gradually become more polished in his manners, thanks to the Copenhagen years and to the lively sociability of Falster country houses and rectories, he still retained a good deal of his old awkwardness, and even if there was no grandeur about Egelykke, still the milieu and tone were different from what he was accustomed to. Not for naught was the lady of the house a member of the Reformist Fabricius de Tengnagel family, a typical embodi-

ment of the prosperous period and its European culture. None
of this was crucial, however. The crucial new thing was that at
Egelykke Grundtvig fell in love, something that he had never
really done before, and at Egelykke became a romantic. These
two occurrences, alike so astonishing to himself, are less so to us
who can look back and see how his inner development and outer
circumstances had predisposed him in this direction, if only the
proper stimulus were applied—and it had been.

> But—now the time had come. I saw a woman, and I, love's
> coldest and bitterest contemner loved at first sight, as deeply, as
> ardently, as is possible for a mortal. The past vanished before my
> eyes, or, rather, coalesced with the present, which appeared in the
> form of my beloved. Yes, I have lived, lived in this world and
> encompassed all around me with love, because all seemed to exist
> for the sake of one and to revolve about the one point where my
> thoughts and feelings converged. Yet brief was this bliss, for I
> needed only to know that I loved to become as unhappy as I could
> be. The decencies stood as an unscaleable wall between us, and
> nature had in addition set a yawning gulf between our existences.

So Grundtvig wrote not many years later to his friend Molbech.
In the diary kept at the time we find: "I came here, I read
in this lovely woman's eyes, and what were all the world's books
as compared to that?" "This lovely woman" was, as we know,
the mistress of the manor, Constance Leth, beautiful and viva-
cious, nearing thirty, and of a buoyant and cheerful disposition.
She was in no sense a notable or a distinguished person, but she
was talented, had literary interests, and above all possessed a rich
and warmly human emotional nature. For her literary interests,
since these were not shared by her husband, she naturally found
an outlet through conversations with the widely-read young tutor,
and Fru Leth also became a member of the reading circle that
he got up among the island clergy. Fru Leth herself hardly
knew, in any event did not fully realize, what a tempest she had
raised in Grundtvig's soul. Her buoyant and cheerful disposition
may well have lent itself to misunderstanding. Several years later
she wrote, in another connection: "I did not go through life
coldly or indifferently. My feelings were too sensitive, my blood
was too warm for that, but I do know that I retained the respect

and love of the persons with whom the world has ascribed to me
the gravest indiscretions." In writing these words, her thoughts
may well have returned to Grundtvig, who for a time undoubtedly misunderstood her nature and in consequence directed reproaches against her, as may be seen from the diary and from a
letter from Fru Leth six years later, in which she says:

> You have no enemies here, nor have you offended me. You
> did often suspect and misjudge me, and this distressed me deeply,
> but if you have become convinced that you erred in your con-
> demnation, I feel relieved and glad, for, God knows, I was and
> am innocent.

The meeting with Constance Leth meant nothing short of
a revolution to Grundtvig. Now he learned what it was to love,
and to possess a heart, but a heart so torn that it gave him no
rest day or night. Here his diary could be of small help as con-
fidant. But it is curious to see how from the first moment Grundtvig "only needed to know that I loved to become as unhappy as
I could be." An insurmountable obstacle stood in the way of his
love for this woman who rightly belonged to another, and not
for a moment does he appear to have conceived of the way out
that would seem obvious in any modern "triangle drama." This
was precluded by his strong, almost puritanical moral instinct—
no doubt an inheritance from strong-willed forbears, an instinct
which likewise asserted itself in his above mentioned reproaches
against Fru Constance. With this road barred, what more natural
than to imagine that his solution could only be the young
Werther's: to succumb to his despair and give life up. But Grundtvig was no Werther-nature. He was made of sterner stuff, and
the Weltschmerz of the age was not for him. But what then?
Where was the road out?

Singularly enough, the solution is suggested in the very first
diary entry that has been preserved from the Langeland period,
written a scant six months after his coming to Egelykke:

> ... but to conquer is not within my power, yet I dare not, cannot
> fling myself back into the purposeless stream where ordinary
> people roll along like leaves in a brook. [There is no going back;

his old world is irrevocably smashed to bits.] Either I must hope
for new power from above, or, like a stone in the water, sink and
be scoffed at by leaves and sticks which wonder why I do not
float as they do. [Here it is Werther's fate that presents itself as
one possibility.] A presentiment bids me believe that this is my
last birthday in this guise. . . . I am then to go hence without
knowing the earth life in anything but an insignificant or a pet-
rified shape, the former until one is bored by this everlasting drag
through the swamp of the finite [so his earlier life now looks to
him], the latter when emotion's stream bursts its dam to merge
with the sister stream anticipated, for then it meets only rocks and
walls. It dare not turn back, but stops, stiffens, freezes, and necessity's coercive law then bids us fling away this empty existence.
Surely this is not such a life as one would be inspired to rouse to,
surely one must be tempted to prefer eternal death to a life whose
bliss one dare only surmise, and whose misfortunes alone one has
experienced. Yet, even so, *I feel within me a longing for life as
strong as, yes, were this possible, even stronger than, the longing
for love.* Were the latter satisfied as far as is possible under the
galling fetters of the finite, even then would the first not be silent
or only be silent momentarily when it mistakenly believed it had
found its goal in love's well-nigh unearthly form. What then?
These two are, must be, one. Love, the highest thing that we in
our limited existence can conceive, and even then not wholly, love
is, love must be, only a spark of the eternal fire which immutably
burns on the other side of what we call death. . . . Now for the
first time do I hear the heavenly spirit speak plainly through Paul:
when all shall have passed away, there still remain faith, hope,
and love.

Being a theologian, Grundtvig naturally clothed his experience in the language of theology. But it was not Paul's faith,
hope, and love that he had found access to. It was a faith in the
human heart's strong instinct for life, a hope for the fruition—if
not the satisfaction, at least the fostering—of the soul's deepest
longings, it was the love which says yes to life in all its power and
all its terror, even if only to be tossed about on stormy sea and
foaming billows with no land in sight. Dared he, and would he,
under these conditions, say yes to life and welcome it? This was
the setting of the drama at Egelykke. Such was the world to

which love had brought him when "his spirit opened its eyes." Here stood the battle line. Often despair seemed to be gaining the upper hand, but the fight was carried on until life was victorious.

This was not primarily what we call a moral struggle against a sinful love. It was that as well, but that struggle was long drawn out, and it would be years before Grundtvig came to terms with his love for this woman who irrevocably belonged to another. No, the drama lay in the fact that the meeting with Fru Constance had awakened within him the life-instinct itself, had awakened a power stronger than even the fires of love. He felt that within man there were powers and forces whose existence he had never before suspected, and which completely shattered his humdrum existence to fragments. Love is a spark from the very furnace of being and points to eternity. But the meeting with Fru Constance had at the same time filled him with hopeless despair. Love had opened like a bottomless abyss before his feet, and he stared despairingly down into it. Across on the other side, to be sure, there rose a new world and a new reality—which had nothing to do with this "swamp of the finite" in which he had hitherto vegetated, but the road led between abysses. Dare he, and will he, travel it? Dare he and will he say yes to life and its fulness even when it shows itself through unhappy love's hopeless anguish? Long did he ask, bewildered: "Where is the haven I will not say that I can reach, but that I can aspire to?"

But within him, despite all, the will to live had awakened stronger than even the craving for love, and he saw that this life-instinct pointed toward life itself and eternity.

O might I drink of Lethe's gushing waters and lose the memory of those lofty strains, then would I be happy! . . . But what are you wishing, fool? Is it not that faint reverberation which constitutes my sole worth? Was it not that which transcended itself when it awakened a presentiment of the eternal in me, and raised me above existence as the sun's harbinger, the reddening sky, lifts the lark above the sultry earth? Yes, so it was, and this is full compensation for the loss of life's joy, even of love's, which as compared with the joy of that higher thing is as the stove's heat to the fire of the sun.—True, the highest bliss would be the ability to warm oneself by the former (love) during life's winter while not forgetting one's longing for eternity's spring, but that is granted to few, and it is better to suffer the shivering cold which one knows must give way to the ever warmer spring than to become firmly attached to that milder winter without hope of something fairer when it ends.

The language is that of a Platonizing romantic, the sort of thing one gets in Schiller, or, here at home, in Schack-Staffeldt's poetry. But what does language matter? The fact is that Grundtvig by solitary nocturnal struggle has fought his way to where he can say yes to life under these conditions, has said yes to life with all the anguish it holds for a despairing heart. Better to have a living heart with an instinct toward life and eternity than to vegetate in the swamp of the humdrum finite. To this yes he steeled his will, thus giving his romanticism a special impress. Psychologically the experience was mirrored to him as the will's gigantic struggle to win and to hold its own as a spirit destined for eternity. Grundtvig thus became creator of a Palnatoke figure whose fundamental law is expressed in the words:

> What man wills, can men and gods
> Hinder, obstruct, it is true,
> But man cannot cease to will.

His romanticism thus found its richest pabulum in Northern antiquity with its heroic deeds and energy of will.

The drama may also be defined in other terms: that through his love for Constance Leth and the anguish which it brought him, Grundtvig realized that his youth's closed, manageable, pseudo-rationalistic world was unreal, since man is a spirit filled with longings for eternity. But the new world was only won at the cost of anguish and misery, since heart, passion, rapture and despair are mighty powers which capsize man, that frail bark on a rough sea. Love led Grundtvig to the threshold of a new world and he had the vitality and will to pass over, even though the road lay between abysses. He was victor in the battle for himself. But from there on it was German romanticism that led him into the promised land. It was Steffens, Goethe and Schiller, and above all Fichte and Schelling.

So much for the actual falling in love at Egelykke. It is not the concrete love story that interests us—eventless, its details for the most part unknown—nor yet Grundtvig's feelings and moods. His personal experiences and his inner life he has, despite the diaries, irrevocably taken with him to the grave, and neither the keenest psychology nor the subtlest historico-literary empathy can make them live again. The thing that makes Grundtvig's affair of the heart on Langeland something more than so many other love stories is precisely the fact that he did not stagnate in his feelings and moods. History abounds in unhappy lovers, and there have been many whose erotic passion has been at least as arresting, and who have given far more poetic and beautiful utterance to it. But the great thing with Grundtvig, what makes him worth listening to, is that for him passion was more than a "passion" of the moment. It opened his eyes to a new world and a new reality, and out of this understanding of human life and its conditions he was able to speak in powerful visions. It is the vision and the actuality, not the feeling and the passion, that have interest.

Therefore—and this observation applies universally to literary research of a pronounced psychological stamp—our gaze should not be directed by way of the diaries and other works toward Grundtvig's own soul and spiritual development. His soul is no more, and we can never make it live again. No, our gaze must be directed toward what he reveals. This naturally does not prevent what little we know about his psychical development from being an aid to understanding, but the goal must be to listen to his message, to the word which stands as an emissary from the world of the spirit into which he has glanced. But here it is undeniably a matter of: he who has ears to hear, let him hear. If one lacks open-mindedness, the meeting with Grundtvig is still interesting literary history and exciting psychology. But for anyone who is himself overwhelmed by life's splendor and terror, the visions become a message to his own life sense; he will understand something of Bjornson's words at Grundtvig's grave:

> His visions after him like sun-clouds pass
> Over the sea-lashed lands.

Grundtvig became a romantic, but romantic is a dangerous word, like so many other clichés. For him romanticism became something more than a spiritual- and literary-historical current. It became a life-pattern. His romanticism varies widely from much else that goes by the same name. It is not a passive cult of yearning and fantasy, a dream of poesy's blue flower, of the mist-enshrouded beauty beyond every mountain. Only in idiom could Grundtvig at times approach this platonizing enthusiasm that dreamed itself away from the earth. Nor was his romanticism a speculative cosmic philosophy which like Schelling sought to comprehend in unity's mighty celestial span everything from stones to deities, from earth to heaven, from evil to good. Grundtvig's romanticism was, to be sure, in some respects the same. Both drew upon poetry and philosophy, but his own road led else-where. Though like Goethe and Schiller he began with poetry, and though he proceeded to philosophy, where Fichte and Schelling became his masters, from there he went on to history and Northern antiquity, where he found poetry's dim presages realized in this earthly life. And from the deeds of the past he drifts to the present, to the people and its fate. Thus instead of ending up in bloodless talk about two worlds and the blue flower, he ended in a direct prophetic revelation to his own day, born of the spirit of romanticism, but with feet solidly planted in actual life. His romanticism was something more than moods and feelings, more than philosophical theories and doctrines. Like everything that he touched, it became life and fire. There are deed and drama in it. It is a revelation of reality and of life's conditions, a yes to human life, not, like so much romanticism, a flight from it.

Grundtvig's romanticism may perhaps best be epitomized by saying that he was alert and faithful to the craving for life which had been awakened in him, stronger than love itself, the craving whose enemy was death, and which had vanquished the death-longing that is always the bitter fruit of unhappy love. Grundtvig might now already have said, as he did say many years later to the German speculative theologian Marheinecke: "Mein Gegensatz heisst Leben und Tod" (my antithesis is life and death), even if he had not as yet fully plumbed the chasm that yawns between these two mightiest powers of existence. It was the craving for life that made death no longer the gentle deliverer but the merciless foe. This craving pointed beyond all barriers toward the land of eternity and of our yearning. During these years Grundtvig had dreams of "the land beyond the sea," of "the land of the living," dreams destined later to take form as one of his finest hymns, *O Christian faith*. Here was a life-instinct which burst all conventional and rational boundaries, which embraced planets and stars, scanned infinite space and the time stream. It caused the earth to roll away beneath his feet, demolished all security and all fixed points. It gave dimension and excitement to existence. And, by the same token, it made Grundtvig a poet. Formerly he had "composed verse," and as time went on his verses had got somewhat better, but now it was verse that possessed him, and not the other way round. He had acquired a life-content to which he could only hope to give form in poesy's obscure imagery and to the metallic clang of the skaldic lyre.

He became a poet because poetry was akin to what his heart sensed. But what then was poetry? He filled many pages of his diary with reflections about what it is that "constitutes poetry." He scornfully dismisses the 18th century's definitions, which, no longer loyal, he formulates as "the art of saying much about little," or "poetry is lines divided into regular foot-measures with a correct rhyme at the end," undeniably not a bad characterization of his own experiments in the poetic art up to that time. But poetry must be something more than "a euphonious agglomeration of words that associates objects with emotion and imagination." He knew better, for he had himself experienced it: poetry is akin to life itself and to the longing for eternity. He must therefore admit that "the latest poets" were right when they said: poetry is anything that bears the stamp of the eternal, just as prose is anything whose tendency is merely finite. Poetry is not something narrowly æsthetic, versificational. It is a life-attitude and it builds on "pure nature-intuition." The terminology is "the modern poets'," but Grundtvig is obliged to accept it, albeit reluctantly. Pure nature-intuition is the ability to view nature's myths with the inner eye and to hear its secret notes, which betray a higher meaning than that which shows itself to common sense.

Poetry is to lend to the finite the stamp of the eternal, is to see one's own and others' lives as an expression of the eternal, as the actuality of ideas.

Poetry is the Greek *theion,* a divine possession under which the poet has presentiments of the higher meaning of things. But when he tries to express what he has beheld, a chasm opens, the chasm between eternity and time. What he would express threatens to die upon his lips, speech is inadequate. Carried away by the divine, he has become a stranger to the temporal. Yes, Steffens had seen truly when he spoke of poetry as "opposed to existence"—something Grundtvig had not taken in at all during the winter of 1802-03—and therefore of a certain morbidity as characteristic of the beginning poet. Was it then only under poetry's divine intoxication that one could grasp life, eternity, and beauty? Must that state always be followed by a bitter awakening to the irrelevant commonplace of existence?—and Grundtvig knew something of how bitter such an awakening could be. Here he had stumbled upon romanticism's specific problem: the question of reconciling poetry and reality. Scornfully had Steffens proclaimed that Goethe had "reconciled himself with existence" and was thereby lost to poetry. It was this very problem that had led to the bloodless talk about the two worlds and about man as a poor pilgrim wandering between time and eternity. In Grundtvig we find: "I in no wise wish to vindicate existence, for to me too it seems a very sorry affair, but here it is and we dare not step out of it." He was made of an all too earth-bound stuff to seek his true life in beautiful dreams, and thus let existence remain an indifferent and empty vegetating. No, he wished unity. The same power must and should permeate both worlds.

"The eternal"—"the spirit"—these were new words in Grundtvig's world, but did they represent an actuality, or were they merely dream jugglery? Confronted by this question, it was Fichte and Schelling who taught him to understand what he had himself experienced under this head. First and foremost, in Fichte's *Die Bestimmung des Menschen* he found understanding of his own life-instinct and its relation to the woman who had awakened it. It was a curious coincidence that Grundtvig in his

Langeland corner should have stumbled upon just this work, the one that more than any other in all romantic literature seemed written for him. In the preface, Fichte had indicated as his goal: "forcibly to draw the reader away from the sensual to the super-sensual," and through three long chapters on doubt, knowledge and belief one is led to a settlement with the 18th century's mechanistic world-view and on to a wholly new conception of one's own world and of oneself as will and power, not a link in necessity's endless chain. For this emancipated ego is traced a higher supermundane goal, a higher will, in which the ego for the first time becomes itself and is filled with flowing life and power. "Man is not a product of the world of sense, and his being's final goal cannot be reached in that world. His destiny transcends time and space and everything sensual. What he is, and to what he shall mould himself, that he must know. As his destiny is lofty, so must his thought also be able to rise above all sensual barriers. That he must do. Where the home of his being it, there will his thought necessarily be also, and the most truly human, to him the only worthy attitude, the one in which his whole power of thought unfolds, is the one in which he rises above all his barriers, the one whereby all that is sensual is con-verted for him into pure nothingness, into a mere reflection in mortal eyes of the non-sensual which alone exists." (Lehmann).

Here were notes that found an echo in Grundtvig's soul. His intuition he dared not forget, but should this continue to be attached to Fru Constance's enchanting form it would slowly break down even the most robust spirit and the strongest body. Could the intuition then be transferred to some other object? To himself?

"First must I then with bold hand lift the veil that rests over the holy of holies, source of the intuition . . . only when I become sensible of the intuited can I separate it from her in whom alone it has so long existed for me, and my own soul become its expres-sion." Then will he be saved, for then he will be above the law that bids man seek the solution of life's problems outside himself. "Then shall I have in the union between my inner being and the most high a satisfaction which leaves the finite farther and farther behind the nearer it climbs to that most high which stands as the ultimate goal." Then life will once more acquire meaning. "I dare not credit myself with the centrifugal force to be able to rise above all so that my life in the higher idea will be unbroken, constant, but at this moment I am looking down on her as a creature wholly isolated from me and from my craving. I look about me. No one can fill her place, but I do not demand that it be filled. In this there is no resignation, no renunciation of passion. The earth rolls away under me, I float where previously I stood, and rise by my own power toward the beckoning height. . . . Heavenly thought, intoxicated not as with drink but with too great bliss I clasp thee to my bosom. So shall all that is finite be cleansed of everything that sullied it, or become identical with its own pure archetype." Then shall life once more be a harmony.

Here Grundtvig had obtained help toward understanding the life instinct within himself. The world was no longer a dead weight, but the eternal stream of power and life foamed and billowed through it. For him the intuition, as he expressed it, was intimately bound up with the life-principle, and he now understood that the newly awakened craving for life, detached from the object which had awakened it, was destined to lead him forth into a new world charged with life and action. In Fichte, he was fortified in his fidelity to his own life-instinct and attained clarity as to its nature. But for the question poetry had raised as to the reconciliation of poetry and existence Fichte's book had no answer. Here Schelling was the man.

Schelling was a remarkable speculative genius, half thinker, half poet. For more than a generation he held practically all intellectual Europe spellbound. The exciting thing about him was his theory of cosmic unity, his understanding of the world as one great organism, from the dead minerals through plants and animals to men and gods. In this bond of union, this all-pervading power, all contraries were reconciled, organic and inorganic, eternity and time, heaven and earth, poetry and reality. Speculatively, he conceived of the world as a creative process, an artistic creation, whose point of departure is the eternal spirit. This finds its organ, its medium of expression, in nature, but only in man does it become sensible of itself. The same life-force pervades everything. Therefore spirit and nature are one. Nature is visible spirit, spirit is invisible nature. In the human spirit the life force fights its way to self-consciousness, and poetry and philosophy are the forms under which this takes place. Philosophy, whether nature-study or historical investigation, and poetry are one, and both of them are religion, the unveiling of existence's holy of holies.

It is easy enough, especially for a sober-minded generation, to see that Schelling's philosophy is an air-castle and that his words sparkle and intoxicate without having actual value. Nonetheless, this was the collective expression of the life-mood that permeated the romantics and related them to existence.

And Grundtvig listened to that talk. This we perceive in the treatise *On Religion and Liturgy,* which he wrote in 1807 as a contribution to the lively public debate over Boysen's proposed liturgy, the whole thing an oblation to the sentimental spirit of the Enlightenment: Life is lived as in a valley bounded by an illimitable billowing sea. In this valley we dimly surmise that beyond the sea there lies a land with fairer vegetation and purer air—our true home. Instinctively we gaze in that direction, but we can not be content with this vague surmise, and in poetry and philosophy we have the two messengers on whom we pin our hope. The one swings well out over the sea but there loses itself in the clouds of heaven, the other must be content to explore the valley here and give rules for the easiest way to get to the sea. But how reach the other side? Here religion steps forward, and *par excellence* the Christian religion: Jesus is born, and with him religion descends again to earth, since the essence of religion is precisely this reconciliation of the finite with the eternal. That is the mystery expressed in the teaching about the two natures. Does not the scripture say: Jesus reconciled man with God? "So now man stands once more in communication with the eternal. The world of poetry has acquired reality and has become associated with existence, which, as philosophy's sphere, is an important cipher in the table of approximations. The identity of poetry and reality is brought out in Jesus's chief commandment: Love God above all else, and thy neighbor as thyself!"

Here Grundtvig very nearly let himself be carried away by the Schelling magic, yet it was not along the road of anemic theological speculation that he actually found his way from the poetry of longing for life to existence, as for the moment seemed likely. When one day he discovered that the Schelling principle of reconciliation likewise bridged the contradiction between life and death, between good and evil, made them rungs in one and the same ladder, albeit at infinite distances, he was through with Schelling, who, as the "father of naturalism," became from then on the arch-enemy. Life and death were for Grundtvig absolute opposites—that was settled. But there was still another reason why in the long run he could not be held by these Schelling-Steffens speculations. Namely, that he lacked all feeling for the natural science which they built on, all feeling for electricity, galvanism, Volta piles, and whatever else was listed in the inventory of natural philosophy's world, for inquiries into the earth's "inner natural history," for geology and biology. Thus he found himself much more permanently attracted by Fichte's virile, ethically toned philosophy of will.

But there was something still to be derived from Schelling and Steffens. Both of them appealed to history, and understood it not as a mechanical agglomeration of details following fixed laws, but as a self-revelation of spirit, and the manifestation of life's hidden powers. "Today," said Steffens in one of his lectures, which had meanwhile been printed, and which Grundtvig read eagerly on Langeland, "I shall start considering history, as in the previous sessions I have considered nature. There we saw a spirit which appears to have permeated all nature. . . . Mass itself, the material, would appear to be this spirit's half-transparent cloak, or rather its eternal organ—and history is its revelation." This struck a note Grundtvig could catch and which set vibrating all those strands that ever since his childhood at Udby had bound him fast to the Northern sagas. Willingly did he leave it to H. C. Oersted to write about *The Spirit in Nature*; for him the spirit in history was the proper field. Now for the first time he understood that the history of mankind was not a determined series of chance events, and that historical research was not a quasi-rationalistic cataloguing or a still more quasi-rationalistic moralization. No, history was the revelation of existence. In it the diligent searcher saw visions which shed clarity and light upon life itself. In the preface to his long poem on the decline of the heroic epoch he says:

> History I view as an unfolding drama which has thus only to be filled in by the creative spark within man and which then appears as the most sacred poetry, where gods and planets move with giant stride, proclaim life's strivings and its goal. .

At the moment his meeting with the giant-force of Oehlenschlaeger, first and foremost in *Hakon Jarl* and *Vaulundur's Saga,* was the great adventure. He abandoned philosophical speculation to find life in history. Here reality met him. Through the dark forests of the *Eddas* he wandered to Urd's spring, there to view life in all the radiant splendor he had dreamed of, had surmised within himself, had sought in poetry and philosophy, without ever really getting existence and the phantasms of poetry united. In Northern antiquity he would seek his intuition as reality. Here, at the Scandinavian fountain-head of human life, it must bear or break. If it breaks, there will be nothing left but to sink to the bottom like a stone, since the visions will have shown themselves to be mere phantasms.

> The present has deprived my life of its meaning, and it is doubtful whether antiquity will restore the lost. I once saw an image of the eternal. Could I, dared I, paint that as it appeared to me, you would kneel and adore. . . . This image floats continually before my eyes. . . . I can not deny having seen it, but its harmonious unity I must rediscover in the ancient North, else is my life lived.

Here Grundtvig found the solution for his situation. It was history that saved him from despair. And with all the energy that was his he set about the task. Meanwhile the unrest of the age invaded his quiet cell. The war with England was in full swing. The fleet had been lost and the outlook was dark. He was sincerely indignant at heart that even national calamity could not rouse the dull and slothful people. Unconcerned, in the very hour of calamity, people went on with their entertainments, comedies and masquerades. The time had come for plain speaking, and in the spring of 1808 he got out the brochure *Masquerade Ball in Denmark.* Here for the first time he stepped forward as the prophetic awakener who with history's authority bids his people halt on the brink of the abyss. Style and tone are not yet sure, but there are metal and power in the poem. The weakness was of course partly that a prophet of the judgment day must himself have firm ground under his feet, and Grundtvig had not. He hardly knew whether to take his stand under the hammer or the sign of the cross. So he ironed out the conflict between Odin and Christ:

> High Odin, white Christ!
> Settled is your dispute,
> Both sons of the all-father.
> With our cross and with our sword
> Is your pyre here consecrate,
> Both of you loved our Father.

Soon the author of *Masquerade Ball* had returned to his quiet work on the Eddas, however, and it became clearer and clearer to him that the road ahead could only lead through the Copenhagen libraries. The time had come to break away from Egelykke and Langeland, something which appears to have been accomplished without any very great pangs, enthusiastic as he was about the future he was entering upon. In Copenhagen he obtained a graduate vacancy at Valkendorf's college, where he now passed two or three happy years completely engrossed in historical and literary pursuits. His daily bread he earned by giving lessons in history at the Schouboe Institute. His scholarly work proceeded briskly—not many have been able to work as Grundtvig did, once enthusiasm drove him. By December 1808 his *Northern Mythology* had appeared, and this, together with a little essay on *The Asa Doctrine* from the year before, constitutes his first and greatest scholarly contribution.

Northern Mythology is a singular mixture of high poetic flight, at times really sustained by the Northern spirit, and arid scholarly reflections, but upon this very mixture the worth of the work depends. The introduction carries an historico-critical investigation of the sources of Scandinavian mythology which marked an epoch in mythological research. With sure instinct Grundtvig had seen that only upon the elder poetic Edda could this be based, while Snorre's Edda, Saxo and the Sagas must rank as secondary. Within the poetic Edda itself he likewise raised problems of source criticism, albeit with less success, for posterity has altogether refused to subscribe to his view of *Voluspa* and the *Sayings of Odin* as the oldest components. The exposition proper falls into three sections dealing respectively with the gods, with the Asa-doctrine, and with the myth-doctrine. Of the three, it is the Asa-doctrine section that becomes the focus of interest. This has justly been characterized as Romanticism's irruption into historico-mythological research. Grundtvig has sought unity and organic coherence in the many fragments of the mythology and, grouped about *Voluspa,* has erected out of them a grandiose historico-cosmological drama: the war of the Asas against the giants under the inexorable law of the Norns with everything leading up to Ragnarok, the great annihilation. But the Sibyl looks even farther ahead. In the twilight of the gods she dimly glimpses the dawn of the eternal day.

In matters of detail many objections may well be raised against Grundtvig's views, but that he has here in the main grasped the fundamental idea of the Scandinavian myth-world none will deny. At the same time, from a purely critical view-point he took a prodigious step forward when he drew a distinct boundary between mythology and history by rejecting attempts to explain the gods as reflections of heroes who had actually lived, just as definitely as he rejected the interpretation of the Scandinavian legends as nature-myths. For Grundtvig the myths were still symbols, but symbols of the eternal which resides in man, a product of our Scandinavian forefathers' spirit. Thus it is mythology that opens the door to an understanding of our fore-fathers' life. And the modern re-poetizing of mythology becomes the great implement for a re-creation of the heroic age which once flowered in the North. Here we come to that which in the last analysis constitutes the greatness of this unimposing little book, and which is worth more than all critical acuity and all religious-historical intuition. The author himself lives in that whereof he writes, "for only deep in the North am I at home," and so con-secrates his life to "erecting upon the grave-mound of heathen times a talking stone," with power, if it be yet possible, to call to life the fathers' spirit and arouse a people dull of heart to new deeds. Scholarly inquiry, poetic beauty, and national awakening here fuse in a most characteristic manner.

Northern Mythology was, however, for Grundtvig merely the prelude. His goal was not scholarly research but popular awakening. It was at this moment that he and his friend Molbech, who, despite all dissimilarity, did share his historical enthusiasm, undertook a walking tour through the storied region of central Seeland. Their tour also took them to the forests at Gunderslevholm whose proud trees hide one of Denmark's largest and best preserved cairns. What an impression this experience made on him, Grundtvig depicted a few days later in a long poem:

> Here among the oaks dwell
> The dead gods of the North.
>
> Through falling tears
> How tenderly I gaze,
> What rises yonder?
> O is it not the altar's mossy stones
> That the branches of the oaks
> So closely overarch?
> It is! O, I tremble,
> I quiver with joy,
> And sanctified devotion fills my breast.
> I hasten, I hasten with winged steps
> To the Asas' altar to fling myself down
> And glorify the dead gods.

These lines must of course not be understood literally as worship of the Northern gods, but they show how violent the "Asa-intoxication" was which had seized upon the young skald during these years. He had felt the heart of existence open before his eyes, and he did not speculate much as to whether the vision should go by the name of the church or of mythology. At one time it even looked as though the Scandinavian name would hold the field.

Then too in 1808 Grundtvig got out his *Invitation to Friends of the Ancient North,* a sort of subscription-prospectus for a largely planned work which was to present in poetic form the most significant episodes from the Scandinavian heroic epoch. The next year, 1809, the first volume of the work was issued as *Scenes from the Decline of the Heroic Epoch in the North,* a poetico-dramatic presentation of the struggle between heathenism and Christianity in the tenth century. The main character is Palnatoke, who, in true loyalty to the spirit of his forefathers, fights his hopeless battle unsubdued, for though men and gods may thwart his plans, "man cannot cease to will." Poetically speaking, several things about the work may be criticized. The verse is uneven and the episodes are more conversations than dramatic scenes. But there is nonetheless a greatness about it, and in these *Scenes* Grundtvig gets a good deal nearer to the Northern spirit than Oehlenschlaeger ever did.

Like the *Mythology,* the *Scenes* are the work of a man inspired by enthusiasm, and therefore deeply in earnest about the whole thing. In Northern myths and hero-life Grundtvig had found an actual world where poetry and existence were combined. His sympathy is therefore on the side of Palnatoke, the champion of heathenism. The South's pale doctrine, and Christian compassion and self-denial, must not be allowed to corrode the life-force. Christianity is accordingly represented in the first part of the work by the base and crafty Poppo. But Grundtvig did not stop there. Heathenism has had its day, and by the laws of history must yield. Rightly understood, however, the Christian faith will likewise show itself a source of power and life. Therefore Poppo is replaced by Bishop Odinkar, a Christian Palnatoke, who like the latter wanders confident through life since he knows that not even defeat can break man's will:

> The power is not slain, even though no more
> Its voice is raised aloud in the clash of arms;
> It is working silent, within
> And daily slays evil giants.

Odinkar has not forgotten that "strife is the hero's life," even though deeds are now of another order. The North's hero-life and Christian works were both of them testimony that the world of spirit, of eternity, has succeeded in breaking through to our earthly existence, that visions could become real. That is why during these years Grundtvig found it natural to unite the "high Odin" and the "white Christ," since both were witnesses to the life of the spirit, the life to which he himself had on Langeland found the way, and which he wished to recreate among the Danish people.

These were great literary projects that were fermenting in the poet's mind. The next year, in the spring of 1810, the continuation, *Scenes from the War of the Norns and Asas,* was ready. But within him the times had changed and another hour had struck. Before these new *Scenes* had gone to press, he was in the throes of a violent religious crisis, and not until the summer of 1811 could the *War of the Norns and Asas* appear—amplified now by additions which everywhere advanced the Christian viewpoint, to the detriment of the work artistically. And with this, Grundtvig for the time being brought his labors with Northern antiquity to a close.

To resume in brief what life had taught Grundtvig during the years since 1805, it amounts to this: an understanding of the life-instinct that had been awakened in him by the meeting with Constance Leth. He was not fated to live a sickly, sentimental Werther-life in dreams of the beloved. Nor was he fated to retreat to the nebulous worlds of poetry and speculation. No, he was destined to lay hold on life as deed and exploit, life as reflected in the heroic epoch of the North. Here a bridge had been thrown across the chasm between poetic yearnings and existence. Life had once more become a unity, not the well-groomed and harmonious unity of the Enlightenment, nor the mist-veiled unity of longings and dreams, but the unity possible to a battlefield. And from the spiritual battlefield the road led to the present, to his day and people. To waken and to warn was his calling, to halt a people which dully stood on the brink of the abyss, amid all its worldliness and twaddle. And here Northern mythology and the Bible's patriarchs and prophets spoke the same language; here, in the spirit's claim upon mankind, the hammer and the sign of the cross could meet.

What sort of claim was it then, and how did his message sound to his contemporaries? The message was that man is spirit, partakes of eternity. Believe not, it counsels, the many who think that temporal concerns are the essential thing, that civic affairs, trade and economy are the content of life. Though civic existence is not to be denied, it must be shaped and permeated by the image of the spirit. And this reconciling of the temporal with the eternal demands fighting and will-power—this applies alike to the individual and to the people. A people can not exist if it is exclusively absorbed in temporal things. It must be awakened to an understanding that its life is also an expression of spirit. Should the reader ask: what then is spirit? there is not much to answer. He who has himself never felt something of the life-urge which bursts all common bonds would not understand, and he who has himself travelled the road would not have asked. The spirit's form of manifestation—this to a slack and dull generation—is strife and deed. Only where there is strife is there life. And the way to lay hold upon life is through memory of the past. Therefore history is not casual and indifferent, a common secular technology like so many others. No, history, saga, is where men and people become conscious of themselves and find their life's archetypes. History is a great continuity of the ages with Christ at the mid-point, an unveiling and a revelation of eternity and spirit, under the conditions, the fighting conditions, under which eternal life is given the world.

Life had once more acquired unity and meaning for Grundtvig. He had found his prophetic calling, to awaken the Danish people. Proud dreams, mighty will-power, filled his soul. But one day he was brought up short. He then discovered that life's deepest chasm is not between poetry and reality, vision and deed—this can be bridged. But behind this opened a new chasm, an abyss—the abyss between life and death, of hitherto unsuspected dimensions. And then he understood that even his own sturdy life-instinct was worm-eaten at its root. That day, his proud, hard-won world collapsed.

III
The Year of Crisis

In the spring of 1808 Grundtvig left Langeland and set out for Copenhagen with the intention of completely burying himself in the past, of devoting his life to study and to a poetic re-creation of the life he had beheld in Northern antiquity. He did not however wholly sever his ties with the present. As alumnus at Valkendorf college he lived a rich life with comrades and friends. With the young litterateur Povel Dons he formed a close personal connection, and through Dons made the acquaintance of several of the literary notables of the day. With the historian, Christian Molbech, he established a warm friendship, doubtless reinforced by the fact that both had experienced the pangs of unhappy love. At the college he was very much attached to the young Norwegian theologian S. B. Hersleb, afterwards professor of theology at Oslo, who introduced him to his fellow-countryman Georg Sverdrup, afterwards professor of Greek. More surprising seems the friendship he formed with the young and highly gifted philosopher F. C. Sibbern. The latter and Grundtvig differed widely, but perhaps felt all the more drawn to one another on that account. For a time they shared a room at the college and had plans for jointly publishing a periodical.

More important perhaps than his friendships, however, was another link between Grundtvig and the present: his relation to his home. Of this to be sure we do not know much during these years, but it is typical that Grundtvig did not send *Masquerade Ball in Denmark* to his old father at Udby, in spite of its being his first independent publication. The explanation is, surely, that his childhood home's piety had retained its hold over him, and that he was well aware that this piety would not mix with the romantic combination of Odin and Christ which figured so prominently in *Masquerade Ball*.

To all this was added the teaching at Schouboe institute, which likewise opened a door to the living present. Moreover Grundtvig put great energy and interest into the work—to this we have the testimony of several of his students. He was here forced to go beyond Northern history into world history, and at the same time was led to occupy himself with the Christian middle ages and with the crusading era in particular. Thus his teaching inevitably brought him to a reconsideration of his own relationship to that Christianity which was after all the basis of education in the school. Placed face to face with young people, for whose education he was, moreover, responsible, he could not be content to view Scandinavian heathenism and the Christian faith as expressions of one and the same spiritual life. The lines must be drawn more sharply and a choice must be made.

It was undoubtedly here that the impulses originated which led to the great crisis of 1810-11. Unperceived by Grundtvig himself, or others, his life was preparing to take a new direction. Any slight impact from without would be enough to start the avalanche. This impact came in the form of a summons from his father to become his curate back at Udby, and proved the starting point of a protracted crisis which conclusively defined his whole existence. In May, 1808, he had written to his friend Molbech—a remarkably poised and harmonious nature: "For me the Norn, I know not whether in anger or friendship, had chosen another course.—My way lies between abysses." What these words referred to was no doubt his harrowing experiences on Langeland, but they would soon be confirmed to an extent which he himself had hardly foreseen.

One day, while Grundtvig was living his quiet life in Copenhagen and dreaming of a shining future as scholar and poet, there came a message from his father at home in Udby, asking the son to return and be his curate. Old Johan Grundtvig had grown too feeble to attend to his duties himself, and retirement would entail serious economic hardship. In this situation, the son would of course "not shirk the sacred duty of standing by a venerable father in his old age," even though it cost him considerable effort to forego the future career which he saw lying bright and shining before him (Letter to his father of March 5, 1810).

By the 17th of March, 1810, he was preaching his probational sermon: "Why has the Lord's word disappeared from his house?" To anyone familiar with Grundtvig's poetry in the period immediately preceding, the Christian finality of this sermon will seem highly surprising. In the preface the question already crops up which an autobiographical note among his papers shows he had long been pondering: "But is it then only the ignorant who stand in need of Christ? Do we ourselves actually hold a chain in our hand which we have fixed between suns in the high firmament? Whoso does, let him pity me! I freely confess I do not." From this belief in the necessity of Christ he castigates with an almost prophetic authority the unbelief of the age and of the clergy. Sermons on vices and virtues, on human sagacity and on pride, have replaced the evangel of Christ and salvation which alone can conquer doubt, comfort the sorrowful heart, and lead man in the narrow way of justice and holiness. The preacher plants his feet firmly on the faith of the fathers and the word of the Bible. It was hard doctrine, but worked out with definite competence. The sermon-judges awarded it the mark of "Optime," and in April the author sent it to the printer. Once out, however, it aroused a storm of indignation. Six Copenhagen pastors complained to the chancellery of this "lampoon." The case was sent up to the theological faculty and the episcopate for an opinion, was continued for the better part of a year, and ended in January 1811 by Grundtvig's being called before the consistory, the university's highest authority, to receive a comparatively mild reprimand. In itself the whole matter is both silly and dull, but since at the time it approached the character of a persecution of Grundtvig, it may well be regarded as a factor of some importance to his inner development.

While Grundtvig was preparing his sermon for publication, difficulties about petitioning for his father's curacy became apparent, and these difficulties he made the occasion for altering his decision. In a letter of April 20, he advises his father not to reckon on his aid, and even his mother's severe reproaches can not shake his conviction that his calling is "to contribute to the Heavenly Father's glorification through scholarship." For the next few months, then, Grundtvig resumed his previous life, partitioned between scholarly, poetic, and pedagogical interests—only interrupted by the not inconsiderable disturbance occasioned by the publication of his probation sermon at the beginning of May.

Upon this agitated spring—again according to an autobiographical note—there followed until well into the summer a period of let-down during which he lay as if dormant. The only literary products from this time are a long funeral elegy on the occasion of Prince Christian's death and the brochure: *Is Union of the North to be Desired? A Word to the Swedish People.* That his attitude toward the question of seeking clerical appointment again altered during these months we see, however, from the fact that in September his father is again reckoning on the possibility of getting his son as curate—a scheme which Grundtvig himself however dismissed because he was sceptical of its ability to pass the Chancellery, and because he preferred to become a pastor himself elsewhere. He therefore petitioned for the vacant post at Præsto, where he thought his prospects were better. Unless I am very much mistaken, the explanation of this new decision to abandon his literary career after all is to be found in the reception accorded his probationary sermon. Grundtvig was always the sort to defy the gale, and when his message met opposition, an inner necessity must have goaded him to battle. Was not battle the life of the spirit? And should he step aside when battle offered?

If the summer months were quiet, autumn was to be all the more tempestuous. By summer's end, his intellectual activity had flared up anew: "Without being able to tell myself why, I all at once had an irresistible desire to read history." It was now the Middle Ages that captured his interest—the struggles of Henry IV and Gregory VII and particularly the Crusades. While reading Kotzebue's *Prussian History,* he was infuriated by the statement that the Teutonic Knights substituted the withered cross for the green oak. He hurled the book from him. He sprang up as if gripped by a mighty spirit which called him to be a reformer. The thought was not new to him, but his reformatory vocation had taken on a far more positively Christian content.

There now followed a month or two of proud dreaming,

when he buried himself in the Bible, first and foremost the Old Testament prophets, and when he roused to an intense intellectual productivity. He prepared a rather extensive draft of *What were we of Yore, What are we Now?* a work never completed, which was to have supplied the connection between the Christian faith and the relics and deeds of our forefathers. At the same time he wrote a series of Crusading ballads, among them *The Pilgrims* and *Peter the Hermit*—probably conceived as preliminary pieces to a great work on the Crusades, the Christian faith's historic exploit. Of his feelings during these days we have clear evidence in the poem that commonly goes by the name of *Today's Crusade:*

> To love and poetize, these have their time,
> Happy the time so allotted!
> But now is a time for war and strife alone,
> For the faith and for heaven's glory.
> A crusade alone can rescue from distress,
> Can ransom souls from endless death
> And keep the kingdoms alive.
>
> Not for the holy sepulchre of Christ
> Must we with the heathen strive,
> The cross does not call us now beyond far seas,
> Today we must all understand
> That the Lord is near wherever we go on earth
> And has his temple in South and in North,
> Wherever hearts are found that yearn for him.
>
> The infidels, they build in our own breast,
> They trample upon the cross.
> They prompt full many a sinful lust,
> And delight but in infamy.
> That is why we are brought to such sore distress,
> And why we are fearful of strife and of death,
> And the kingdoms fare so badly.

The poem goes on to say that now is not a time to sleep, but to act, lest there come a night of weeping. Strength has as yet not ebbed from the North, but this is a time to turn back:

O, let us turn back to God,
O, let us heed his holy word
And love our father's kingdom.

A fatherland have we as old and proud,
As may be found on earth;
But diseased is its body, its heart is cold,
Seldom is strength now put forth;
For this reason, the holy word of the Lord,
And our fathers' deeds, in the North are forgot,
Wherein only is strength to be found.

They must therefore look back to their forefathers, and from them let their gaze wander into their own hearts:

O look ye then into your own hearts,
And see if ye there can find
The living courage, the quiet mind
That our fathers had in theirs!
And if these are not there, then mark it well,
That without these twain no good can come
To men, or to countries either.

Two books there are to every man in the North
That are as kinsmen dear,
One is the holy word of the Lord
That faith in our hearts doth kindle;
The other is the tales of our fatherland
That lift and strengthen the mind of each man;
O, would we but had them in hand and heart.

Nothing could surpass this poem as giving an insight into Grundtvig's state of mind from the autumn of 1810 on, when he felt himself called—as prophet and reformer—to mount a crusade against the unbelief of the age, called to halt his generation in its wanderings toward the abyss by placing the Lord's word and the testimony of past ages as two flaming torches before their eyes. Even his friends evidently felt that something new had come over Grundtvig. Molbech scarcely knew whether he dared approach

this smoking volcano. Nonetheless it would be absurd to suppose
that Grundtvig spent his life that autumn in a constant visionary
enthusiasm, in an abnormal mental state, let alone in an ecstatic
intoxication which robbed him of self-mastery. Outwardly there
had been nothing much to attract attention. He attended to his
work, managed to get two small poem collections ready for publication, *Idunna* and *New Year's Night or a Glance at Christianity and History*. In the prefaces he took leave of his "Asa-intoxication"; as Christian prophet he now had more important matters
to attend to. Indefatigably he digs into the Bible itself, above all
into the Old Testament prophets, yet in the midst of these violent
prophetic strains, the simplest childlike piety is at times audible,
as in the Christmas carol about the Three Holy Kings:

> Beautiful is the heaven blue,
> A joy it is to look upon,
> Where the golden stars twinkle,
> Where they smile, where they beckon
> Us to leave the earth and come up there.
>
> Upon that Christmas midnight,
> Every star was shining faintly,
> All at once there came in view
> One as clear in heaven's vault
> As a little starry sun.

The poem goes on to tell how it had been a tradition from
ancient times that when this star appeared there should be born
a king without equal. Therefore the star-wise sage set out with
his king and his king's son to seek this king, and they came to
Bethlehem and found their way to the hut:

> Here was no kingly throne,
> Only a poor woman sitting,
> Rocking her babe in her lap.

But the sages of the East knew that the child was the true Christ,
therefore they bowed down joyously and offered what they had
brought. So must all little children do even today:

You too have such a star,
And, if you follow it gladly,
You will come to Jesus surely.

This star bright and gentle,
Which can never lead astray,
Is his heavenly word so clear,
Made manifest to us
For a light unto our feet.

It has sometimes been thought that these sharp antitheses in Grundtvig's emotional nature, the swing from the highest prophetic exaltation to the most childlike simplicity, should be taken as testimony that he had passed the bounds of the normal. By now it is very hard to draw the line between normal and abnormal, particularly so with a mind such as Grundtvig's, but we have no evidence that his friends regarded his condition as abnormal previous to the final break in his health in mid-December. Even as late as December 16, Molbech mentions in a letter that Grundtvig is to preach the following Friday. That Grundtvig's mind was anything but well-balanced is another matter. In the preface to *New Year's Night* he might be carried away by his proud dreams, and in a language half natural-philosophical, half poetical present a prospect embracing both the life of mankind and his own life. At other times he might gaze up with childlike piety at the stars of heaven. And again with a magnificent calm all his own he might write a dedication-poem to his old father at home in Udby (the prelude to *New Year's Night*.) He was master of a wide range of styles and could vary his instrumentation to suit the feelings he wished to express. But there was still nothing to indicate that he had lost control over himself or his actions.

During this period of prophetic exaltation Grundtvig read the Bible daily, the Old Testament in particular. Then, in the nature of things, a day came when the Word which he was studying for use in chastising the sin and unbelief of the age recoiled upon himself and crushed him under the question: Are you yourself a Christian, have your own sins been forgiven?

Then was the pride in his own heart smitten. He had desired to be his people's prophetic awakener, and had therefore with Christian zeal seized the harp and searched the Scriptures: "All that I deemed to be un-Christian I had put from me, excepting pride, which had fixed its habitation within me, and which had now merely changed its cloak when it made me believe that I was a holy man, pleasing in the sight of God, and by him chosen to set Christianity on its feet again or at least testify plainly like the Lord's bygone champions. This pride on the one hand, and, on the other, some eccentricity of my nervous organism brought me to the point where I thought I was having strange and marvellous visions. Undoubtedly I should thus have become one of the proudest visionaries that ever walked the earth, had not the good God taken pity on me and torn away the veil which the powers of evil had hung before my eyes. Suddenly it was as if scales had fallen from the eyes of my mind, my pride and uncharitableness stood incarnate before me, and no remorse or repentence was to be found in me for my past sins. Now was I nigh to despair, my reason trembled, but my heart remained hard and cold"—thus did Grundtvig himself describe his experience some months later in a letter to a friend. Like a "hammer-blow" the Word had struck him and had shattered his proud prophetic dreams.

In all probability it was two scripture texts in particular that had gripped him: "What hast thou to do to declare my statutes, or that thou shouldest take my covenant in thy mouth? Seeing that thou hatest instruction, and castest my words behind thee" (Psalms: 50, 16-17) and the words of the apostle Paul: "And though I have the gift of prophecy and understand all mysteries, and all knowledge; and though I have faith so that I could remove mountains, and have not charity, I am nothing." (Corinthians, 1, 13, 2.) These words compelled him to look into his own heart, and here he saw only "hardness of heart, coldness of heart"—here opened an abyss of pride, selfishness and trust in his own strength. And yet God's message—the message of love— stood implacably as his judge. Many years later, in *New Year's Morning,* he himself described his experience in telling words:

I felt that, beaten
From field to hill,
By shadows beguiled,
I stumbled at nightfall;
Swept away was my strength,
And slain was my peace,
From the dark it thundered:
And had you the faith
Mountains to move,
It could not avail,
When stone-hard is the heart and cold.

I felt that the staff
Over me had been broken,
To worse than the grave
By the Lord cast off;
My dust I despised,
My soul was my all,
I gazed upon death
In ghostly form,
With death in my heart
I felt not a qualm,
But shuddered and paled at myself!

Then learned I, poor wretch,
In midwinter cold,
That light without warmth
Is the torture of hell;
I could not weep
For God or friend,
Only shudder and ponder
And shudder again,
I would fight my way
To the spring of Love,
I would make myself over!

You earth-clod, you sinner!
What do you ponder?
What the flesh begins,
Must the spirit disdain!
Will you do without God

Until you are like him?
Nay, give him his glory,
And he will help you!
From death unto life
To but one was it given,
To wing his own way!

Here life had become dualistic in earnest. The chasm, the only crucial chasm, had opened, between good and evil, between life and death, and Grundtvig found himself irremediably on the side of sin and death. Then he sank to the depths of despair. The inner tempest became so violent that it produced sickness of soul and body. But it was no doubt also a fact that a manic-depressive tendency in his constitution together with impairment of health by excessive work and late hours had done their part toward making the crisis come as it did and assume so violent a character. Here what is primary and what is secondary are hardly to be disentangled. Without doubt, psychiatric inquiry is correct in asserting that Grundtvig's psychic life oscillated between manic and depressive states, and that this is the hypothesis for the whole course of the crisis. A marked anxiety-sense, and the trait of feeling himself plagued by impure thoughts particularly point in this direction.

At any rate, one morning shortly before Christmas, Grundtvig was lying in bed in such a perturbed state that his friends at the college sent for his maternal uncle, Professor Bang—who declared that here no physician was needed, since Grundtvig was not troubled by any bodily ailment but engaged in an inner struggle for his soul's salvation. A few days later he had calmed down sufficiently so that his friend Sibbern could accompany him to the parsonage at Udby, in the hope that there he would regain strength. On the road, the two friends stopped overnight at Vindbyholt inn, where Grundtvig sat up to write a farewell poem to his students at the Schouboe institute, while Sibbern went to bed. Late in the night, however, Sibbern awoke to find Grundtvig on his knees in a corner of the room and praying in a voice loud enough to attract attention on the premises. Sibbern succeeded in calming him, but it took a long time. The next day, in the coach, Grundtvig told how during the night he had "felt the devil as a snake literally wind himself about his body."

The old Udby parson took the matter calmly: " 'My son has temptations,' he said, showing that he knew what he had to deal with" (Sibbern's Notes). In his childhood home, to the sound of Christmas carols, his troubled mind soon regained some degree of calm, and before New Year's came round he had gone back to Copenhagen to re-petition for appointment as his father's curate after all. His illness had created quite a sensation, and had aroused sympathy, since many associated it with the persecution launched against him in connection with his probationary sermon, and this fact may have contributed toward predisposing the chancellery more favorably. In any event, he received an affirmative answer soon afterwards, took his catechetical examination in Copenhagen, and in May was ordained as his father's assistant.

But neither his illness nor his spiritual crisis ended with those few days in December 1810. Well on into the year 1811 Grundtvig is still complaining in letters of his weakness, inability to work, and above all of "impure and presumptuous thoughts" which he cannot get the upper hand of. He himself ascribes his state to the temptations of the devil, but is still not blind to the fact that it is also a matter of some "singular process in the nervous system." His convalescence progressed, however, and by late summer he had in the main regained his power to work. By early spring he was able to get out the as yet unpublished *Scenes from the War of the Norns and Asas,* with the additions already mentioned The interval in Copenhagen before his ordination he utilized for solid historical studies as preparation for a world-chronicle. Immediately after his ordination he took up his pastoral duties at Udby with zeal and energy. Spiritually he came to rest in the old-time Lutheran belief in the forgiveness of sins.

The chief symptom of this crisis of Grundtvig's had been a violent and sudden experience of the reality of evil—a phenomenon typical of depressive psychoses. Life had actually become dualistic, and Grundtvig felt himself in a personal struggle with the evil one. Time after time this appears in such minor poems of the period as exist among his papers:

When Satan catches hold of me
With his serpent-teeth,
And when in the dark night
He horridly besets me,
Then cleverness and art help naught,
Only Thy word is not in vain,
It alone can bind him.

At least on one occasion, the projection of the evil one was so violent as to take the form of hallucination—that night at Vindbyholt inn—but his fight with the devil was, so to say, daily bread to Grundtvig during these tempestuous months. The world he had won through the battle of his youth on Langeland had been irretrievably shattered. Life's myth had changed. The myth of Romanticism might roughly be phrased as: The world is in its essence life and spirit, fire and power, and the human soul is a spark of the eternal fire. Therefore the demand life lays on man is that he unconditionally say yes to the life-instinct, the divine within himself, that he commend his life and longings to it, follow his impulse forth toward that great unity which alone can give life fulness. This myth had been shattered to bits—the life-instinct, worm-eaten as it was at its very root, did not span the chasm between life and death. The actuality about the human heart was different and spoke its own pitiless language: hardness, pride, coldness, selfishness—and behind the heart's death and coldness stood the evil one himself.

And from all this there was no escape, since the last extremity was the word of the law which thundered its: Die or do what a sinner can not do. Confronted by the law's stern command, he knew that the thing required was not life-development, but to obey God's holy will, not power and fulness, but obedience and love. He knew that light without warmth, rapture without love, were torments of hell. Here was a realm beyond man's will, for of re-creating himself man was incapable, and nothing less was sufficient. This experience led, however, to a wholly new understanding of human life and its conditions: man is not an eternally divine being, a spark of the divine life itself, destined to return to its eternal source, but is God's creature. He is as clay

in the potter's hand, and God is his sovereign lord, with authority
to give orders and to pass sentence. Life is not man's own possession, but God's gift, to be received in humility and obedience and
lived in love. Therefore selfishness and pride—the desire to be
his own master—were rebellion against the creator, and the re-
bellious man was cast off to worse than the grave. In this, man's
extremity, there existed only one place of refuge: with him who
had overcome sin and death and who had lived the life to which
the creature had by the creator been appointed.

Now the old question: Can human life be lived without
Christ? assumed a new character. Now it meant: Can I in Christ
find salvation for my soul, or must I perish? The answer to this
he found in an old-fashioned Lutheran faith in Christ as saviour
and reconciler, and reconciliation did not now mean reconciliation of existence and poetry or of the temporal and the eternal,
but meant to give up all reliance on oneself, one's strength, one's
righteousness, one's vocation, one's morality, and only "put one's
trust in that humble man who was counted among malefactors."

Not until we acknowledge our profound impotence and incredible
corruption will our proud heart bow and confess: I can not. And
here we stand at the momentous forking of two narrow ways, one
of which is short, and leads back, yes, irrevocably back to the broad
way which leads to corruption. Down this have many wicked
dreamers strayed because of not having repented in earnest. They
have fancied that what we cannot we need not. They have felt that
if they wished to renounce the world they could rely on merit alone
without having recourse to the throne of grace. ... The other road
is long, but leads to God's kingdom. This have all God's children
travelled, for when they felt that they could not do what they
must, they heard the Lord's voice: without me can ye do nothing.
Then it was brought home to them that faith itself is the work of
the Holy Spirit, and they ceased from all righteousness in their own
conceit, and denied themselves, and took up their cross and followed Jesus. That, my friend, is the way and the truth and the
life. If we acknowledge our own impotence and unworthiness,
and the necessity of becoming altogether new human beings
through spiritual birth, of becoming members of Christ's body
who will have no life, no salvation except in him, then shall we
sigh until we learn to pray, think until we learn to feel. We shall

journey and repose with the thought that God sees us, that only Jesus can save us, that only the Holy Spirit can enlighten, move, and strengthen us. We shall obey God's call as servants until we learn to obey him as children, pursue our vocation according to our conscience as best we may until power and love are bestowed upon us from on high. So shall we journey and wait upon the Lord's loving-kindness with patience, and none shall wait in vain.

Here we get a typical Lutheran "experience of conversion," where the thought of man's impotence and sin and of God's sole efficacy is central. What mankind must but could not, that Christ did. He came not to loosen the law but to fulfill it, and he fulfills the law not only *for* but *in* his believers when he draws them into his own divine life, as members of his body, so that "now I live no more, but Christ liveth in me"—an apostolic word which Grundtvig often takes as typifying the Christian life:

> O, try thou but once more
> In my name to pray!
> I have bought thee, thou art mine,
> And canst thou believe, then I am thine,
> I well can shelter thee.

This stanza dating from the crisis-period is not melodious, but it phrases the matter clearly: only he who in faith is one with Christ and a partaker in his life is thereby saved from judgment and death. This is the secret of the atonement, that the believer lives not his own life but a Christ-life which is bestowed upon him from above.

But where was Christ to be found? This is necessarily a prime question, and Grundtvig answered without hesitation: In the word of the Bible. On scriptural ground he, as a Lutheran preacher, took his firm and, as he believed, immovable stand. Therefrom he launched an unsparing campaign against the unbelief of the age and against rationalism, which would set reason and human intelligence in the place of simple faith. "The true system, the true fabric, is the Bible, since this is the word revealed in the flesh, this is Christ's spiritual body"—so far he was able to go in his Bible-Christianity, but it would be wrong to speak of a "book-religion," since for him the book derived its value only from Christ, who in and by the word of the Bible was livingly present. Christ was pivotal, not the book. There might consequently come a day when the scripture's mighty fortress would be shaken to its foundations, but when the Lord of the scripture would stand unchallenged. This belongs only to a later period, however.

Grundtvig was clear in his own mind that during the winter of 1810-11 he had been at life's borderland, where last things are visible. Romanticism's myth was shattered to fragments and instead life's drama now became creation, the fall, and salvation. And all three links were equally important and alike sharply dissociated from romanticism. But did not the romantics mention a creation? Yes, as idealistic philosophy has always done, they talked of man as an emanation of the divine all-life. But the Christian myth spoke of God as creator and of man as creature, of an I over against a Thou, of an antithesis never to be resolved. Here and now man stands not over against the "divine" but before his Lord, whose categorical demands must be fulfilled. Here the question is not of an eternal striving to realize his destiny but of obedience or disobedience. Here in the matter of the first article of faith is the critical dividing-line between romanticism and idealism on the one hand and Bible-Christianity on the other, and here for Grundtvig the new concept of life began. It was meeting God as absolute monarch that opened his eyes to his heart's pride and coldness. Then he saw that sin and guilt were something other than the soul's downfall and submergence in the material and in sensuality as discussed by idealistic philosophy ever since Plato's day. Then he saw that sin was not imperfection or weakness, but rebellion against the creator, desire to be one's own master. Salvation was therefore not to be found in the yearnings of poetry, in the Jacob's-ladder of mysticism, or in deed and exploit born of manly will-power. Salvation was only to be found in Christ, who reconciled man with God, created man anew to be his child.

This was not, as many may perhaps be inclined to believe, merely a new theological labelling, but constituted a wholly new conception of reality, of human life and its conditions. Grundtvig was in sober earnest about not being his own master, and it became a commonplace that his life could not be lived without Christ and Christ's atonement as mediated to him day by day through the word of Scripture. This apperception, as is typical, did not however remain a private experience, something only applicable to his own inner life. No, it was, in the fullest sense of the word, actual. He was convinced that it expressed the truth not only about his own life and its conditions, but about his people's and his generation's. It was human life itself that cannot be lived without Christ if it is to escape perdition. For Grundtvig this was a concrete reality in a wholly different sense from that accepted by his age. When he viewed his people and his age it was therefore impossible for him to doubt that life was being lived on the edge of the abyss. Thus far the visions of the previous autumn had been true enough:

> On shadows I gazed,
> But not on vanity.
> Thought was confused,
> But the vision was true.
> With shadows I fenced,
> It was what I could do
> As an echo from the land of shadows.

Thought had lost its way, and he could not turn his visions into reality, since he himself was only a shadow. But the thing itself was right enough. And now that he had returned from the uttermost bounds, now that his life had been properly placed, he felt called more strongly than ever to summon and to awaken by holding before the eyes of his generation the words of the Bible and the testimony of history. Owing to his concept of human life, however, this call necessarily brought him into the sharpest conflict with his time. That Rationalism and the Enlightenment-philosophy must be an offense in the eyes of one fighting for Bible-christianity and simple faith was a matter of course, but Grundtvig felt himself no less sharply opposed to Romanticism as crystallized in the Schelling nature-philosophy, "Naturalism" as he always called it. Where Rationalism preached reason and morality, Naturalism preached man's self-sufficiency and wiped out the distinction between creator and creature, between life and death, between good and evil. As early as 1810, Grundtvig had begun an article, never completed, attacking this whole view, which in after years was to represent his most dangerous enemy. Meanwhile here in Denmark Rationalism and Romanticism were the two directions which prevailed in church and culture. Thus Grundtvig's experience had made him "the Bible's lone champion," called in the midst of an unbelieving generation to declare the Lord's word.

IV
Lutheran Christianity

"Feelingly do I thank the God of heaven who has plucked me out of the whirlwind," wrote Grundtvig in 1811 in his long poem to Udby-garden, whence his life had sprung, to which he had time after time returned, and where he now found his safe haven after exile and years of storm. He felt as if rescued from a cyclone when, at home in his childhood's world, he gradually settled down to a simple faith in the forgiveness of sins. Along with this faith, however, he also achieved clarity as to many things in his life, and thereby obtained light for the road ahead. First there was his relation to Constance Leth, still unresolved. Though love had awakened the life-instinct within him and had brought him to the dark world of the sagas, his unhappy passion was by no means conquered when he left Langeland. On the contrary, it blended in a strange visionary way with his historico-prophetic dreams.

> Life is of double nature,
> Whole only in man and woman.
> If cruelly divided by a wall,
> Life from both must vanish.

So he wrote as late as 1809. It was only when his life had become integrated through belief in Christ that he could for the first time not only break loose from his infatuation but even take an attitude of heart-felt friendship toward the beloved. This is attested by the poem that he wrote in 1811, as every year, for her birthday on April 11:

> I stand before you on Maundy Thursday morning;
> So stood I on that first birthday,
> When, met beneath your friendly roof,
> I greeted you in song's cold tones——

But this time I first stand here as your friend:
I greet you, but with gaze in full faith fixed
Beyond, on Him, the Saviour of us both.

But when Grundtvig had thus settled accounts with his
Egelykke period, the cheerful days of his youth at Torkildstrup
and Gunslev on Falster came back to him. He had then been as
good as engaged to the youngest of the dean's daughters. The
older sister, Bodil Marie, was now married to Poul Egede Glahn
and installed as pastor's wife at Olstrup, only a few miles from
Udby. Here Grundtvig occasionally went to call, and here once
more met Lise Blicher, to whom he became engaged in September 1811.

Equally essential, however, was the fact that the road ahead
now lay quite plain before his eyes. He was called to be a pastor
in the spirit of Luther, and entered with the utmost zeal upon
his pastoral duties. To him the principal thing was preaching,
and he took great pains with his sermons. These were decidedly
"biblical"—as he himself called them when he brought out his
Biblical Sermons in 1816. They were biblical not only in the
sense of being consciously designed to reiterate the testimony of
the Bible, that is, to be not "original ideas" but "reflections," a
rethinking of the Lord's word and the precepts of faith, but also
in that their language, imagery and mode of thought were derived
from prophetic and apostolic prototypes. They teem with biblical
quotations, but even when not quoted it is the Bible that shapes
the style and mode of thought. Polemical his preaching was as
well. Sternly he condemned the unbelief of the age and its contempt for God's word. A year or two later when he came to
preach in Copenhagen this sharp polemic would make him many
opponents. Yet it was neither the biblical nor the polemical
quality that gave the young curate's sermons their special stamp—
as distinguished from almost all other preaching of the day. It
was rather what might be termed their "annunciatory" quality,
the fact that they contained a revelation, a proclamation of judgment and of the gospel, for belief or for a vexation. Of reasoned
reflection and argument there is but little, and it would be absurd
to call these sermons edifying in the usual sense; psychological
understanding or spiritual guidance are essentially remote from

them. The preacher stands there like a herald who has been entrusted with a message which must be shouted in streets and market-places—and woe unto those who will not hear it.

Sermons were, however, only one side of his pastoral responsibility. Grundtvig put no less zeal into instruction, both preparation for confirmation and superintendence of the schools, where he made a special effort to improve the teachers and keep them on the job. He also looked after the poor. He wished his faith to show itself in life, not merely in words. It is told of him that during the winter he had given away the rectory's seed-corn which was kept in the loft. When this was discovered late in the spring and his father asked for an explanation the son is said to have simply replied: "Well, father, what do we preach?" He was priest heart and soul. In letters to friends he mentions how it had been granted him to speak words of consolation to a poor old woman about to die: "O what is any earthly joy by comparison? How flat is the picture that even the sacredly inspired poet evokes of faith's perfection and eternity's splendor beside what at such a moment not only meets our eye but comforts and warms the heart."

Yet his pastoral duties at Udby were not everything to him. He felt that he was called to something more, that he was responsible for the unbelief of his day and generation, that his task was to combat this. Hence his thoughts were constantly directed toward a pastorate in Copenhagen, whence all new currents of opinion spread through the country. Hence too he busied himself with large literary labors. But hence also he followed with the utmost attention the two spiritual magnates whom he correctly saw as destined to assume leadership in Danish culture, namely the poet Adam Oehlenschlaeger and the pastor Peter Jakob Mynster, at whose side he heartily wished that he might fight. But Oehlenschlaeger's poetry had taken a new direction since the writing of *Hakon Jarl,* and when the zealous young clergyman wrote him a long letter, disclaiming any ambition to compete with "the poet of the North," but at the same time reproaching him for "making light of spiritual things" and attaching more importance to outward splendor and honor than to inspiring his brothers to God's worship in spirit and in truth, and taking him to task for his ambiguous attitude toward Christianity, it led to a complete break between them. "After this mutual explanation I should hardly think that we two had much more to say to each other"—so did Oehlenschlaeger conclude his letter to the curate at Udby. The letter was marked not only by a fair share of pride and wounded vanity—the much admired poet was unaccustomed to such plain speaking—but by sheer lack of understanding as well. What happened to Grundtvig in relation to Oehlenschlaeger was to happen many times after that. Grundtvig spoke straight from the heart, often harshly and sternly, but almost never from motives of personal ill-will or bitterness. On the contrary it was his very love and sense of inner solidarity that impelled him to reprove those he really prized, and all his life long he continued to believe that he could attack such persons and tell them home truths while still remaining on good terms with them. In most cases this method of approach led only to breach, suspicion, at best to cool reserve on the part of the other. If things went badly for him in 1811 in the case of Oehlenschlaeger, they went even worse when he sought to make personal contact with Mynster.

There is something tragic in the mutual relationship of these two men. Indeed, one might perhaps call it *the traged*y of Danish 19th century church history. Grundtvig and Mynster. These are unquestionably the two most illustrious names in the ecclesiastical life of the time. They differed widely and never learned to understand one another. Yes, Mynster scarcely reached the point of even respecting Grundtvig.

Jacob Peter Mynster was born in 1775. By nature he was sensitive and poetic, with a strong introspective bent. As was natural, he had in his youth been an enthusiast for freedom and the French revolution, at the same time coming under the influence of contemporary materialistic philosophy, ill adapted though it was to satisfy a nature such as his. It was Kant who emancipated him from that materialism against which his instinct had rebelled but which his understanding had been unable to dismiss, and from Kant he found his way to romantic poetry and philosophy. On this basis he became vicar of Spjellerup in south-eastern Seeland in 1802. Here, however, he experienced in

the summer of 1803 a spiritual awakening whereby the categorical
imperatives of conscience and duty as these find their expression
in Christ's words were brought home to him. This experience
was in actuality a break with the romantic and a return to that
which constituted the kernel of rationalism's piety, but for
Mynster it became the starting-point of a fruitful development
which ended in historico-biblical Christianity. The peculiar thing
about Mynster's conversion—as opposed to Grundtvig's—is that
it did not cause him to repudiate all that he had previously lived
by. He recognized how much the best both of romanticism and
of rationalism had meant to him. Therefore he broke no staff
over the older generation but regarded the purely rationalist
clergy with a certain sympathetic understanding and lived in a
continuing interchange of ideas and in close friendship with
several of romanticism's leading spirits. It was thus that he obtained his great influence, particularly in the polite world. He
was no iconoclast, not one to preach awakening and repentance,
but—through sermons and devotional books—he became spiritual
guide to a whole generation. He had the ability to meet people
at their own level, to build on whatever there was to build on,
and thus conduce to their progress without ever abandoning the
Christian dogma. Consistently with this his sermons are more
reflection than revelation, more edifying than awakening, more
"meditative than believing," as Grundtvig wrote of them as early
as 1812.

The moment Mynster published his first sermon collection
in 1810, Grundtvig was aware of this. Whatever one may think
of his judgment in other respects, he did have an amazing ability
to discern what had worth and what was equivocal. So with
Mynster. Though Grundtvig saw that among the younger men
it was "he, who, as oldest and early sure of himself, had broken
the ice for a defense of the ancestral faith and the state religion,"
he still felt doubtful. He missed the sharp break with the past
that had marked his own development. Late in 1811 he decided
to take a short-cut. With a view to establishing a personal acquaintance with Mynster he rode the four or five Danish miles
from Udby to Spjellerup. The visit was not a success. "Other
visitors had just come to me," writes Mynster in his autobiogra-

phy, "but I still found opportunity for two hours or so of conversation, which did not edify me in the least." Grundtvig spoke with his customary violence even about matters upon which he was not properly informed, and this jarred on the correct and circumspect Mynster. The Udby curate for his part found his host "singularly cold," and they never got round to discussing the questions that he had on his mind. Shortly afterwards Mynster moved to Copenhagen, so that there was no opportunity for further meeting, but from Copenhagen, through letters from friends, Grundtvig received conflicting reports about his preaching. Now he was lauded for his Christly warmth, humility and love: here was a preacher who was not ashamed of Christ's gospel. Then again the letters would speak of "correct, moral discussion, which neither uplifted nor gladdened thinking, believing Christians."

Now it might of course be asked: what business was this of Grundtvig's? He had not been appointed his brother's keeper. And yet he could not exist in uncertainty. During the year 1812 he was preparing for the great battle against contemporary unbelief. There was nothing singular about his wanting to know where that man stood whose gifts and capacities no one could doubt and who had so definitely sounded new Christian notes. Was he friend or foe? Such considerations lay back of the letter he sent Mynster on December 1, 1812. Here he mentioned the contradictory impressions he had gained in various ways regarding his attitude toward Christianity and ended with the direct question: What at heart is your opinion about the Bible and belief in Christ? Mynster however dismissed his aggressive correspondent with coldness and offended superiority. He referred him to his public utterances and plainly wished no private approach, intimating that he preferred to leave open for the present the extent to which their ways should coincide. Nothing further was gained by a second letter from Grundtvig, which Mynster left unanswered. Grundtvig had here done what he could to create a relation of personal confidence between them, but, as so often, had gone about it in the most unfortunate manner conceivable, and the result was as might have been expected.

It was natural that Grundtvig during these years should have

been on the lookout for like-minded persons desirous of fighting
the same battle as himself. For he not only meant to conduct the
campaign from the pulpit in Udby church, but was preparing
for a great coup, to be fought with history as weapon. As a
teacher in Copenhagen he had already had plans for writing a
concise, easily read world-history. This project was now combined
in a peculiar way with his desire to campaign for biblical Christianity against contemporary unbelief, and the result appeared
in his *Short View of World History as a Continuity,* with the
motto: "The kingdom, the power and the glory are God's for
eternity." This little book created a tremendous sensation and
will always stand as a milestone in Danish literature. It had
obvious faults. In the first place, it was a hurry-up job, marred
by grave mistakes and omissions. Nor had it been carefully worked
out with respect either to style or to structure. This is plain from
the one fact that 250 of the book's 363 pages were devoted to
the Lutheran period, and were disproportionately thorough about
Danish affairs into the bargain. But with all its defects the work
is still something of a feat. For the first time in Danish historical
writing an attempt had been made to present universal history
not as an accumulation of dry facts but as an organic continuity
activated by a guiding principle. Through his own experience
Grundtvig had arrived at the conviction that human life cannot
be lived without Christ. Thus he now also became convinced—
in grateful memory of Steffens—that Christ constituted the focal
point of the ages and their unifying element; history proved that
all true virtue springs from belief in the Crucified, and that it
is in company with this belief that spirit down through the ages
has wakened or slept, power been dissipated and renewed, and
that states have fallen and risen. It is the Christian faith which
is history's heart-beat. And at the same time history bears witness
to Christianity's miraculous ability constantly to regenerate itself.

But Grundtvig did not content himself with this. He was not
merely desirous of educing a philosophy of history, but was
preacher as well. Thereby he weakened his own work. He did
not have it in him to let events speak for themselves, but was
everywhere present in person, as reasoner and as the one to pass
biblical sentence on men and epochs. And the nearer he got to

the present, the more sternly he stood as preacher of repentance, chastizing the quick and the dead with equal severity. Pietism and "godly" congregations found no favor in his sight, but with "that impious Zinzendorf" he was simply furious: "he held fast to his heart's uncleanness, and yet wished to be called apostolic, he feigned zealotry and profaned what was holy well nigh as often as he took it upon his lips"; yet it was not to be denied that many sincere Christians had lived at Herrnhut and from there had gone forth to declare the glad tidings of the Crucified. As was to be expected, doom fell heaviest upon the 18th century philosophy of enlightenment and upon rationalist Christianity. Had Grundtvig stopped there, he would doubtless have won the approbation of a good many modernists. But with almost equal severity did he condemn romantic religiosity and the Schelling nature-philosophy. Only one thing could save the age, namely, for Bible-Christianity to be reborn like the phoenix from its ashes.

It was primarily the harsh judgments upon men still living, without respect of persons, that aroused animosity at the time. These judgments showed how isolated the young preacher of repentance stood. Nor does it alter the case that a later age, approaching the whole matter with more detachment, has, if not corroborated, at least given substantial consent to these judgments passed by Grundtvig upon men of his day. In them he showed a surprising sharp-sightedness, an ability to distinguish husk from kernel. Taken as a whole the work's strength is its almost intuitive clear-sightedness as to a multitude of small points, the ability to isolate details and observe their significance to the great interconnected whole. His own age characterized the book as a lampoon, and many later critics have been of the same opinion. Grant that this characterization is in some degree warranted, it still does not prevent the reader with a sense of history from discovering that here is an author who is a citizen of the world of history, even though his gifts may not as yet have reached full fruition.

In the literary world of Copenhagen the book caused tremendous excitement. Old Bishop Balle wrote Grundtvig that it would hardly profit him "with the mighty": "It is making a great sensation, is bought and read from hand to hand, but bitterness, mockery, threats, echo from mouth to mouth . . . that is, Dr. Hornemann wants to start suit, and lawyers are urging him to do so. Numerous opponents are arming themselves, whether merely with pen or otherwise I know not. . . . A certain poet is supposed to have said: 'It grieves me that so excellent a head should have taken leave of its senses.' " The jurist Anders Sandoe Oersted, one of the best intellects of the time, read the book in foreign parts and wrote home: "This man's unreason and bad form pass all bounds." The most official notice, Jens Moller's in the *Danish Literary Times* was critical, yet calm and fair, in its comment. Sharper was the onslaught of Molbech, the friend of his youth, who did not share Grundtvig's religious view of history. The two friends carried on a somewhat extended polemic, which ended in a complete break, but which gave Grundtvig an opportunity to summarize his position in brief: "If a Christian writes history, he must write it biblically, must flatly and without further proof call all doctrine that goes against the Bible false-hood and fallacy. But, you say, such judgment must not be called history: it is philosophy of history. Properly history is the vera-cious narration of what has occurred . . . but is the narration no longer a veracious narration because in addition a veracious judg-ment is passed upon men and achievements relative to the Bible and Christianity—why, in that case, Christ and the Bible are liars." His position is clear enough, but in the eyes of contem-poraries it constituted the most dogmatic narrowness, and those stern judgments passed for an expression of intolerance and priggishness.

The result of *World History* and the ensuing debate was therefore Grundtvig's ostracism from that good literary society where he had previously been on the point of winning himself a place of note. Early in 1813 his old father died, and when not appointed to succeed him at Udby, Grundtvig, late in the autumn of 1813, moved to Copenhagen, where for the next seven or eight years, with no regular employment, he maintained himself by his pen. His actual presence in the small community of Copen-hagen, however, only made a bad situation worse. During the first months he preached often, now in one church, now in another, as a rule to a considerable following. These sermons were, naturally, not lacking in sharp diatribe against contemporary unbelief, and they contributed still further toward confirming the impression of him as a proud zealot. Yes, it got to the point where more and more of the clergy were barring their churches to him, until at Christmas in 1815 he himself resolved never to enter a Copenhagen pulpit again unless legally called to it by the authorities.

During these years, had any Copenhagen clergyman, university instructor, or member of the literary world been asked what sort of man Grundtvig really was, the question would practically everywhere have received without hesitation the same answer, namely: that Grundtvig was a gifted young theologian, but unfortunately of a distinctly morbid disposition, perhaps even on the way to the madhouse; that through a violent inner crisis he had arrived at a severely orthodox position, coupled with an unlimited ecclesiastical narrowness and fanaticism that found expression in intolerance, pride and morbid over-valuation of self; that with this zealotry was coupled a dangerous leaning toward sectarianism and a failure to understand man's intellectual life and cultural values. Yes, it was even to be feared that he desired to make himself spokesman for a purely medieval dogmatism that would utterly demolish scientific freedom and bring back heretic-burnings. Such, roughly, was the verdict upon Grundtvig—and yet nothing could have been more mistaken, even though it is not difficult to see how this verdict was arrived at.

A Bible Christian, an orthodox Bible-believer, Grundtvig was—yes, he had appropriated the whole unhistorical inspiration-theory of orthodox times and he maintained the literal truth of every word found in the scriptures. Before the word of scripture human knowledge must bow, even the natural sciences. "I am no astronomer," he says in a newspaper article, "but if, as a theologian, I should find reason to believe that it is actually stated in the Bible that the sun moves, and be so convinced, then all the astronomers in the world could not make me believe the contrary." Such utterances were enough to cause consternation to quite a few. But Grundtvig's Bible-Christianity was, all the same, of a special kind. He was convinced that only in the words of scripture is Christ present and so becomes the focal point of human life. That Christ is lord of life can thus mean nothing else than that the Scripture is such. Nonetheless, Grundtvig was far removed from what is customarily termed "Bible-Christianity." This immediately suggests the Pietist-Herrnhutist awakening or a strictly circumscribed ecclesiastical Christianity. In some such circle it was indeed thought that Grundtvig properly belonged. Early in the game he was discovered by the awakened who hoped to find in him the leader they so desperately needed. It is surprising, however, to observe how coldly Grundtvig received the advances of these pious folk—the more surprising since these were the very years when he was standing more and more alone and when this solitude weighed heavily upon him. Undoubtedly he was hungering to see fruit from his works, to have the voice that had sounded in the wilderness win response in the ears of men; in any event he was thirsting for human warmth and understanding. And yet he dismissed the conventicle folk; he refused to join them, let alone be leader of their faction. What then was responsible for his attitude of dismissal?

Grundtvig had in 1810-1811 learned something new about human life, namely, that God in Christ had revealed himself as truth and grace and that without Christ man is lost. On this point he and the awakened were at one. But for Grundtvig this realization was not merely a truth concerning the soul and the inner life, not a specialty for small circles of the pious. No; it had validity for human life in all its aspects: the Christ of Scripture was and must be the focal point in both poetry and history, in science and philosophy, yes, even in politics. Nothing was more remote from him than a biblical positivism for which belief and knowledge, religion and culture, respectively fall apart, and where the pious cut themselves off from the life of the world. One might far better call him a humanist in the sense that nothing human was indifferent to him. He could not rest content with his newly won understanding of human life and its lot and at the same time accept a view of history, poetry, science, philosophy and politics which asserted man's sovereignty, and for which the human spirit was in the last analysis the highest reality.

What he wished was nothing less than a rebirth of the whole

Danish people and its spiritual life through Christ becoming lord
over it. This could not be accomplished by taking it as it was
and then adding a little Christianity on Sunday. He had not forgotten his youth's dreams and poetry, his love of history and of
the fatherland, his musings upon the ultimate questions—but the
whole of this was to become something new, because it was to
be made Christian. Thus his opposition to the Enlightenment's
reason-worship must be keen, but even keener was his antagonism
to nature-philosophy's deification of man. He by no means contemplated breaking down the culture-life as Oersted and many
another of his opponents believed, but he did wish to remodel
it, and was unwilling to accept the norms and ideals of Romanticism.

"Inevitably," he had said in 1811 in the preface to the poem-
collection *Saga*, "when my eyes had been opened, I must account
all things as loss beside the excellence of the knowledge of Jesus
Christ my Lord, I must account them all as dross that I might
win Christ, might know him and the fellowship of his suffering
and the power of his resurrection. As such I account them still,
but I have learned from Saint Paul that one may with clear
conscience win the goal in many ways if only one remains of
steadfast mind. The harp which I had hung above the Lord's
altar He Himself returned to me, when he had consecrated it
his, and with free heart I pluck the new-voiced strings . . .
nothing, neither history nor meditation nor song, is unclean
except to him who thinks it so, for God has sanctified all things
in Christ, and they are all clean if they are used with thankful-
ness, so that God is glorified in them." These words are applicable
in an amazing degree to Grundtvig's own work. He by no means
confined himself to a purely biblical message, a "re-thinking."
It was not the harp alone that was given back to him. All that
had replenished him in the days of his youth, he now recaptured.
The great goal which remained ever before his eyes was to
awaken the Danish people to live a Christian life—but this life
was to blossom not in the church alone, but in poetry and literature, in historical research and philosophy, and in purely civic
life.

In other words, Grundtvig was no pietist. Later than 1811

he said as much in an essay on "What is Poetry?" In the preface
to *New Year's Night* he had written: "A remnant of the divine
image was permitted by the Creator's eternal love to survive the
fall, so that the poor race of men should not wholly sink into
the finite and forget its kinship with the divine. This remnant
is nothing else than the hidden and without the evidence of
scripture the inexplicable longing for more than the visible, which
at its strongest became poetry." Therefore all poetry is by definition religious. Its object is not "to divert earth's fallen children";
nothing was farther from Grundtvig than "art for art's sake."
The poet has a vocation and a responsibility. Graciously is he
chosen to be God's mouthpiece and prophet, to see clearly and
tell truly of human life and its lot. Therefore he chastises the
skalds of this sorry day who think that they can sing fast and
loose about what they will, provided it moves hearts and sounds
well to the world's ear. They believe that they will be called
equally good skalds no matter whither they turn hearts or what
fire they kindle.

> Skalds! Skalds! Remember
> Your high calling and election!

And the skald-life's election is to be seers who look down into
life's deep springs, and who in myth and song are able to re-
create what they have seen.

> The garden that God gave us here below
> Borders on the Lord's Eden,
> In spirit to us wafted
> Through the openings of the lattice;
> And by surmise we catch
> Perfume from what is therein.
> Rejoice thee tremblingly, O skald!
> This thy choice is, and thy calling:
> Through thee shall be imaged forth
> What thou sawest in life's spring,
> Through thee shall be spread abroad
> Rose-perfume far and wide.
> Thou art life's chosen reconnoiterer,
> Thou are the Lord's collaborator.

The poet's goal lies not in the purely artistic, but in revelation. He lives by rapture, by mysterious inspiration. Therefore his utterance is often dark as the Sibyl's voice of prophecy. Clarity lies far ahead as his beckoning goal, clarity regarding human life.

> O despise not this strange voice!
> To be a skald partakes of miracle.
> The voices from above we hear
> **In that secret accent;**
> What we say, ourselves we know not;
> But woe unto the skald who questions!
> God must know what God has said,
> He created what the skald's eye sees.

Grundtvig therefore treats with sovereign contempt all questions of poetic form and technique. He is convinced that "what is worth anything comes in its proper vessel" and that "it is much better for the mould to crack than for the vision to be broken." What matters in a poem is "the beholding," and "by its truth and life, power and clarity do I value it."

As with poetry, so with history. For Grundtvig, history-writing was not primarily a learned, antiquarian affair, and although he was not blind to the importance of critical detail-work, he was still aware that accumulation of details could never create a work of history. No, history must never set itself a lesser goal than this: to understand man and his existence. "If we thus regard history, we can readily see both that it should be closely questioned by every truth-loving student, and that it should be able to give sure and significant answers, since it is an exploit in which man must of necessity express his true condition, and a statement in which truth must needs pronounce its judgment on man's plans and practices. Only in history do we find man complete, insofar as he has hitherto been revealed, only in history does man reveal his substance and true shape, which may not there be concealed from the eyes of posterity." Thus history is the root of all true human knowledge. Only history opens the road to a true philosophy of man. History and poetry belong together, and life's interpretation is the task of both. Of the existence of such a kinship between poetry and history, Grundt-

vig gave a demonstration in his long poem *Roskilde-Rim,* a sort
of versified survey of the history of Christianity in Denmark,
even looser in composition than the *World History,* and harsher
in its verdicts. Truly, the reading of it is next door to a wandering in the wilderness, yet in the midst of these thousands upon
thousands of lines of verse one stumbles upon the two poems
Bishop Wilhelm and King Svend and *Master Ole Vind,* which
will forever remain two of the pearls of Danish poetry. It was
characteristic of Grundtvig's form of genius that he could sit and
write page after page of, to put it mildly, half-bad verse, and
then suddenly and incalculably toss off something quite perfect.

Things looked very dark for Denmark during these years,
and humanly speaking there was little ground for hope. Due to
the king's disastrous constancy, 1812-1813 found the country still
ranged on Napoleon's side. The result was that England, Russia
and Sweden could do about as they chose with our kingdom.
The domestic picture was one of national bankruptcy and general impoverishment. Small wonder that most people were a prey
to discouragement. But not so Grundtvig. In 1813 he wrote his
little *To the Fatherland,* a fiery popular preachment which insisted that the real peril to the country was not alien weapons
or plots: "No, our own unbelief is what we have to fear, that is
what will destroy us." If the people will repent and rely on God,
they shall not be put to shame, but rather shall the rulers and
potentates be put to shame. Full of courage, he prophesied of the
future, but the war ended sadly with the peace of Lubeck and
separation from Norway, which Grundtvig had loved more than
most and where he had long hoped that he would find his life-
work as professor of history.

And yet Grundtvig did not lose courage when defeat became
a fact. Quite the contrary. Now he felt that the call was greater
and the responsibility heavier. Now was the time to build a
spiritual Dannevirke. Originally he had seen his task as that of
a prophetic preacher of Bible Christianity, and his words had
fallen with judicial severity and thunderous bombast. He had
then conceived of himself in a general way as chastiser and
preacher of repentance. But gradually as all avenues were closed
and his hopes disappointed he took it as a sign that his road lay

in another direction. Not that his view as to Christianity and its
significance had altered, but he knew that the roads were many,
and that one of them lay through awakening the people to
spiritual life by confronting them with their forefathers' deeds
and exploits. Therefore his whole activity for the next few years
is naturally focussed in the periodical *Dannevirke,* published
from 1816 to 1819. This gave translations of historical documents
and sources, numerous ballads in Grundtvig's adaptations, and
a series of peculiarly interesting historic-philosophico-literary
essays. He wrote every line of the magazine himself. His object
was a spiritual defence of the Danish people, whose existence
was threatened. Grundtvig was sustained by the conviction that
no other European people had "as great legitimate possessions in
the realm of the spirit" as the Danish people had, but that a
Dannevirke was most necessary, not in any sense to prevent intercourse with foreigners, but as a defence against foreign inva-
sion. His whole love of Denmark and the Danish people he
poured forth in the columns of this periodical, and his utterances
took on an unfamiliar mildness and gentleness, coupled with a
certain wanton gaiety. The impetuousness and bombast which
had earlier stamped his work now disappeared almost entirely.
He had learned to walk softly, and he knew that he was working
at long range. He could therefore bide his time.

To open his fellow-countrymen's eyes to the rich spiritual
inheritance that lay in the people's past, to transform that inheritance into living power was the goal Grundtvig had set himself. He therefore undertook also during the years 1815-1821 the
gigantic task of translating the ancient chronicles of Saxo and
Snorre. Into the bargain he did the English *Song of Beowulf,*
which an Icelander had recently published. In itself this was a
major undertaking, one which made stupendous demands in the
matter of historical and philological research. Yet that was the
least of it. His ambition was not to make a literal translation but
to re-create these works in the contemporary idiom so that they
might act as a living power among the people. To succeed in
this, he must abandon the literary-academic idiom which held
full sway in the world of books. He must speak the people's
own language.

He who the folk would reach
Effectively here in the islands,
With the folk must yelp,
If they can not bark!
He who for it would sing,
Must borrow its own tongue
And learn to breathe with that!

In the servants' hall where common people sit and speak their mother tongue naturally is the place to learn Danish. In folk-song and heroic ballad, in the ancient rhymed chronicles and in proverb collections he had listened for the people's own idiom, and what he learned had fused with childhood memories derived from intercourse with Seeland and Jutland peasants. His problem was nothing less than to create a new idiom, and it took time to solve. In many ways his endeavor was comparable to what has been happening to the Norwegian language during the past generation or two. The translations which resulted from these many years of toil are in a broad, sonorous and figurative language. But undeniably the style at times becomes needlessly debased and the language at other times is affected and strained. This does not mean, however, that Grundtvig was anything but victorious in his struggle.

The translations themselves may be open to dispute. In the first place they by no means acquired the popular significance he himself had expected. Yet to Grundtvig those many years of intensive study meant a tremendous enrichment. Here he learned "to speak truly of small and great, and simply of everything exalted." Here were laid the foundations of his popular poetry— both hymns and patriotic songs. Here he learned his verbose, slightly chatty style that is so typically Danish. But here he also learned to compress a clear and simple thought into an aphorism that is almost lapidary. These pithy Grundtvigian sayings have in many cases lived on the lips of the people—often with no suspicion as to their origin. "He has never lived, no matter how wise he be, who has not first known love"—"We shall have gone far in the matter of wealth when few have too much and fewer still too little"—"Each sows his own here below, and the tares jostle the wheat"—"Let freedom be our watchword in the North,

freedom for Loki as well as for Thor"—to quote only a few of
the best known. It is good proof that a man has hit the people's
mood and tone when his words are thus remembered and comprehended by young and old, by learned and simple.

Often Grundtvig felt cramped during those years of solitary
life in the "burial vaults" of history, busy with pen and ink,
carrying on his unobtrusive labors. Little encouragement did he
get from without, and for a man with his need to feel life pul-
sating warm and strong, this hermit-life with books and a few
good friends was a wretched existence. "Daily my longing grows
to preach God's word," he says in a letter of 1819. He had not
forgotten that he was a pastor. But the sacrifice must be made
and he made it. Nor was the sacrifice in vain. During those years
he found his way to the heart and tone of the people; then was
he trained for his future work.

Skald, poet of history, that is what Grundtvig was. But this
calling led him to take a harshly critical view of the educated
world of the day. That world responded with coldness and contempt—at times coupled with sympathy for the poor man who
could not get a post and plainly did not know whither to turn.
Conflicts were always occurring, but these many literary feuds
need not be mentioned here. The most memorable took place
between Grundtvig and the renowned physicist Hans Christian
Oersted, a typical representative of speculative romantic religiosity. Not without reason was his most read work entitled *The
Spirit in Nature*. The points at issue were many, and the battle
was long. Most important was the opportunity it gave Grundtvig
for a thoroughgoing settlement of accounts with the Schelling
philosophy and contemporary religiosity.

Even less reason is there to dwell upon the many purely
literary controversies that Grundtvig flung himself into. Literature was to him no matter of indifference. He set his own requirements for anyone who aspired to the name of poet, and if
the requirements were not met, he was merciless in his judgment—even upon the much admired Oehlenschlaeger, whose
later development caused Grundtvig such bitter disappointment.
For the day's brood of younger poets he had no great partiality.
The one exception was B. S. Ingemann. In a curious way, the

robust Grundtvig felt drawn by the gently feminine and deeply sensitive elements in Ingemann. But here he also encountered a poet who had drunk deeply from the chalices of romanticism and nature-philosophy, and who at the same time had clearly kept aloof from all pantheism. Finally, Ingemann was probably the only one who understood anything of Grundtvig's dreams about a popular awakening based on history and the mother-tongue.

During the long, hard years from 1815 to 1821 Grundtvig time and again sought some modest religious post in Copenhagen but was always disappointed. He had come irremediably into disrepute, and old Bishop Balle had proved only too correct in his fear of what "the mighty" would say to the *World History*. Economically, the young litterateur remained in extremely straitened circumstances. Not until 1818 did he obtain a modest subsidy from the crown for his translation job, which at length enabled him to marry Lise Blicher—they had been engaged for seven years. Finally in 1821 something unexpected happened: without previous solicitation Grundtvig was called to the charge of Præsto and Skibbinge. Personally he was not glad to be leaving the capital, but he felt confident that his stay in Præsto would not be unduly long. And now his long "night sessions" in history's burial vaults had ended. He was coming out among men again, to active work. And thus a new period in his life began.

A glance back over the decade that had elapsed since the great crisis shows that a notable change had taken place in Grundtvig during this time. Young and enthusiastic, but inwardly immature, he had desired to fling himself into a reformatory campaign. He undoubtedly expected great things to come of it.

Quite likely he expected persecution and opposition, but these did not frighten him. He was ready to pay the battle's price. And at the same time he expected that the campaign would really succeed in awakening the people to Christly deeds and exploits. Everything went wrong, however. The persecution was indeed not lacking—but it did not come as a sensational martyrdom; in complete silence all doors were closed to him, he became a pastor without a church and a preacher without a voice. And as for the awakening, it need only be said that very few took any notice of his work at all. The influential and educated shook their heads most at his impetuous and unrestrained zeal. Circumstances drove him back into the cloister cell instead of out into the strife. But here in the calm existence of the study he ripened. Here he came to understand that it was vital to know something of human life and its conditioning factors. One was that it had its foundation in the word of the Bible—and of this word's fixity he was firmly convinced—but at the same time it was requisite that man attain clarity as to his own being. During these years, therefore, Grundtvig began a "stroll in the grove of mankind" which was not to cease as long as he lived.

After a digression on truth and beauty, we find, in an article in *Dannevirke:*

But more of this later, when we have *set ourselves right as to those human matters* which we interrupted to get mind and feet in good order for a stroll which is not so easy to take as one might think from seeing how every second author for centuries past has walked there as anthropologist, psychologist, or pedagogue, still in slippers and night-cap, smoking his morning pipe. From the corporeal side, it is plain enough that this practice is precisely my own, yet from that side it was far from being the practice of those others, who as to externals went in curls and ringlets and cocks' combs and tufts and tassels and Hungarian boots and French coats and Prussian hats and all sorts of German caps, yet inwardly made boast of what their fathers took home on week-days, and this practice I can ill endure, since it is at bottom beggary. And so, outwardly, slippers and night-cap, and inwardly healthy night-thoughts and true morning-dreams and a little old-fashioned morning-prayer and morning-reading too: these I maintain to be the best preparation for a stroll in the maze of the grove of mankind. For though it may be far from conducive to seeing all that one might wish, or understanding all that one sees, still in this way one does not easily transgress or trespass, does not go astray and get either into mud up to the knees or into water up to the neck like those who rely upon their high boots and their ease in swimming, with the result that their boots generally stick in the mud so that they must go home in stocking feet. . . . We, on the contrary, shall leave the mud alone and merely measure the depth as well as we can with our staff; and above all we shall leave the water alone, *look down as deep as we can in still weather at sunrise and let time make clear the rest.* Before leaping into the air with a certain few and the boys among us . . . let us take good care to look to our slippers and to observe how the newest air-machines as well as the oldest feather-cloaks float empty on the surface of the water without having reached either the sun or moon or any star, far less the spirit whose powers shine in them. Let us instead *view in friendly fashion all in which life stirs, and not walk so buried in thought that we hear not the singing bird, run not from the buzzing bee, or let the forget-me-not hide itself unregarded.*

It was to this stroll in the grove of mankind with its contemplation of all in which life stirred that Grundtvig devoted the years 1810-1820, and once begun, the pilgrimage never ended as long as he lived. And he himself was changed from the blustering prophet of doomsday into "life's chosen reconnoiter" and the ardent lover of Denmark and what is Danish.

> Yes, maidens and swains,
> This must I confess:
> That war *is* hard;
> When glittering swords
> Clash at my shoulder,
> I stand and smite;
> But if I hear singing
> On the waves so blue
> In Denmark's tongue
> The mermaidens small,
> Then the spirit moves
> So deeply my heart
> That my hands drop down,
> My cheek is wet,
> Then must I begin,
> Like the mermaidens small,
> To swim and to hum
> On the blue waves out yonder;
> Yes, can I not sing,
> Then I shall hum,
> In the tongue of our times,
> In the speech of the Danes.

In a poem of the year 1817 he has Denmark address the skald:

> By night you roved
> Through my castle purlieus;
> At the portal stoutly you knocked,
> Singing troubadour songs the while.
>
> You knocked and you wooed
> The long night through;
> Your breath on my window pane
> Suddenly thawed it clear.
>
> You wooed my heart,
> Like to amber and red gold;
> You wooed the taper
> Shining up from the mould.
>
> You wooed the flowers
> Whose pattern in ice you saw;
> You wooed the summer
> Which lay under the snow.

So did he knock and woo the heart of Denmark and her people the whole long night, and his steadfastness was rewarded. Not, however, until other things had happened.

A Lutheran Bible-Christian had Grundtvig remained all these years, nor had it ever occurred to him to doubt the basis of human life as defined by this doctrine. There came moments, however, when even this firm foundation appeared to totter. Not so much on account of scholarly criticism. This he could still disregard. Doubt came rather from within: Christianity ought not to be a book religion, and Christian life the study of a book; it should be life and power and warmth. Yet often it almost seemed as though Christ himself were on the point of being lost, even though the word of Scripture still stood as firm as ever. Then his heart would sigh:

> Jesus, where hast thou gone?
> The heart seeks thee in vain,
> Even where the apostle's pen
> Thee with heavenly art hath drawn,
> As a helper in all need,
> Lord over life and death,
> As you walked and stood down here,
> Easy to find, and good to pray to.

Such must Christ still be today: easy to find, good to pray to, lord over life and death. But the book was only a report, however excellent, of something that had been in the past. And what was true of the Bible was likewise true of the chronicles. Even the best popular book is still powerless to awaken and revive. It began to dawn on him that only the living word on human lips could create life out of death. He therefore felt more and more that his stay in the burial vaults was a dead man's existence. It was such reflections as these that were interrupted by Grundtvig's new call to a pastorate, and this assisted him enormously in finding a new foundation both for his own life and for that of the people.

V

The Historico-Ecclesiastical View

On Palm Sunday, 1821, Grundtvig was installed, and preached his inaugural sermon from the text: "This is the day which the Lord hath made. Let us rejoice and be glad in it. Save now, we beseech thee, O Lord. O Lord, we beseech thee, send now prosperity. Blessed is he that cometh in the name of the Lord: we have blessed you out of the house of the Lord." (Psalms, 118:24ff.)

The text could not have been more appropriate. Now life was to begin anew for him who had sat for so many years immured with pen and books. Once more he was to be a pastor and proclaim the word of God unto the people. The gospel to be proclaimed was unaltered: "The Cross and the evangel of peace may be to the world an offence and a folly, but they are by the power of God for the salvation of everyone who believes." His message was essentially the same now as before 1815, and he had the encouragement of preaching usually to a full church. He discharged his pastoral duties with great zeal, taking special interest in preparing the young for confirmation. And meanwhile he put the finishing touches on his translations of Snorre and Saxo that enabled both to appear in the autumn of 1822.

On the whole those were happy days at Præsto, and it is there that his eldest son was born. But the pastorate was not destined to be a long one. By the autumn of 1822 his wish for a charge in the capital had been fulfilled: he applied for, and and was granted, the perpetual curacy of the Church of Our Savior in Christianshavn. Here too his preaching drew a large following. And in it he set himself a double aim, on the one hand "to preach the word as to a Christian congregation, for the instruction, edification and consolation of believers," and on the other to fight against unbelief and error—which meant that his preaching took on a marked polemic and "apologetic" character. But at the same time he was evidently becoming more and more sure that it was not the Bible as such that constituted God's word, but only the teachings of the Bible as informed and brought to life by the spirit. Not for nothing had Grundtvig experienced the deadness of the written word. And now that he had become a preacher, "the living word in the mouths of men" which he had dimly surmised was proving to be an indubitable reality. The word and its hearing rather than the book and its reading became Christianity's presentative form, and divine service, the congregation's fellowship of the sacraments and the word, thus became the focal point of the Christian life.

The first year in Copenhagen was, none the less, a dismal time, and Grundtvig almost lost hope. Out of several contributing causes, the underlying one was undoubtedly a certain drought in his own soul, which seemed to be lying dormant while it gathered strength for the tremendous development that was soon to come. He himself associated his discouragement with the spiritual torpor that he found in the capital:

> During that period, I recall, a period which history likewise tells me is one of the most spiritually dead it ever knew, things got deader and deader year by year, and it seems to me that I myself contributed as much to this state of affairs as did my antipodes, and that in the natural course of things if one lived out one's span one must expect to see the time when one preached if not to empty pews at least to snoring auditors and wrote only for oneself and for one's censor. Everywhere I look I seem to see in the realm of the spirit only the Seven Sleepers, and somnambulists, skeletons and ghosts, until I could almost believe that I too am only some knight templar or old Lutheran preacher walking again in me.

It is possible that back of these pessimistic utterances lay Grundtvig's disappointment over the failure of his historical writings to bear more visible fruit, but on the other hand it is indisputable that the early 1820's were a sad and sterile period in Danish spiritual life. It seems curious that his large audiences did not cheer Grundtvig more. He was not a man to be dazzled by numbers, and it afflicted him that his preaching did not succeed in creating a true congregational and communal life. At the same time he was greatly oppressed by the state-church relation-

ship that obliged him to administer communion and perform
other church offices for purely worldly persons, "known scoffers
and profligates." It was in this connection that his doubts were
first awakened as to the justification of the state church.

To all this was added his seemingly hopeless battle against
rationalism. With all the rest, he now found it difficult to win
even a firm fighting position. The orthodox view of scripture he
had abandoned, but if the word of the Bible be not letter for
letter pure truth, where then is one to find ground under one's
feet? He began by making distinction between the divine and the
human in Scripture, next between the Old Testament and the
New, then between the words of the Apostles and Jesus' own
words, then tried to isolate a single text (John 3: 16 in particular:
"God so loved the world . . .") as the sum of the whole, but
nothing came of his efforts. Yet battle was more urgent than
ever. "I nearly worked my head off," he says in the preface
to *New Year's Morning* (1824), "trying to figure out some way
in which a ripple might be produced on that Dead Sea. To that
end I labored with all my might on an apologetic for Christianity
which should show sun-clear both how defensible Christianity is
and how utterly indefensible are all objections to it and indifference as well, and this work was by no means wasted, for it disclosed the tepidity in my own breast and gave this its death-blow.
But with the form I could never be satisfied, for no matter how
dryly I began, it soon became so poetic as to seem to me quite
unsuitable for use on the Dead Sea, and when at length I succeeded in getting it lucid I saw to my horror that the life had
gone out of it."

Numerous fragments among his posthumous papers show
with what diligence he had worked during those months trying
to find the right defence for Christianity and the right way to
reach his contemporaries, but how the thing had refused to take
form for him.

It so happened, however, that toward the end of 1823 he
passed through one of those violent periods of ferment when
mighty creative powers unfolded within him. While preparing
his sermon for Advent Sunday he read these words in the Epistle
to the Romans: "The night is far spent, and the day is at hand,"

and then it "flashed through" his mind that these words were reality. The toilsome grind at apologetics had not been in vain, for even though what he had written remained dead, he himself had come alive, had been filled with hope and courage. As a preacher, he noticed this during the Advent season of 1823. A new warmth and power had come into his preaching. "As a writer," he says, "I first felt it when I grasped the rhymer's wand that had now long lain idle among all the other antiques that I expected to carry with me to the grave. Then did I first have the delightful feeling that for me a blessed New Year's morning had dawned at the height of summer, whose rays I, now so long accustomed to the grave's night and cold, had for a time sought to outshine with my own little rush-light, with weak, tepid meditations and a thousand misgivings as unprofitable as they were superfluous."

In the midst of this tremendous experience he received from Ingemann the great epic hero-poem *King Valdemar and his Men*—testimony that the spirit of history was not dead in Denmark:

> Rise from the grave, O dead generation,
> Proclaim your fall, tell how you offended,
> Warn us concerning the doom of annihilation,
> And show us whence your salvation came.
>
> Then the soul doth tremble, the spirit wakes,
> The heart takes strength, the hand weapons takes,
> For the Danes, for great and glorious deeds—
> To Denmark's rescue in the hour of need!
>
> What Denmark was, it again can be:
> The spirit of our fathers liveth still.

To Grundtvig this was like an echo of the life that stirred in himself, "a heroic-resurrection, the start of a new series of heroic deeds for the Danish people." Now he saw the hope he had long cherished being fulfilled from without, and he greeted the event with a matin-hymn, the 312-line poem *New Year's Morning:*

God's peace! where ye build,
On field and on mountain,
In the beech's shade,
By the river's spring,
God's peace on the waves,
Where sail the ships,
Which anchor, raise flags
On festal days,
Which even display our fathers' flag.

God's peace, as 'twas found
In our fathers' breasts,
God's peace as 'twas won
By the Saviour's arm,
God's peace as 'tis throned
Where love abides,
God's peace as shown
In cabins of sod,
As I myself have it—
This wish I and offer
My brothers and kin of the North.

New Year's Morning constitutes a knotty problem in Grundt-vig's literary output. Opinion upon it has varied greatly. His own time took little notice of it. This may have been partly due to its obscurity, for obscure it is, often to the point of being absolutely unintelligible—as Grundtvig himself afterwards acknowledged. Nor has the literary criticism of a later day always been favorable. On aesthetic grounds objections may easily be raised. Yet I shall venture to claim for it a place among world literature's major works. It sprang straight from a living human heart and was penned by a skald who may not have conformed to the rules and regulations of the poets' guild but who had an ear for music and who was able through tone and rhythm to stir the mind. This poem should not be read line by line with exegetical reflections but "traversed in eagle-flight" to get the total effect—provided one has ears to hear the song of life which reverberates from it. To attempt a summary would be hopeless—in the main it is his own life-myth that we here find mirrored, together with Scandinavian and biblical motifs. Several stanzas have already been quoted. I shall single out just two more, in which he prophesies concerning the new day which he sees for the Danish church as well:

> Proclaim that o'er the forest
> I now create day,
> Proclaim that on the billow
> I unfurl now a flag
> Like Dannebrog patterned
> With flowering staff,
> With champions hedged round
> Who roam the seas,
> At each corner lightning
> Which reaches from eagles
> To the serpent down under the sea.

> Proclaim that of birch
> I build in haste
> A roof for the church
> Where laths were broken.
> Proclaim that I roof
> With rush and with bark
> Which the gale shall not snap
> On mountain or field.
> Proclaim that I light
> A candle which burns
> Despite all the water in the womb of the waves.

Nor did this prophecy prove empty. A candle was indeed lighted which burned brightly and threw its light afar. Day with deed and exploit followed the glow of dawn.

What had happened to Grundtvig during those winter months? This is difficult, indeed impossible, to fathom. But this much is certain: morning had dawned in his own mind, and he saw before him "the land of the living," that land he had dreamed about ever since he wrote *Of Religion and Liturgy,* and to which he believed he had found the way when all his powers unfolded during the Romantic saga-intoxication. Now for the first time did he understand in earnest that life is God's gift, and that quickening is exclusively an act of the Holy Spirit. Now he dared to believe that night was past, and that day was approaching and would triumph even in the dead Danish church. From this period dates his poem *The Land of the Living*—which, more briefly and more accessibly, says about the same thing as *New Year's Morning* and which will perhaps serve better than anything else to give an impression of Grundtvig's grandeur:

I know a land
Where the hair turns not gray, and time has no tooth,
Where the sun does not burn, and the waves do not beat,
Where the autumn embraces the blossoming spring,
Where the evening and morning dance always in step
With the splendor of noon.

O promised land!
Thou art greeted on morning's mirror-clear strand,
When the child mayhap views thy shadow full fair,
And dreams thou art found where the woods are green,
Where a child may share with the flowers and the reeds
His smile and his life.

O, delusive dream!
Thou shining bubble on time's stream!
In vain the poet with lips and with pen,
Out of glimmering shadows would create thee again;
When the shadow is likest, the little ones sob
Who gaze thereon.

O, spirit of love!
Like a child let me kiss thy outstretched hand
Which reaches from heaven down to earth's mould
And touches our eyes with fingers of gold,
Until blue in the distance beyond the roaring strand,
Rises that beauteous land.

O, miracle-faith
That throwest the vaulted bridge across the deep,
Where the ice-drift defies the roaring strand,
The bridge from death's abode to the living's land!
Sit lower down with me, thou high-born guest!
To squat is best.

O, light-winged Hope!
God-brother, in holy baptism reborn!
For many journeys made to the land beyond the sea,

For tidings good, for comfort given by thee,
May I so thank thee that Joy I descry
   Now that Hope has gone by.

   O, Love itself!
Thou tranquil source of the river of the powers!
He calls thee Father who doth loose our bonds,
All life-force in the soul is a remnant of thy spirit;
Thy kingdom is where one bids death defiance;
   To us thy kingdom comes.

   Our Father so faithful!
Willingly throned in the temple of clay
Which the spirit builds in the Advocate's name,
With smoking altar set within human reach,
With thy remnant's heaven-bright house in a secret place—
   Builds to thee and to thy son.

   O, Christian faith!
Thou pourest into our hearts what the world knows not of,
What we but dimly glimpse with widened eye,
But it lives in us, of it we are well aware;
My land, says Life, is Heaven and Earth,
   If so be love dwells there.

He was in high spirits, confident of what the future had
in store:

Of what I am to do from now on, it is perhaps as yet too early
in the day to say anything sure, for while one of course wishes
during the day to see his morning dreams happily fulfilled, one
must still realize that this is not to be expected, particularly when
the dreams are, like mine, a trifle grandiose. Yet I now feel myself,
with God's help, prepared to proceed with the North's ancient
chronicles, renovate and I hope augment our stock of old-fashioned
Danish hymns, and by and large with the aid of my rhymer's-
wand rescue a good many old friends from the grave, in the hope
. . . that they may gather strength for a new lease on life. This is
about what I intend, and I ought to be profoundly ashamed when
after all that has happened to me I can still sometimes feel doubtful
of finding a little kindly spot where I may have peace and cheer
for this my day's work. . . . Soon, God willing, the stone that has
for many years lain heavy on my heart will be rolled away, and

then, when I have preached the gospel as well as I am able in
Denmark's capital, I shall, methinks, be as free as a bird in the air
and can alight anywhere in the North where God shall have prepared me a place! Truly that is my hope . . . that God will give
me a little spot where I can preach what I believe, sing what I
think, and tell what I see, without being afflicted by . . . the self-
conceit of the poor in spirit . . . that whole death in life which is
the pestilence of our day. . . . How vain it is to wrestle with the
ancient sorceress whose true name is indifference, spiritual insen-
sibility, Thor learned long ago at Udgaard-Loki's, but that is the
sort of thing nobody believes until he has experienced it. . . . Now
long I right fervently for a little circle of kindly fellow-workers
who without worrying about the witch will lean on God and keep
their eyes fixed on the great goal which He surely wishes to see
attained, namely, the revival of the Northern hero-spirit to Christly
exploits along lines suited to present needs and conditions.

Thus did Grundtvig envisage his future, and in its main
lines this picture accords with the fact. History and hymn-writing
indeed became his life-work, he did find such a circle of friends
as few have had, and in Vartov church was granted a peaceful
spot where he could preach what he believed and sing what he
saw. But it all came about quite differently from his imaginings
of 1824. Extraordinary were the twists and turns his life-course
followed.

One of the effects of the renewing of his spirit was that
Grundtvig now felt himself ripe to take the field against the
whole 18th century "enlightenment in the matter of salvation."
With spiritual weapons he would wage "war unto the death"
with it. Consequently he said yes to a proposal that he join two
of the most learned and most gifted among the younger theologians, Dr. A. G. Rudelbach and Adjunct J. C. Lindberg, in
publishing a *Theological Monthly* which should lead the fight
against rationalism and serve as an armory for old-fashioned
Lutheran Christianity.

Grundtvig's battle ardor was further fanned by another cir-
cumstance. In the Kaerteminde district on Funen a strong pietistic
revival had taken place and had met with bitter opposition on
the part of the rationalist clergy. By invoking the Conventicle
Act the latter had got the authorities to intervene against the

Awakened with prohibitions, fines and imprisonments. Now Grundtvig was anything but a votary of Pietist conventicle-Christianity. The godly assemblies were in his eyes but a poor substitute for the life of the church. Church history had taught him that a certain morbid pietism is often coupled with distorted fantasy, contempt for the office of teacher, and ultimately for the written word itself. He had therefore never recommended but had on the contrary deprecated them. Yet he was not blind to the fact that essentially they did adhere to the old Lutheran faith, and that therefore it was an intolerable state of affairs in the church for these simple believers to be persecuted by non-believing pastors who had no right to be in the church at all. Eagerly he hurled himself into the breach on behalf of the conventicle folk with a number of newspaper articles.

This whole episode contributed mightily toward opening Grundtvig's eyes to the necessity of finding a firm position from which to combat rationalism. But this could not be the word of the Bible, where there would always remain the question of correct interpretation, and which must always bring the humbler folk and the minors of the congregation under the papacy of the theologians—the theologians, who were never even in agreement. No, there must exist some infallible testimony to true Christianity, so constituted that no scholarly quibbling could shake it, and such that even the simplest could comprehend it. It was during these cogitations that Grundtvig made his "matchless discovery," found his way to the historico-ecclesiastical view. This had not as yet been vouchsafed with the quickening of 1823, but that was what put him on the road to it.

How he got light on the subject, he described many years later in *The Ecclesiastical Mirror:*

I had been in deep thought over the desperate state to which Christ's congregation, and particularly its children and unlettered members had been brought through the fact that not only were holy scripture's origin, scope, authenticity and correct interpretation much in doubt, but the church's fundamental doctrines of the Trinity, Christ's divinity, and the redemption, were not, if one had command of the original tongues and looked into the matter, anywhere to be found in the Bible, which, to all Protestants was

nonetheless their faith's sole authority. However convinced I myself might be that the Rationalists' Bible-criticism and scripture-
interpretation were about equally unfounded and dishonest, I still
could neither overlook the fact that Christian children and laymen
were alike at a disadvantage nor forget that even my own Bible-
knowledge would not have sufficed to defy the testimony of those
legions, had I not also had a knowledge of church history and possessed, above all, the spirit's testimony within me, able to defy the
testimony of all the world.

On the basis of thoughts such as these he became convinced

> that in the church there must exist some far stronger and more
> valid testimony to the true, original Christian faith than a literary
> document could in any sense be for women, children and all the
> unlettered. As I now ceaselessly pondered, read and wrote, along
> this line, with prayer and supplication, lo and behold, it struck me
> in a blessed moment that the matchless testimony I had so labori-
> ously been seeking all over the spirit's world had been audible like
> a celestial voice all the time and throughout Christendom in *the
> Apostles' Creed at baptism.*

The creed, always spoken at baptism in token of incorporation
in the church, was the sun-clear mark of true Christianity, was
common to all Christians down through the ages. This was the
"discovery" that gave him a firm footing for the fight against
the Rationalists.

The first time this new view of the church came clearly to
the fore was in the clash with Professor H. N. Clausen. The latter
belonged to the younger generation of theologians and was one
of its most eminent members. He was son of the old diocesan
dean H. G. Clausen of Our Lady's Church, one of Rationalism's
best men. He himself, during a trip abroad, had been strongly
influenced by Schleiermacher and was, if anything, developing
away from Rationalism toward a deeper concept of Christianity.
As a university teacher he exercised a considerable influence upon
the theological students. In August 1825 he had brought out a
big book on *Church-government, Dogma and Rite in Catholicism
and Protestantism*—a quite solid and competent work, albeit
stamped with the author's own uncertain theological position.
Barely a fortnight after Clausen's sizeable work came out there

appeared in the bookshops: *The Church's Answer to Professor of Theology Dr. H. N. Clausen,* by Nik. Fred. Sev. Grundtvig, Curate of the Church of our Saviour—a little pamphlet of 47 pages. This pamphlet contained an attack of unprecedented violence:

> It can surely not astonish anyone who has read Professor Clausen's just published book ... that I appear against its author not as a reviewer but as an ecclesiastical opponent, for he has in the book placed himself at the head of all the enemies of the Christian church and scorners of God's word in the country. Even though the professor has no name, I believe, as a writer, nor any power to become a leader, still his position as priest-teacher and his reputation as exegete among the young theological students give him an ecclesiastical importance in the Danish church that it would be indefensible to overlook. To indicate this, to draw attention to the fact that on my side the quarrel is absolutely impersonal and by no means merely academic, but as purely ecclesiastical as possible, I have called this challenge the church's answer, thereby removing the case from the strictly scholarly realm to the court of Christendom at large. It is therefore the priest who, as teacher in the Christian church, here accuses the theological professor as priest-teacher in the church-school, and maintains that as an honest man he must either make the Christian church a formal apology for his un-Christian and scandalous teaching or lay down his office and drop his Christian name. This is my irrevocable demand in the name of the Christian church and congregation, and if Professor Clausen will do neither, then I hereby declare him, on behalf of the church which was, is, and shall be, and whose doctrine lies clearly unfolded and familiar in its history, on behalf of the one true, historical-Christian church, a false teacher who misuses the name of Christian to confuse and seduce the congregation so far as he is able, and who strives to undermine the church which he proclaims that he would serve and perpetuate.

So says the preface, which ends by explaining that if the attack had not before been made with such severity this was due to the fact "that I have but recently arrived at a clear understanding of what constitutes the immovable and unalterable foundation of the Christian church." Previously he had never ventured to pass so severe a sentence on the false teachers because his own exegesis, however sure it might seem to himself, still did not give him an adequate footing. But now that "the Christian principle has been clearly recognized, the church door is so barred against false teachers that none can open it, and so opened to all believers that none can bar it."

Briefly stated, what the "Christian principle" amounted to was this: that Grundtvig had become clear in his own mind as to what the church is. Over against Clausen's somewhat sublimated church-concept, his "air-castle," Grundtvig sets "the historical church which calls itself Christian and which incorporates into itself through baptism and holy communion only those who renounce the devil and confess their faith in God the Father, Son, and Holy Ghost, according to the three articles of faith which scholars call the Apostolic Symbolum." It is an absolutely indisputable historic fact that at all times there has been a Christian church on earth recognizable through its creed, whereby it has proclaimed and does proclaim belief in Christ as the only way of salvation, the way that leads through baptism and communion to God's kingdom and the land of the living. Whether this way be true, whether it does lead to salvation, may be challenged, but that such is the way of the Christian church there is no denying:

> Only consider how one would go about challenging the principle that the means of grace with its corresponding confession of faith, which is the only thing all Christians in all situations, in all congregations, at all times have had in common, the thing that has both identified the church to friend and foe and united the congregation, which has thus indisputably been both its distinguishing mark and bond of fellowship, how deny that this is the foundation which has till now met the charge our Lord laid upon the rock which, despite the gates of hell and the powers of death, should bear his church always, until the end of the world. How challenge this principle whereby we are merely placing the church mentally on the basis upon which it has demonstrably stood and beyond question will stand as long as a single human being, myself for example, voluntarily embraces the confession and declares himself united through the means of grace with all the true believers who have been, are and shall be born, reborn in the same faith, of the same spirit, through the same baptism, to the same hope!

It is therefore time for all true Christians to rally around what is basically Christian and let be all theological differences reconcilable with it, "but then not budge a hair's breadth either for open enemies or for false friends."

This was the "matchless" discovery, which did indeed become a candle that spread its radiance far in the Danish church. This was the heart-beat of Grundtvig's whole historico-popular concept of Christianity. A construction frequently put upon the "discovery" is that, between reading Irenæus and himself pondering what there was essential to the church which could with authority be used against the Rationalists, he had stumbled upon the apostles' creed as an exceptionally precious and ancient historic testimony independent of the word of scripture, and that thereupon he and his disciples had assumed about the same attitude toward the creed that the scripture-theologians maintained toward the Bible. It is easy to understand how such an impression might have been created just because Grundtvig first stated his ecclesiastical view in the little polemic against Professor Clausen. The *Church's Answer* itself in a certain sense completely overshoots the mark. It is both unjust and unfair in its treatment of Professor Clausen, while at the same time it easily gives the impression that the ecclesiastical view's chief function was to implement an effective combating of the rationalists. Quite likely Grundtvig himself in writing the *Answer* had regarded this as the main thing. But he was soon to be taught otherwise. It was not as a weapon of war that the matchless discovery gained its importance. *The Answer* did not become, as its author had expected, the signal for a great sorting of belief from unbelief in the Danish church. The Professor did not apologize, nor did he resign his office as priest-preacher. Instead he started a libel suit, and after long debate Grundtvig was actually found guilty and for the future placed under censorship.

To the above-mentioned misunderstanding of the matchless discovery another factor has also contributed. There were actually quite a few of the Grundtvigians who regarded the creed about as the orthodox regarded the Scriptures, and they were borne out in this attitude when the ecclesiastical view was gradually amplified by a most unfortunate "theory"—originally conceived by

Grundtvig himself, later elaborated by Peter Christian Kierke-gaard, and with such success that for many the theory became one with the ecclesiastical view itself. The theory was that, his-torically, the creed had not originated with the apostles but was "that little word from our Lord's own lips," that it had been conveyed by Christ himself to the apostles during the 40 days between the resurrection and the ascension. Any such thing was still a long way off in *The Answer,* which merely mentions the "so-called apostolic confession," and where the age of the con-fession is not discussed at all.

There is more to life than theories, however, and the historico-ecclesiastical view had its value quite independently of the un-successful and in many ways unjust attack on Professor Clausen. That is, Grundtvig had experienced—as a starter, in 1821, much more powerfully in 1823, continually thereafter—the fact of a living *congregation,* which incorporates persons into itself through *baptism* and assembles about the *communion-table,* these being, along with its confession of its Lord, the invariable distinguishing marks of the Christian congregation. It had long since dawned on him that the written word, yes, even the word of the Bible, rich as that might be, was of itself dead.

Now it came over him that in the congregation, and only there, is heard the word which creates what it names, the living word, which is our Lord Jesus himself, his living presence. This is not the written word, for that is always dead. No, this is the word that has lived in the congregation in unbroken oral tradi-tion, on its tongue as the confession, in its hearts as faith. To know what Christianity is, one should ask not scholars and lin-guists, but the congregation, where the Lord himself is present in the word of life. Only therefrom does life proceed. This oral word of the confession has always been spoken in the congrega-tion, beginning with baptism, where a man becomes Christian, and it always will be; it is the real secret of God's kingdom:

> The most prodigious thing on earth
> Is Christ Jesus' kingdom,
> Its splendor so exceeding great
> That there exists no equal.

> Invisible as soul and mind,
>   Yet easy to perceive,
> Like a city on a mountain-top
>   To all the world revealed.
>
> Its riddle is a word divine
>   Which creates whate'er it names,
> Which fills up vales the world around
>   And makes rough places plain.
>
> With this is baptism consecrate,
>   Blest is Jesus' cup,
> Yonder springs the hope of life
>   Which here refreshes us.

This living word, our Lord Jesus himself, was in the church before scripture existed, for church is older than scripture, and scripture is only written testimony concerning God's true word. One should therefore not build the church upon the scripture, the altar upon the Bible, but should rather lay the Bible open upon the altar-table. This is the main thing in the matchless discovery: the sense of the congregation and of its living only by virtue of the Lord's presence as he speaks his word to men at baptism and communion and holds commerce with them, gives them rebirth and nourishes their Christian life. "The Word" has here again become drama and myth, not judgments of reason, or moral precepts or edifying observations, no, the word is the bond between heaven and earth, the bond which only God and his spirit can create, but which man may experience in the congregation:

> Here is the key, cunningly wrought,
> To God's house and heaven's gate,
> Here is the light on the golden stick
> That makes night as clear as day.

Or:

> Never more must the North forget
> The church of living stones:
> Which through the power of God's word
> Faith and baptism have joined!

The spirit itself builds the church best,
Leaning as little on king as on priest:
The word alone hallows the house.

In contradistinction to Rationalism's moral-reason Christianity and to Orthodoxy's Bible-church and theology, Grundtvig had discovered the historical congregation which always had existed and would exist by virtue of the fact that the Lord himself is present in it, and there has lips and voice. There and only there does God give man rebirth through baptism and nourish his Christian life through the communion. This is an act of the Holy Spirit, but the Spirit works always through the word. As man's spirit makes itself known through speech, as the people's spirit lives in the mother-tongue, so also is God's spirit active through "the word"—that word which makes baptism baptism, and communion communion, namely the creed and the words of institution. This word Grundtvig calls "the word of God's own mouth," which, at any rate originally, had no connection with any theory of the historical origin of these particular words, but expressed what constitutes the essential basis of the church, namely that in and through these words God speaks his creative word to us. He therefore speaks his word "only at font and at table."

Only at font and at table
Hear we God's word *to us,*
But ever through this life-word
Sin and death we can defy;
For the spirit attends on the word,
In the voice of God life surges
Pure and sacredly sun-clear.

Jesus Christ, heaven's mouthpiece,
Himself the eternal word of God,
By word of mouth to *us* comes down
At his font and at his table;

He, our Savior only,
Clearly covenants with us:
By my word you now are pure,
Baptism's word *to you* was said,

The Father-word, the prince of life
Says *to us* beside his table:
If you hunger, if you thirst,
Spirit and life are these my words.

So *to us* with the word come
Light and life from our Lord's mouth,
Earthly spring and heaven's summer,
All on the ground of love;
On that ground from sin we are washed,
On that ground with life we are fed
In our Lord Jesus' name.

There has for most people been something incomprehensible about this limitation whereby God's word comes to us only at font and at table. But Grundtvig means just what he says. He precisely means *to us,* to me the individual. Scripture is only testimony as to what happened of old, preaching is only the testimony of another person, which, like scripture, serves to throw light on the Christian life—but man cannot live by the testimony of others. The ecclesiastical view was for Grundtvig the completion of his insight of 1810, namely that human life without Christ is cast off to worse than the grave. Man is saved only by *God's* covenant *with him,* but that occurs at baptism, and his Christian life can only be preserved by *God's* sustaining and nourishing it, but that happens at communion. Therefore the words there spoken—as opposed to the words of scripture or preaching—are not human words, but *the word of our Lord's own mouth.* Therefore baptism and communion are the creative factor in the Christian life, token that the church is neither a reading-circle nor a moral educator, but Christ's continuing life, into which he draws his believers.

This is not the place to discuss the correctness of Grundtvig's ecclesiastical view. On the other hand, it is essential to establish the fact that, from 1825 on, this was his fixed position, never abandoned, and that this view was basic to his whole future accomplishment in church, school, and nation. Therefore there is no use dismissing it as *only* a theory, for it has stood the test, it has shown that the power of growth was in it. On many points Grundtvig might gradually change his opinions, and on many points he perhaps never reached clarity at all, but in his view of the church and the word of our Lord's own mouth he never wavered.

Through his own development in youth, Grundtvig had come to know that life could neither be lived by the Enlightenment's optimism nor by Romanticism's longings and dreams; all this led only to defeat, since it could not span the chasm between life and death. Only One could bridge this chasm and thus save and regenerate human life to the end ordained for it by its Lord and creator, and that one, namely Christ, should be sought neither above nor below, neither in a distant past nor among the dead leaves of the Bible. He was only to be found in his congregation, where he was present in and through the living word as spoken at the Christian life's beginning in baptism and at its renewal in communion, the word which created what it named, which brought man rebirth into a Christ-life, which alone threw a bridge between heaven and earth. Here was the heart of the whole, and nothing could be farther from a new humanism or romanticism.

> This whole world does not outweigh
> What we believe and what we know,
> Heaven we here on earth possess
> In our Savior's love.

Yet this love does not grow in human hearts, but only in the congregation, where the spirit ever maketh Christ to live.

The line runs straight from his youth's question: What then of Christ? through the awakening of 1810 to the "matchless" discovery, but from that point it fans out into poems and hymns, into free school and high school, into historical view and popular awakening, into demand for freedom in church and society, into temporal competence and initiative on the broadest front. Grundtvigianism became a swift and powerful stream of humanity and culture which influenced and renewed Danish life in practically all its aspects. This subject will be discussed in subsequent pages, but what must not be forgotten is that the source of the whole was the concept of human life and its conditioning factors which Grundtvig himself had reached in the year 1825.

VI

The Years that Followed

The author of *The Church's Answer* saw himself as a reformer
called to arouse the church to fight for belief against unbelief.
Without doubt he expected and hoped that Professor Clausen
would be forced to lay down his office, forced to cease being a
priest-teacher. But things had not gone that way at all.

The little book, to be sure, created a tremendous sensation.
In a week no fewer than three editions had been printed. This
did not mean, however, that Grundtvig was gaining support—
at any rate not outside a very limited circle. In the cultured
world, Clausen was perhaps the most popular of university professors, an intrepid advocate of freedom in science and in the
church as well as in civil life. Grundtvig, on the contrary, had
from of old been regarded as something of an obscurantist—the
clash with Oersted was still fresh in memory—and his attack on
Clausen could scarcely escape being taken as an attack on religious and scientific freedom.

Even a man like Mynster, who was theologically remote from
Clausen, still took his part, and in a way that wounded Grundtvig
deeply. In a sermon "concerning Christian wisdom," he mentioned persons of divided nature who will accept today what
tomorrow they will reject, undertake today what tomorrow they
will regret, and thus, in spite of knowing and meaning better,
become enemies of the cross of Christ, in that they rouse vexation
and strife. This sermon was immediately printed and no one
could doubt to whom these words had reference. A week later,
in Our Saviour's Church, Grundtvig preached a sermon "concerning Christian strife":

Let the world's priests and prophets cry: Brothers, we must have
peace, the world's peace, at any price! Let them reap the world's
praise for gentleness and meekness, for wisdom and love. Let them

sanctify and bless the world's hatred and indignation against us
for that we, like the Savior, bear witness that their deeds are evil.
... Calmly and frankly we reply: Brothers, we must, we will have
strife in the Lord's name. We will, not because strife is pleasing,
not because we lack the high wisdom that it is far more comfort-
able, while the foe rages, to sit with our hands in our laps ... but
because we see from the Lord's word and from the Christian people's long career that strife is unavoidable.

Behind these words one may sense how it had rankled that
Mynster, whom, despite the difference, Grundtvig had always
regarded as a fighter for the faith, should have openly sided with
unbelief.

Clausen answered the attack by suing Grundtvig for libel.
The latter had expected something quite different, and felt this
to be unworthy and depressing. He was conscious only of having
acted officially, in accord with his priestly vow—and yet he now
found himself involved in a vexatious libel suit, without any
serious consideration having been given the question of the truth
or falsity of the allegations. How, then, was one in future to fight
against unbelief like a true priest? It is no wonder that under
these conditions all Grundtvig's earlier misgivings about the state
church and its uncleanness cropped up anew. It was also becoming more and more clear to him, as he wrote Ingemann, that he
was only "fitted to be a preacher, not for everyday pastoral life,"
that he was the religious revealer, not a spiritual adviser or parish
priest—an observation that was perfectly correct.

Then came the drop that filled his cup to overflowing. In 1826
the thousandth anniversary of Ansgar's coming to Denmark was
to be celebrated. Grundtvig had long been interested, had, among
other things, published a rather long poem on "King Harald
and Ansgar." Officially nothing had been done beyond decreeing
a festival service for Whitsunday. For this occasion, Grundtvig
had a pamphlet printed containing three hymns of his own composition, among them "That Blessed Day." The church authorities intervened, however, to prohibit the selection of hymns outside the Hymn-book. This led to painful discussions with the
diocesan dean and the bishop, with the—to outsiders, at any rate
—astonishing result that, before Whitsuntide, Grundtvig had sent

in his resignation. "If people can't sing my hymns, neither shall they hear my preaching." To resign his post was, for a man of Grundtvig's age, with wife and children, a very serious step. His friends did their utmost to dissuade him, but his wife never lost courage: "Well I know what pains you, that you are troubled about wife and children. Forget us and do faithfully what our Lord bids you! He surely knows how he shall give us bread," she said to him in those difficult days of decision. And she proved to be right. In some strange way his resignation was a preparation for his future work.

Quite likely Grundtvig imagined that the extraordinary step he had taken would cause the libel suit to be dropped, but in this he was disappointed. It was carried through, and—after varied literary discussion—ended in a verdict of October 30, 1826, whereby the offensive terms were declared null and void and Grundtvig was ordered to pay the costs of the action together with a fine of 100 rigsbankdaler. What was worse, the judgment carried the rider that he was to be subject to censorship in future—something which he felt added insult to injury. Nor did this verdict settle the matter. The fight was passionately continued by Grundtvig's close friend, the above-mentioned Jakob Christian Lindberg, who was unwearying in his attacks on Clausen and the rationalists. The most important thing about the whole debate was that it again and again forced Grundtvig thoroughly to consider his attitude toward the church and toward ecclesiastical freedom, and in the process his position underwent a distinct development.

As in 1813, so now a full stop had been set to Grundtvig's ministry. With reason has it been pointed out that the swell which now swept him into the ministry, now left him stranded in the market-place, was of major significance in fitting him to act as "awakener" in two directions, both ecclesiastically and nationally. Had he been only a pastor, the intervals between his church appointments—and this time the interval was to be even longer than the last—would have constituted purposeless parentheses. Now, instead, they became rest periods when he had time and tranquility to go broad and deep and master human life in all its abundance.

Out of the pulpit, it was a matter of course that Grundtvig

must create and act through his pen—and thereby procure the necessities of life as well. A new "hibernation" in the study began—richer than the previous one.

For the *Theological Monthly* he wrote a series of articles in which he developed his ecclesiastical view theologically, together with a somewhat extended treatise on religious freedom, the final section of which was suppressed by the censor. Of greater importance, however, was his collection, revision and publication of sermons from the years of his pastorate at Our Savior's Church, which resulted in *The Sunday Book*. This came out in three thick volumes (1827-1830) and found a considerable and ever expanding circle of readers. The fact was that under outward adversity Grundtvig's circle of friends grew. An increasing number, even among the cultured, had been perceiving the element of power in Grundtvig's personality. By 1828 one already encounters the since so oft repeated and not ungrounded charge of an exaggerated personal devotion on the part of Grundtvig's friends. For the first time the appellation "Grundtvigians" also crops up. During these years, no doubt primarily on the responsibility of his tireless armor-bearer Lindberg, and strictly against Grundtvig's own wish, the nucleus of a Grundtvigian sect was formed, which, again through Lindberg's agency, and half against Grundtvig's will, came near joining the circles of the awakened that were found all over the country, especially on Funen.

Personally, Grundtvig again felt himself drawn to Northern antiquity. Through the *Song of Beowulf* he had made the acquaintance of Old English literature. And despite bygone hostility (1807) he still could not forget that it was Northmen who had settled in England and had there kept alive something of the hero spirit. He was convinced, and rightly, that glorious treasures still lay hidden in English libraries. He therefore petitioned the Crown for a travelling fellowship, and when in the spring of 1829 he was actually granted 2000 riksbankdalers he expectantly started westward. Nor were his expectations disappointed. This is evident from the fact alone that in the next two years, 1830 and 1831, he crossed twice more to the isle of coal. From the scholarly viewpoint, to be sure, his journeys failed to yield the expected dividends. Not Grundtvig, but English research-workers, presided over the publication of Old English literature, and his acquaintance with that literature left only very limited traces upon Grundtvig himself, chiefly in a series of hymns that may be described as free adaptations from the Old English.

What was it, then, that drew him to England, and led him even as late as 1843 to make a trip there? In addition to his scholarly expectations, he had gone with exalted ideas about the Anglican church. Was it not in many ways related to his own ecclesiastical view? During these years he himself still had firm faith in the clerical office and under the influence of Irenæus had interested himself in the subject of the apostolic succession. It is not unlikely that he may have expected to find some response to his message among high-church Englishmen. In this he was obviously disappointed, however. Whether the fault lay with Grundtvig or elsewhere is an open question, but certain it is that in the Anglican church he found only rigid torpor and empty forms. On his last English visit, in 1843, it was if anything the Methodists who interested him, but in general the significance of his English journeys is as little to be sought in the ecclesiastical realm as in the scholarly.

No, the determinant was something of a quite different order. In England he had learned to view with admiration the energetic civil life with its restless industry and its practical initiative. Steamships and railways, docks and factories, foundries and shops and smoking chimneys—all these manifestations of the secular life he had learned to admire and understand. Naturally he was not blind to the worldly motives that constituted the driving power, to the selfishness and lust for profits that lay back of the urge for action. And from of old he had been wary of natural science and mechanics as promoting poverty of spirit. But, granted all this, from great effects one must still infer great causes, "from the steam-engine's thousand horse power, human grandeur and the Northern hero-spirit in its inventors." He understood that this whole motley display of energy in industry and trade belonged to "what the noble call life's joy," and that these were now the realms where the old Northern hero-spirit performed deed and exploit. What he thus came to see in England, at first with a certain consternation, gradually with wonder, and finally with admiration, stood, however, in marked contrast to the dead calm that prevailed here at home. Copenhagen was a peaceful, drowsy provincial town as compared with London. He could not help asking himself what made the difference. To this question he soon found the answer, and it proved of vital significance to his whole understanding of human life: Freedom, personal and national freedom, was the underlying principle of English initiative. From now on it became an axiom in Grundtvig's total view of human life that only in freedom can spirit live and unfold.

Thus his residence in England served to broaden his understanding of life, and became a major premise to his whole later national accomplishment. In England he became a realist: there he learned to turn from the past to modern life and to understand the latter as also deed and exploit even though the form of expression might be different. But still more important: in England he became a liberal. Without the lessons learned from England he could scarcely have written the preface-rhymes to *Northern Mythology* in which he sings of thought's and faith's and learning's land, where alone life stirs in strife:

> Where, even when it wraps itself in steam,
> Clearly power proclaims: my life is in strife!
> Thought's and faith's and learning's sea,
> Which without freedom is the Asas' grave,
> But which, when powers there compete for place,
> Is like unto a blooming, billowing mead.

The intervals between his English visits and the years immediately following, Grundtvig spent in his study at home, diligently reading and writing. The 1830's were one of his great productive periods, when his energies seemed to know no bounds. Besides a long series of topical tracts bearing on the current ecclesiastical debate, he completed during these years one immense work after another: *Northern Mythology* (1832), *Handbook of World History* (I, 1833; II, 1836; III, 1843), the first volume of *Hymns for the Danish Church* (1837), the lectures *Within Living Memory* (1838).

And yet he by no means lived in isolation as during the period prior to 1820. The circle brought together by his preaching at Our Saviour's Church felt, after 1826, like a flock without a shepherd; it more or less attached itself to the catechist of the German church of Saint Frederik in Christianshaven, Lorentz Siemonsen, who had been a good deal influenced by Grundtvig. When it was reported, however, that the German services were to be discontinued, a not inconsiderable group planned to lodge a petition with the king that St. Frederik's Church be made available for the services of a free congregation with Grundtvig as pastor; under these conditions he would have been willing to return to the ministry. Temporarily, however, the plans were shelved on account of Grundtvig's third trip to England, and in the meanwhile his friends in Copenhagen began holding "godly assemblies" at Lindberg's home. In these, however, Grundtvig upon his return refused to participate. On November 24, 1831, the above-mentioned petition was therefore lodged with the king in earnest. It was, however, definitely refused by the authorities. As a result, Grundtvig now determined in spite of everything to speak at Lindberg's meetings, which began to bulk much larger. There was uneasiness in high places, and after long debate the Bishop of Seeland, sober-minded and scholarly P. E. Müller, succeeded in having Grundtvig permitted to preach at Danish evensong in St. Frederick's Church, on condition that he use the authorized ritual and the Evangelical-Christian Hymn-book—and without leave to administer the sacraments. This was not what they had wanted. The plan had been to form a free congregation outside the state church. But Grundtvig accepted such freedom as there was in the hope that this might be the first step to something better.

Home from England, Grundtvig first set to work on his great *Northern Mythology or Symbol-language historico-poetically developed and elucidated,* which has, not without reason, been called "the most interesting book he ever wrote." In any event it is one of his chief works, opening as it does with an extensive introduction in three parts, namely, "The Science of Universal History," "Myths and Mythologies," and "The Northern Hero-spirit," which gives his view of human life, mythology and his-

tory its most comprehensive expression, while at the same time
sketching in rough outline his educational ideas. Then, too, preceding the introduction there is the magnificent "Rhymed Epistle
to Scandinavian Relatives," a fragment of which was earlier
quoted, but whose main section remains to be transcribed at
this point:

> Yes, ye sons of hero-birth!
> Let us construe our good aright!
> Each of us shaped on his own last,
> Freedom is what will serve us best,
>
> Freedom, but not like fire and water,
> Pest and hunger and wasteland,
> Freedom, but not like wolf and bear,
> Only like the grown man-children we are.
>
> Let freedom be our watchword in the North,
> Freedom for Loki as well as for Thor,
> Freedom for the word in a world new made,
> Which it for itself has created under the sky:
> Thought's and faith's and learning's land.

The fundamental idea in the *Mythology* itself is that a
people's myths figuratively express the folk-mind and the people's
concept of existence, its conditions and goal. It is observations out
of nature and human life that are symbolically expressed through
myths, these being permeated in the case of the Scandinavian
myths with the Northern hero-spirit. Thus the myths often become an anterior image of the people's history, and to interpret
and explain them requires possession by the Northern spirit. That
is why poets and thinkers are far better able to interpret them
than philologists.

The *Mythology* was scarcely finished before Grundtvig was
in full swing with his *Handbook of World History According to
the Best Sources*. He here breaks away completely from the views
of the *Chronicle* of 1812. History is here envisaged as humanity's
life-course on the earth, which unfolds, like the life of the individual, through youth, marked by fantasy (Antiquity); man-

hood, characterized by a strong sense of active power (the Middle Ages); and old age, where intellect is the dominant quality (Modern Times). The progress of history is mirrored in the development of the leading nations, and the others are taken account of only to the extent of their importance to these. The leading peoples of antiquity were the Hebrews, Greeks, and Romans. Subsequently the Anglo-Saxons and Northmen became so. The theological viewpoint has been completely abandoned. The work is a political history, even if not in the modern sense. For its fundamental idea is that every people has its own character, its folk-spirit and individuality, out of which it acts, and which alone makes possible an understanding of events. Nations behave almost like independent entities. Therefore here as in mythology it is not the scholarly investigator who reaches the kernel of the matter, but only the inspired thinker and poet.

This whole historical view is held even today in Grundtvigian circles, but it is hardly an accident that it should never have been adopted by the historical profession. There is something inspired and to others inspiring in the poet's views, but it is neither as historical research nor as historical narration that the *World History* has succeeded in holding its own. Its enduring greatness—as with the *Chronicles* of 1812 and 1817—rests on the many valuable single observations and on the sound universal judgments that constantly reappear.

In the midst of work on the *World History,* however, another question, one that had long been on Grundtvig's mind, presented itself with renewed force, namely, hymn-singing in the Danish church. In 1798 the *Evangelical-Christian Hymnbook* had received exclusive authorization for church use. Of this work it has been said, perhaps too harshly, that it is neither evangelical nor Christian, but it does constitute the typical expression of the era of enlightenment's emotional, highly dilute, and rather shallow Christianity. Grundtvig had hated this hymnbook ever since his first years in the ministry, and his sure eye was not long in perceiving what treasures lay hidden in the older Danish hymn-poetry, all the way back to the Reformation, and especially in Kingo. On the other hand he could plainly see that times were too much altered for Kingo's hymnbook to be restored out of hand. In addition, he had ever since the days of his youth himself felt a mighty urge to regenerate hymn-tunes in Denmark.

> May God with his grace crown me,
> So that I may know the joy
> Of feeling the old hymn-tunes
> Reborn within my breast!
> Then shall sons sing hymns
> Fit to gladden a mother's heart,
> Touch its very depths.

So had he written in 1815 in a poem to his mother. He had then already made various attempts, with but partial success. Only the Christmas carol of 1810 about the three holy kings has been able to hold its own. During the next few years, as occasion offered, he wrote hymns that gave clear evidence of his abilities in that direction, the most noted being "That Blessed Day," "A Child is Born in Bethlehem," and "Should any perchance Remember." Again and again he had seriously entertained the thought of rewriting and adding to the old stock of hymns. But he was always putting it off and might never have got around to it at all if his friends had not brought so much pressure to bear. Pastor Gunni Busck was particularly persistent and in 1835, being well-to-do, offered Grundtvig 1000 Rbd., "provided that will suffice, and more if it be not enough," to enable him to devote a year to the hymns. Grundtvig accepted the offer, and two years later, in September 1837, there appeared *Hymns for the Danish Church,* collected and edited by Nik. Fred. Sev. Grundtvig.

With its 401 hymns, this volume was something altogether unique. And what was more, the author had the temerity to put on the title page: "first volume." That same year he was already at work on a second volume, *Hymns for the Danish Church-school,* which he did not manage to complete, however, until many years later (1870). Posthumously, this was followed by three more volumes, so that the *Hymns* consists, in all, of five thick volumes, containing in all between 1400 and 1500 items. Of the 401 hymns in Volume I, only about a good tenth had been printed before, and three quarters were not even composed until the years 1836-37. About 50 of the hymns are a recasting of older Danish hymns. These are invariably the least successful. Brorson in particular has suffered seriously. The special pietistic note of quiet, introspective meekness Grundtvig simply did not get. The first group consists of hymns brought over from the hymn-books of foreign nations, Hebrew, Greek, Latin, English and German. But actual translations these are not. It is more as though Grundtvig had drawn his inspiration from the original poems and out of this had created wholly new Danish hymns— often far better than the originals. Though the hymns are thus remade in Grundtvig's image they nonetheless serve to bring a certain whiff of the ecumenical into the Danish church. Finally, about a third of the hymns are entirely Grundtvig's own. This group surpasses all the rest. Here one finds hymn after hymn that has lived and continues to live on the Danish congregation's lips.

The first volume of the *Hymns* was scarcely off his hands before another exacting task made its bid for attention. Over and over again his friends had urged him to give historical lectures, and in 1837 when the censorship of his work was at last lifted he said yes to the proposal, and in the summer and autumn of 1838 gave at Borch's Collegium in Copenhagen a long series of lectures which he entitled: *Within Living Memory*. In these he disclosed what had happened on the world scene during his lifetime, characteristically tying his own fortunes in with these large events. June 20, 1838 has with justice been called the natal hour of the living, spoken address in Denmark. It was not a lecture that Grundtvig gave, but a fresh, personal, living talk. His model in many ways had been Steffens's famous lectures of 1802-3, but the tone was far more Danish than had been the case with Steffens. With a mounting attendance the series proceeded, and it ended with a grand ovation to the speaker "for every inspired word that had issued from his mouth to awaken our dormant yearnings, for all his fiery and spirited talk, for all the glory that had declared itself through him as a heritage from our glorious forefathers." If nothing else, these talks contributed greatly toward strengthening Grundtvig's faith in the living word as a medium for educating the young.

A direct result of the addresses at Borch's Collegium was the formation in 1839 of the Danish Society, whose object was "the

use of the mother-tongue for living discussion of the circumstances of Danish national life." Here Grundtvig wished to get
beyond the talk; to arrive at "the living conversation . . . which
alone can thoroughly clarify and illuminate one's ideas." He himself, as we know from numerous witnesses, was a master in the
art of conversation. I need only call to mind the words of the
Swedish dean Wieselgren: "I have almost never met with a
greater skald at conversation. Every thought was like an inspiration. His heart was in every word." Yet the "conversations" had
but an indifferent success. They became mostly lecture, just as
later happened in the high-schools. Very few high-school men
have had the faculty for getting pupils to participate in conversations.

And, amazingly enough, during the very years when all the
monumental works above mentioned were coming along, Grundtvig still found time and energy to develop in a series of smaller
works his educational ideas, as cradled in *Northern Mythology,*
and as destined later on to mature in the high-schools. In 1836
came *The Danish Quatrefoil,* the next year *To Norwegians, on
a Norwegian High-School,* and in 1838 *The School for Life* and
The Academy at Soer. To the subject-matter of these pamphlets
we shall return later.

In 1839 a radical change again took place in Grundtvig's
situation. It started with his applying for permission to confirm
his own sons at St. Frederick's Church. The application, like so
many earlier ones, was rejected. This, together with his desire to
be able to join his friends at baptism and communion—and very
likely economic worries as well, though he never let them weigh
on him—now set him seriously considering the possibility of re-
entering the service of the state church. And when the post of
minister at Vartov, a foundation for aged women, fell vacant,
Grundtvig applied for it and, with the king's support, obtained
it. Mynster, who in the meantime had become bishop of Seeland,
approved the appointment, on the ground that Grundtvig would
do less harm there than as a free agent. Moreover he was now 56
years old, and the fact that he was approaching the evening of
life might well be taken into account. Had Mynster's calculation
hinged on anyone but Grundtvig, it might easily have proved

correct, but in his case things were different. For him, his life's
high noon was now just beginning, his full vigor was only now
unfolding. He, the man of 56, still had a ministry of 33 years
before him!

In the humble little chapel belonging to Vartov hospital, there
grew up during the next few years a congregational life that was
destined to have significance for the whole Danish people. In 1839,
when it appeared that Grundtvig could not get permission to
confirm his own sons, he had, in an hour of sadness, written his
poem on the sparrows in the royal garden:

> Of what do you twitter, you sparrows gray,
> So late in the king's garden?
> To ease my pain please prophesy
> A gem of a New Year's present,
> A swallow-nest, a sparrow-shelter,
> Where my young can celebrate Christmas,
> And grow their feathers to fly.
>
> This little one's nest, this sparrow-shelter,
> With the altar for the priest,
> I have wanted full many a Christmas
> And hoped for trustingly;
> But prudence says: You won't get it,
> For giants bar the road to church,
> Which is free by the grace of God!

The giants had not succeeded in barring the road to church, and
at Vartov his dreams reached fulfillment—far beyond his expectations. What young ones they were who gathered in the nest
and grew feathers to fly all over the country! The nucleus of the
Vartov congregation had been humble folk and average city
people, in large part drawn from his following at Our Saviour's
and St. Frederik's. But they were soon joined by a number of
the best theological students. Several of these had their Christian
awakening at Vartov, and a good many pastors went out from
there who continued to look to "the old man" at Vartov as their
father. A better brood of pastors it would be hard to imagine than
that first brood of "Grundtvigians," either the older ones who had
received appointments before 1839 or the younger who grew up

at Vartov. The congregation was constantly growing, and quite a few of the leading men of the time in business, politics and the arts met beneath Grundtvig's pulpit. And yet it was not his preaching that constituted the mainstay, though he did preach with great power, and though his personal bearing made a strong and compelling impression on people.

What a stranger coming into the church would first notice— and of this we have ample testimony—was the hymn-singing, which sounded much stronger than what one usually heard. When attempts to create a new hymnbook to supersede the *Evangelical-Christian* still got nowhere, Grundtvig brought out a little folder of *Festival Hymns,* which he introduced at Vartov. This was constantly being enlarged, and ended as a complete hymnbook which was long used at Vartov and in most of the elective and free congregations. But if upon a first visit it was the hymn-singing that perhaps made the strongest impression, one did not need to attend very often to discover that what the congregational life at Vartov really centered in was the word of the Lord at baptism and communion. And the older Grundtvig got, the more definitely did communion become the climax of divine service. His sermons got shorter, but to make up for this he prefaced the communion by a confession talk that may well have meant more to his listeners than the sermon. That into this congregational life a certain unhealthy worship of "the old man" may have injected itself is patent, but we possess any amount of concordant testimony to the effect that with all its weak points there was a singular radiance about the church life which had its hearth at Vartov. Otherwise it would scarcely have become the undisputed point of assembly for so much of what took place in the next generation all over the country.

Meanwhile Grundtvig did not forget the people for the church. Just then, during the 1840's and 1850's, the whole school problem was under discussion. Political and national issues were even more in the limelight. For the better part of a generation there had been a "liberal" movement in Denmark doing battle for a free constitution. This, Grundtvig had not joined. In 1838 he was still an absolute monarchy man, and hopeful that accord might be reached between "the king's hand and the people's voice." In monarchy he saw the best guarantee of a free national development. He therefore greeted the consultative assembly of estates with joy, while remaining highly skeptical of parliamentary majority rule. He feared that the latter would lead to the lowest living high at the expense of the capable. On the other hand he had an immense confidence in royal prerogative. He soon saw, however, that, as things were shaping up, the era of popular sovereignty was at hand: "Do what we will, the reign of peasants and the masses is at our door," he wrote in 1848, and from this drew the conclusion that it was now more urgent than ever to implement his idea of popular enlightenment and education by means of a school for young people.

The awakening of the people was prerequisite to the assumption of power by the people, and in their awakening he put his trust. He therefore entered politics. And therefore not as a National Liberal. That party thought of the victory of freedom and folk rule as meaning the transfer of the common people from the tutelage of absolute monarch and officials to the control of the country's clever and cultured champions of freedom. The people itself these champions did not know, nor did they believe in the people. With Grundtvig it was different. From childhood he had been on intimate terms with the farming population and all through his youth had looked toward a popular awakening. Now he knew that the time had come. In England he had learned what freedom meant to a people's competence, and so when he took his seat in the constituent assembly he became the most radical member of the house. With unswerving consistency—often, too, with little sense of the realities—he remained a fanatical champion of freedom in all spheres of life, not merely in church and school but in business and trade as well, in government and legislation. He was both too impractical and too biased to exert a direct influence on political life. But he was like a bad conscience to the rest, and his demand for freedom had the future on its side. On a number of points he may be said to have staked out the roads that Danish politics would follow for the next two generations. That was due not to his political efforts, however, but to the fact that he was at the same time the skald and folk-teacher who knew how to plant liberty in the nation's affections,

the only place where it could so take root as to grow and with-
stand time's stormy blasts. For him, popular education and political freedom were only two sides of the same thing.

That his fight for freedom had been in earnest he had occasion to demonstrate in his extreme old age. In 1857 he had closed
his Rigsdag career, but after the defeat of 1864, when reaction
had the wind in its sails and a revision of the constitution in a
reactionary direction was preparing, the 82-year-old joined in the
fight. He was elected to the Upper House and spoke with
great energy against "privilege, money-bags and arithmetic," and
prophesied that the new motion would bring a sad future to king
and people. When the act was nonetheless passed by the parliament, Grundtvig together with Tscherning sought access to the
king to entreat him to use his power of veto. They were not received, however, and things took their course, but "the old man
at Vartov" could console himself that he had done what lay in
his power to avert calamity.

To Grundtvig the fight was a popular cause and therefore
national as well. And in the development of the national movement his contribution acquired unique significance. During the
1840's he had already written a number of patriotic songs, and
the wars of 1848-50 and 1864 gave his genius air under its wings.
In the years after 1848 he published the periodical *Danskeren
(The Dane)*, virtually written by himself. This was one of the
most valuable items in the whole national effort. The very motive
force of the effort was his firm faith in Denmark's future, a faith
which no defeat or calamity could subdue. Amid "the winter's
darkness" he continued undismayed "to preach Denmark's success" and thus contributed toward creating in the people that
tough energy which weathered the hard times. In a later connection we shall return to this side of Grundtvig's work, the side
which in a certain sense may be said to sum up all the rest.

Just as his practical national activities continued into extreme
old age, so with his literary work. A number of important
writings date from the 1850's and 1860's. For the periodical
Kirkelig Samler (Churchly Collector), he wrote during the years
1855-1862 a series of related articles which appeared in book form
in 1868 as *The Christian Catechism*. Here for the last time he

sought to explain his ecclesiastical view in its entirety. One of the foremost Grundtvig experts has finely said of this book: Here we see before us an elder in the congregation seeking to enlighten his Christian friends concerning life's deep and simple truths with a fatherly love like that of the old apostle John at Ephesus. His discourse has changed from an illumination of life to a testimony out of the life which speaker and listeners know from common experience but which the old preceptor desires to make yet clearer to his friends before being taken from them. Nothing new is here arrived at, but for the purpose of familiarizing oneself with Grundtvig's conception of Christianity the *Catechism* is a principal source.

Grundtvig had long contemplated following up his *World History* with a church-history. In his early youth it had struck him that the seven letters to churches in the Revelation of St. John contained a survey of the future history of the church and described the principal churches yet to be, and that the sixth, that at Philadelphia, was the Scandinavian. On the basis of this "view," he now wrote *Christianity's Pleiads: A Churchly Saga-Song*. The value of the view itself may be seriously doubted; considered as sober history it scarcely has greater interest; but the importance of the work, as Grundtvig himself saw, did not stand or fall thereby. The essential thing about his concept of church history is "that the Christian life is throughout regarded as a spiritual folk-life that has stood in living reciprocal relationship to the distinctive development and mother tongue of all the leading peoples to whom the Christian life has revealed itself in Christian confession, preaching and songs of praise, and that this reciprocal influence is both the basis of the Christian people's strangely complicated career and the master-key to all the so-called Christian state churches with all their confusion." During the years 1860-1863 he sought to further clarify this view of church history in a series of addresses at his home, chiefly for theological candidates and students. As late as 1871 these lectures were published as *The Church-Mirror, or a Survey of the Christian Congregation's Life-Course*—a worthy close to his long career as a writer.

Only his purely personal affairs remain to be mentioned. His

marriage to Lise Blicher had in the main been happy. Bravely
had she weathered with him the evil days. She had borne him
two sons and one daughter. By temperament, however, she was
too mild and "womanly" to quite keep up with him. Moreover
she became more and more moody with the years and the two
seemed to drift farther and farther apart. When she died, in January 1851, death came if anything as a release. By October of
that year, Grundtvig had already married again, the widow Marie
Toft of Ronnebaeksholm manor whose acquaintance he had
made some years before. She was, as he himself expressed it in
his obituary, "a strong, magnanimous and democratic noble-
woman," and in his life with her he found all that he had hitherto
lacked, a strong and independent personality who could fully
share his life with him. Together they experienced a short but
exceedingly happy marriage. Although nearly 70, Grundtvig
found youth again. But his happiness was to be of but brief dura-
tion. On May 15, 1854, Fru Marie bore him a son, and barely
two months later she died. He himself now expected to follow
her soon. He felt his powers waning, but the life-force flared up
anew, and in his extreme old age he had the good fortune to meet
a woman, the widow Asta Reedtz, who was willing to share his
last years with him. They were married in the spring of 1858,
and she cared for him faithfully until his death. On Sunday,
September 1, 1872, he stood for the last time in the pulpit at
Vartov. The next day he quietly fell asleep, with no death agony,
as he sat in his arm-chair.

✸   ✸   ✸

The foregoing chapters have given a biographical sketch of
Grundtvig; we have sought to follow his life's remarkably crooked
course, we have followed his restless activity of nearly three generations with lips and pen, we have tried to throw light on his
inner psychic development. The problem was difficult, and has
yielded only most imperfectly to solution—though it is hoped that
the reader has managed to get some impression of the amazingly
rich and vigorous segment of human life that lay concealed
behind the name of Grundtvig. The longer one occupies oneself

with this man, the more one feels oneself drawn, the more strongly does one sense the element of mystery which pervades all human life, but which stands out so much more strikingly in connection with a personality of such gigantic stature and of so special a character. Historians and men of letters, psychiatrists and theologians, have each made their contribution, and still one is often tempted to doubt whether research ever gets at the real power in this remarkable human life.

In view of so well-grounded a scepticism, it is worth while to remember that in the last analysis it is not the man and what he experienced that have value for us. His experiences Grundtvig has irrevocably carried with him to the grave, and we can never re-experience them. Let his personal stature be never so gigantic, let his abilities be never so great, his mental life never so interesting, it is still not for these that he continues to live today and shall continue as long as there exists a Danish people. No, the vital things are the visions he saw and the account he gave. Because he was clear-sighted and sharp-eared as Heimdal himself, and because he lived his life with a unique frankness and intensity, he sailed several degrees closer to the reality which is common to us all than we other mortals do. He got out to life's boundaries, and there beheld the last things, and what he saw he was able to bring alive in the word, in revelation. It is the revelation that is the truth—if he has seen aright, if he is not a false prophet—it is the visions and the revelation that live; the man himself is dead beyond recall. For this reason we cannot stop at the biographical. That is only a means toward grasping and making one's own the mighty message that this man managed to convey. A book on Grundtvig can therefore not leave off at this point. It must make an effort to clarify the understanding of human life and its conditions that the seer and skald attained to, must hearken to the account of reality that he brought out of his tremendous experiences—whether they were inside the bounds of normal mental life, or outside, does not matter—for he preached as he did in order to confront us with life's own reality—not with the mental life of Grundtvig.

VII

The Human and the National

A Dane Grundtvig was before all else. Born on Seeland, growing up in Jutland, sprung of ancient burgher and priestly stock, early familiar with the common people's speech and way of thinking, his roots deep down in his country's history and literature, he was surely equipped as no one else for summing up and expressing all that is Danish. A shrewd literary critic once said of Grundtvig's work that it constituted not the clearest, perhaps, but the mightiest expression of the battle of the Danish people and the Danish genius for self-consciousness. In his often diffuse chatter, pointed up at intervals by a pithy saying concise as an epigraph, in his mingling of graceful lyric and rattling bombast, in his at once childishly simple and darkly enigmatic speech, coupled with a particular type of humor, he summed up widely diversified aspects of the Danish folk-mind. Take his gift for coining expressions that have the proverbial quality, and which for generations have been able to hold their own on the people's lips as witticisms, until they have become common property. It is a good test of whether a writer has hit his people's tone and temper when his words can thus be apprehended and remembered by all, from the simplest to the wisest, from the man in the street to the cultivated litterateur. But it is not alone in sayings of this sort that Grundtvig's words become the natural expression of what we feel and think. In the great national gatherings that have particularly marked the past few years, we have again and again returned to "Mother's Name is a Heavenly Sound," a song in praise of the Danish language, with the refrain:

> Sweet in joy and sweet in need,
> Sweet in life and sweet in death,
> Sweet in after-fame.

And none of the Danish patriotic songs can rival in power "Our Native Land":

> High above the sun,
> On his royal throne,
> Though the skies burst,
> Sitteth loving and firm
> He who has watched over Denmark so long,
> Still his bow has strings that twang,
> And his bow will never recoil,
> True as gold is the Ancient of Days.

Least of all could Grundtvig be spared in the chancel. There is no one whose hymns are found in such numbers in the hymn-book or are sung so often, whether at the regular Sunday services or at the solemn rites of infant baptism, marriage and burial. Whatever one may think of the song's content, it is not to be denied that Grundtvig has been able to sing so plainly and so Danishly that his song has become common property and a firm link in the nation's total life.

This did not happen by accident. Almost no other author has so consciously striven—even to the point of sometimes being both tiresome and irritating—to be Danish in all life's connections, "ultra-Danish" as he liked to call it. This has sometimes caused him to be accused of "nationalism" in the bad sense, of over-rating, yes, of actually deifying what is Danish at the expense of everything foreign. Often such an accusation may even appear well founded. For Grundtvig was a pronounced warrior type. He was always conscious of his own position as opposed to, nay, rather, as in open conflict with, some foreign one. His Danishness therefore took shape through constant polemic. In his youth, before the English journeys, his most violent stand was against English worldliness and utilitarianism. The English were truly a nation of shopkeepers, a people without soul or deed. Later on he took the field against "the Roman spirit," against the Italian or French enlightenment with its shallow rationalism, and against the whole un-national Latin culture. When the battle of nationality began in South Jutland, the hyper-nationalism of Germany and its genius for unrealistic rumination became the enemy.

This sharp polemic calls for proper understanding, however. Nothing was farther from Grundtvig's intention than to reject foreign culture entirely. He had himself learned too much both from Germany and England and from many other countries for that. "Birthright for Danish alone, but guest right for all on earth," says one of his many apophthegms. But it was through these violent sallies against the foreign that the distinctively Danish clarified itself for him—and this was the main thing. Let it first be firmly established that "the Scandinavian spirit is not a courtyard sprite to the imperial German reason but a lord in its own right, with many great achievements to its credit and more to come," and he will then be willing to admit that the German in and for himself is as good as the Dane. Of deifying the Danish or lauding it as the only thing worth while there was never any question. The Danish, as he himself said, had validity only in one little corner of the earth, and only in time, not for eternity. But he believed beyond question that in the little spot called Denmark, and for the people who lived there, only Danishness did have validity and vitality, and "idle is all foreign talk."

What then does Danishness mean, and why does it alone have validity and reality in Denmark? To answer this question it will be necessary to explore Grundtvig's process of thought somewhat further. "What is man? Whence is he sprung, what is his fate, whereto is he ordained?" These are the words that open an 1811 manuscript lecture that he considered giving on "Man's Condition." It was not by chance that he had chosen as the theme of his lecture this ancient question which has kept coming up ever since there were men on earth at all. The answering of this question, the solution of this riddle, constitute the grand objective of all human inquiry and meditation, of all knowledge. For Grundtvig it had been a live problem ever since his youth, but after Langeland he indignantly took up arms against that spiritless science which believed everything had only to be measured, weighed and computed and the end of the road would be reached. This was what he had attacked as "the Latin spirit," the "Roman" and "Gallic" enlightenment, or "German" reason, and now simply lumped together under the one word, "puerile-erudition." It was the knowingness about life that has since signalized itself as Positivism and Darwinism, as Marxism and Freudianism. Grundtvig was indignant with anyone who wanted to reduce man to some sort of machine, to a higher animal, or to a sterile rational being. He found it outrageous that these people should have no eye for life's overwhelming fertility and enigmatic abundance, for its mysterious depths. And with the same, indeed with perhaps even greater, wrath did he turn against the orthodox Lutheran theologians who on the basis of a rigid dogma concerning the Fall of Man maintained that no good at all was to be found in man, that he was sheer sin and depravity. It was on behalf of reality that Grundtvig here protested and demanded a hearing.

But what then was a man? All his life long, Grundtvig struggled with that question, and the answer he found is given its most explicit statement in the introduction to *Northern Mythology:* "Man is no ape, destined first to ape the other animals and then to ape himself until world's end, but is a matchless and marvellous creation, in whom divine powers are to reveal, unfold, and clarify themselves through a thousand generations as a divine experiment to demonstrate how spirit and matter may interpenetrate and be transfigured in a common divine consciousness." Man is a divine experiment! This means that life is not something we have given ourselves, which we ourselves are lords over, or can mold and remold at will. Nor is human life the same as the life we see in outside nature, in animals and plants. It is something more, something matchlessly, mysteriously beyond that. Man is "neither bird nor fish," but neither is he a performing ape that has merely put on clothes. No, he is spirit and clay, linked together by command of the Creator, neither more nor less. Hence life's mysteriousness. This is why it is too unwieldy and impenetrable for clarity to be made the point of departure for any discussion of it. The lucidly clear people whose wisdom may be learned by heart in an hour and even made plain to a clever hound, all the dogmatists who believe that life may be covered by some few theses, have no respect, any of them, for life's own mysterious abundance, as expressed in the words: Man is spirit and clay.

This is the understanding of human life that attains its

supreme expression when the Bible speaks of man as created in God's image. But the Bible's word is not needed in order to grasp it. It was Grundtvig's conviction that if every human being would be open and honest about his own life he would see that there is something mysterious—call it what you will—which lifts man above all creation. The word of Scripture coincides with the heart's own story. What he had experienced in his youth was not vanity, his visions had not been false—even though he had lived among shadows—when he discovered that he possessed a heart with longings and instincts which pointed out toward eternity. His visions had not been false when he grasped what it means to belong to a people, to be answerable for it, and to be torn by its fate. At that time he had learned from experience that the soul

> Has room in its low hut
> For longing deep as the ocean,
> For hope that even higher swings
> Than souls, or eagles on their wings.

Yes, any man who grasps at all what it means to live will also know something about spirit and clay.

What then is meant by this talk about spirit? Is spirit anything but a word used to cover an inner void? The question is well founded. For what spirit is can not be defined or determined, any more than anyone can say what life itself is. There is, moreover, a connection between the two things, since the human spirit is simply the life-force which dwells in man and which lifts him above the animals. What it is and whence it comes science can not explain, yet its effects are clear enough, namely the whole of human life, and it declares itself in speech. Spirit is the invisible life-force that reveals itself in the word, in human speech, something which even the most highly developed animal cannot grasp, much less produce:

> Dumb as horse and hound
> Live all the beasts in torpor,
> But earth's Creator gave to men
> Speech, that they might talk with him.

The word is the spirit's means of expression. It can link human beings together and transmit the spirit's power from one to another, can put one thing in the minds of all:

> If all the birds with beak and claw
> Were to lay their heads together,
> They still could not think up the smallest word
> Which belongs to the race of man.
>
> Human-spirit is a word
> Which none of us can fathom,
> Yet human life is still its work,
> And the words by man's lips spoken.
>
> Souls and bodies by the thousand
> Can the human spirit bind,
> Pierce them with words like lightning,
> Making all of a single mind.

Word and speech are the saved remnant of God's image: "Man is in God's image made, with living words on his tongue; among trees and beasts he can therefore, with the gods have speech and make song"—or, to quote a few verses more:

> What if I be a man, who like the flowers must die,
> And, sad to say, no doubt of death deserving:
> Human life on an isle in the ocean of time
> Is matchless still for fullness and for power.
>
> The word in the ear and the word in the mouth
> Far transcends what strikes our eye:
> Its mother dwells in the depths of the sea of sound,
> Its father is God's spirit from on high.
>
> Here is a bird without its match on earth,
> Laughs at every marksman and plays about his hand:
> With the winged word man can get
> Lightning from heaven and joy of life in his soul.

In another poem the thought stands out even more sharply:

The sound of the word upon our lips
Resembles in small our maker's voice,
Is still from that other world,
Utters power in the spirit's name;
Low and gentle, it on earth
Has more effect than a clap of thunder.

Still as in God's image made,
Figuratively we all can see.
Heaven's light can its luster spread
In parables of clay;
For through our words, though poor they be,
God's word can find its way.

Here Grundtvig was demanding a hearing for actuality, which spoke its own unmistakable language as to the greatness of human life. He refused to be duped by all the too clear and too clever chatter. Grant that "spirit" is a dark word. Its conduct in speech is an established fact; the word has might like no other. Its effects are obvious in the whole of human life as it is lived on earth. If any choose to deny this and to withdraw into the closed world of reason and enlightenment, where they can sit hemmed in by computation, doctrine, and dogma, there is no use arguing. Let them wait until some day their own world bursts in pieces before them, as had happened to Grundtvig himself on Langeland when through the meeting with Constance Leth "his spirit opened its eyes." Then will they discover that all their science and all their rumination leads only to the border. And when they understand that, they will also see that clarity cannot be the starting point or the pilgrim staff, but that it is the goal which beckons onward.

But what then? What course does this road to clarity take? It leads through listening to human speech and through watching human life, which are the spirit's work. From their effects shall causes be known. The road leads through history, which is not just one chance technique among many, but the crown of all knowledge, and directed toward a universal-historical view of existence. "The explanation of human life in all its natural and historical connections is the lofty goal which ennobles science and unites all alike, from mathematician to poet, from the word-gatherer to the idea-collector, and its objective must needs be a universal-historical view of life in all its fulness, even though man can never reach it. The edifice is like Aladdin's palace, which never got its last window put in. For this ultimate clarity is not attained bit by bit, but is realized only in the God who is father of light, and who yet dwells in darkness."

We have now reached the point of departure for Grundtvig's ideas on education, but before going into these more closely, something further still needs to be said about human life.

For Grundtvig, the human always exists only as something national. Humanity is not an abstract idea, something cosmopolitan, international, but always something tremendously concrete, namely, being human in a particular place and among a particular people with its own history and its own speech. Just as there exists no abstract human language in a general sense, but only a German, an English, a Danish language, and the like, even so does the human exist only as something national. It is flight from reality to skip the differences between French and German and Danish as though they were minor matters, as unrealistic as it would be to make light of the differences between man and woman. The cosmopolitan, the international, is always unrealistic. Whereas, if the national is given free rein, and every nation defends its own independence and liberty, the conditions for a fruitful reciprocity between nations are created, for a true reciprocity among nations each conscious of its own independence, not for a deadly levelling and smoothing off, where all gradually become one.

It is a certainty that any nation which forgets that they are *human beings* and that all their affairs should be conducted as *humanly* as possible, will in nowise become gods thereby but beasts or devils as the case may be, and in our own day a little of each. When I speak of the national as the supreme in every land, it is by no means as opposed to the human, but only as a mark of distinction from what *is purely national in other lands,* and only as opposed to whatever shall by force or guile render a people *alien to itself,* without, in the nature of things, being able to make of it either another people or pure, unadulterated human beings.

. . . Not since mankind was divided into many "peoples, races
and tongues" has there been any possibility whatsoever, humanly
speaking, of a mere human being, unless in the naked wilderness,
for elsewhere one finds only national human beings, be they
Hebrew, Greek, English or Danish. Therefore when some one
people, Egyptians or Chinese, Romans or Germans, declare themselves to be the only rightful human beings, after whom all other
nations must either pattern themselves or be regarded as dumb
creatures, toil like domestic animals or be hunted like wild ones,
mark you, it merely proves that the Egyptians or Chinese, Romans
or Germans, can themselves have very little humanity in them.

The word "nationality" itself is a key-word with Grundtvig.
For modern readers it is sure to cause some difficulty. He himself
put it into circulation, and to him it meant something quite different from the "popular," the intelligible to all; it had of itself
nothing to do with the "democratic," nor is it to be identified
with the "nationalistic." Nationality is closely related to folk-
spirit. Both words are an expression of the conviction that just
as human beings are more than food and clothes, so is a nation
more than "population, soil, and seacoast." In man there dwells
a living power which expresses itself in speech, and which fashions
human life—the human spirit. This is no less true of a people.
A people is not merely an assemblage of human beings living
in a particular area and bound together by social, economic and
political ties. A people is no mere "sociological phenomenon."
It is that as well. But if you go no farther than that, you have still
not grasped the essential thing: that in a people there exists a
life-power—mysterious, like everything living—which permeates
the people from within, which has created its history and fashioned its life—the folk-spirit. This discloses itself in the mother-
tongue:

> The mother-tongue is the power's word,
> Which lives in the people's mouth.
>
> The mother-tongue is the rose-chain
> Which entwines both small and great,
> In it alone the fathers' spirit lives,
> And there alone the heart can beat.

> The mother-tongue is our heart's speech,
> Mere idleness is all foreign talk;
> It alone in mouth and book
> Can arouse a folk from torpor.

Only the human voice, the living word can arouse a man to recognition of life and its conditions, but this word is spoken not in a universal language, but in the mother-tongue, and though foreign speech may be comprehensible to us, it will forever remain artificial and lifeless. The mother-tongue and Denmark's saga were therefore the two pillars of the school for the nation which Grundtvig wished to build.

Nationality ties the human to earth and time. That man is a linking together of spirit and clay does not mean solely that he is spirit, but just as much that he is clay, which is earth-bound. Man is not an eternal, timeless soul that can get along as well or as ill in one place as in another. By his discovery of the national, Grundtvig became one of the few who have freed themselves from the individualism, the "spiritizing" of man, which has ridden Europe like a nightmare ever since the Renaissance, and which is perhaps in the last analysis a heritage from Hellenism. Human life has again become a well-rounded whole, not merely a psychic phenomenon. Man is not an "ego" but a link in a great national continuity whereby he is joined not to timeless eternal ideas but to a particular concrete history. And body is included as well as soul. Therefore the national means something far more than a sense of history and poetry; it means temporal competence along the broadest front for deeds of might, and it means initiative. After the middle of the past century it came to mean reclaiming the heath, marling the earth, draining the marshes, the cooperative movement, the agricultural school, and much else of a similar nature.

This temporal turn taken by a "spiritual" movement has frequently been regarded as a nonessential by-product, yes, sometimes as simply "off the track." And quite unjustly. All this was part of "what the noble call life's joy." It was the result of a human awakening to the understanding of life and its powers, it was one unit in the battle against death in all its forms. It was

this that made Grundtvigianism a broad practical national movement. Grant that as a result it often spread itself thin, grant that
much initiative had a worldly motive at bottom, the pursuit of
money or power—essentially it was still something else: it was a
manifestation of faith in the nation's vital power and its future,
of belief that the splendid past to which history bore witness
could once more become reality, of belief that not alone in the
oldtime heroic era was the Danish folk-spirit capable of performing deed and exploit, but that the very same thing was destined
to occur in our own day, even though the deeds would now
assume new forms. It was an extension of Grundtvig's own
shining faith in Denmark and its fortunes, of the belief which he
himself and his friends had preserved through the years of dis-
aster. In this belief did the Grundtvigian generation of Danish
peasants and small farmers carry out the program set forth in
the words: "Let outward loss be inward gain."

Meanwhile, from all of the foregoing, one very important
consequence ensues: if it be true that man is a union of spirit
and clay, that there exists something which is termed the human
spirit; if it be true that in like manner there exists in a nation a
spiritual power, then life, whether individual or national, can
only be lived in freedom. For freedom is the spirit's natural element, and without it the spirit stifles. As applied to Christian
faith, Grundtvig had seen this very early. This was why he had
campaigned for the godly congregations' freedom back in the
1820's:

> Compulsory belief is random talk,
> Shrewd is the heart in self-defense,
> Compulsory shamming, like the Roman yoke,
> Compels but unto lies and sin;
> Only to hell can one be driven,
> To heaven one must be rung,
> The spirit of truth follows freedom.

This was why he waged constant war against all compulsion
within the stiff state church. Little by little it dawned on him,
however, and here his English visits meant a big step forward,
that what was true within the church held good for national life

as well, for here, too, spirit was involved. In his rough draft for the first of the free lectures at Borch's College in 1838, we read: "Freedom on both sides (i.e., on listeners' and on speaker's) is the basic requirement; but this holds good not only at this one point, but in the whole realm of spirit, since freedom is the spirit's element, whereby its living reality stands or falls, has its beginning and end." Compulsion always costs money, yes, much more than money, whereas freedom costs nothing but yields ineffable returns by creating an inner contentment and joy and a stir of life in all directions."

> Only in drawing freedom's breath
> Do we feel bold and glad and light,
> Able to live and to suffer.

With a never failing enthusiasm he now professed freedom in all its forms. Freedom of belief and thought was the main thing:

> Scot-free shall be
> Among heroes here in the North
> Thoughts and words alike,
> However deep they may cut.

But next came freedom of education and association, freedom of press and print, nor did he shrink from bringing the principle to bear upon civic and social life. He demanded freedom of commerce and trade, abolition of the old guilds, and so on. It was this uncompromising consistency of his in arguing the cause of freedom which gave him his independent front in Danish politics, and made the old ladies' pastor parliament's most radical member.

Now there can be no doubt that as a liberal politician Grundtvig was a child of his time. Not in vain did he live during the decades when liberalism broke out all over Europe, and his own demand for freedom must be viewed in connection with the general ideas of the time. But in making this statement one must add that basically Grundtvig's freedom derived from a source other than that of the Liberals'. With the latter, the demand grew out of a belief in man as a world-citizen with eternal rights, out of a belief in the principial likeness of all human beings.

Liberalism was a child of the 18th century's Enlightenment. But not Grundtvig's liberalism. He carried his zeal for freedom so far as to set his face against every tyrant, "whether he goes by the name of Napoleon or the Equality-principle." To freedom even equality must yield. Another curious fact is that Grundtvig's ideas on freedom had been fully worked out long before his political affiliation with the Liberals, while he was still by personal conviction an out and out old-autocracy man. This is plain from his great and oft-quoted "freedom manifesto," the epistle-in-rhyme which prefaces *Northern Mythology,* 1832. Here the demands for freedom do not stem from Liberalism's concept of human rights or from a belief in human equality, no, they are based on one particular concept of human life and the laws which govern it, namely that life is ultimately a question of spirit, and that it must therefore be permitted to develop through strife, since battle is the spirit's present form of manifestation. Without freedom the new world will be no more than a grave, but if free competition is permitted to the powers, then the world will be a blooming, billowing field, with castles and sky-high mountains, then it will rise above

> what hands can reach,
> And even what eagles high aloft can see,
> Will awaken, like the Ases' domain in the North,
> Awe profound for the living word.
>
> Free be Loki as Bragi and Thor,
> Giants but prison the winged word,
> War-gods all, when stung by a jest,
> Are roused from torpor to glorious strife!
> Freedom for all that derives from spirit,
> Which is not altered, but irked, by bonds.

In the spirit's world it is the word, not force, which holds sway. Command and compulsion are useless for waging war against non-spirit.

This was Grundtvig's view and it naturally led him to co-operate with the "National-liberals." But he never got to the point of feeling at home among them. His understanding of the national was too different from theirs for that. National-liberalism's best men all belonged to the cultured upper class and they did not forget it. Their position was one of condescension to the people in order to act as its guides and counsellors, if not its guardians. At heart they were quite un-national. In Grundtvig there resided an instinctive realization that the best guides and counsellors, yes, even the best rule and the wisest laws can accomplish nothing unless they succeed in arousing the nation to living deeds. He believed in the nation and its vitality—that was the form the national took for him. The popular and the national were only two sides of the same thing—both presupposed a particular understanding of human life and its conditions.

The circle is now complete: we have got back to the Danishness with which we began this chapter. Let us hope that the intervening pages have answered the question we set ourselves, namely: What did Danishness mean to Grundtvig? Properly understood, the national never leads to that nationalism which sees as its main task the digging of trenches and the setting of barriers between peoples. During the past 150 years, even here in Denmark, there has been more than enough of that form of national sentiment which is out to find something or other that will somehow enable one's own people to rise superior to, and feel itself better than, other peoples. The national, as distinct from the nationalistic, always ends in the inter-popular, not in the international, the cosmopolitan, which is a form of unrealism, where all cats are gray and alike. The national brings us to frontiers where we meet the rest, whether they be called Poles, Germans, or Jews, and meet them not as enemies but as fellow creatures, subject to the same conditions and the same requirements as ourselves. A person who has understood what national life is in his own land will approach other nationalities with a deference for life and reality.

There are still two things to be added.

First, Denmark and the Danish never stand alone for Grundtvig, but always as one branch of the Scandinavian. We in the North have in common not only blood and birth, but even our folk-spirit. Therefore, while it may be important for little Denmark to seek right relationship with the great outside powers of Europe, with Germany and England, still, in order to succeed,

Denmark must first of all take cognizance of her own nature, and of this the Scandinavian is a part: "If we are not to get more harm than good from an acquaintance with foreign languages, literatures, and institutions, then we must first of all know and appreciate our own, which we shall then not lose through association with foreign ones, but profit by, and improve or enhance. In this connection it is of the utmost importance that, while not regarding our own as *less* than it really it, we still recall that *Danish* and *Swedish* and *Norwegian* are just as much parts of a *Scandinavian* whole as Saxon and Frankish and Swabian are parts of the German, or English and Scotch part of the British. . . . In the matter of speech, literature and natural thought-processes, our North is by nature just as closely, and perhaps more closely, united, and I may add that although our North is far out-numbered corporeally by Great Britain, to say nothing of boundless Germany, the Northern spirit is still a match for any of the other so-called folk-spirits one might care to name."

Not in vain had Grundtvig from his earliest youth felt an attachment for Norway, and not in vain had he lived in Northern antiquity, where the entire Northern people formed a whole in a quite different sense than now. It had made him believe in community between the Scandinavian lands. Though the prospect might often seem dark, and confederation remote, still to be of the same spirit and stock does more to unite than all else can do to divide. Therefore, with an inner consistency, his ideas on education were likewise extended to include the whole North.

So much for the first thing. The second may perhaps be more difficult to make clear. Even a person who has grasped what the Danish and the national mean in Grundtvig's view of human life will time after time when reading the skald's own works be appalled and astonished at his eulogies of Denmark and the Danish people and his confidence regarding the country's future. The Danes are "love's-lineage," marked by freedom and truth and justice. He is convinced that Denmark not only holds an important place in world history, but in God's vast world-plans as well. He is therefore sure that "the Ancient of Days" will never abandon Denmark's cause. He is convinced that the divine experiment of uniting spirit and clay that the Danish people is will be carried by God to completion. And one could go on citing passages which appear to show a quite unwarranted idolization of all that is Danish.

The explanation of this is a quite simple one, namely that he has been so bewitched by the Danish spirit that whenever he meets Danishness, whether in nature or history or speech, he sees mighty visions which so overwhelm him that his eyes brim with tears, and his tongue must sing, must praise and extol. Had any-one argued with him about his visions and challenged their veracity, he might have beaten some such retreat as: well, suppose my visions are preposterous, suppose that my eulogizing of Dan-ishness for its love, righteousness and goodness has no basis in reality, suppose that all my expectations for the future are put to shame, the fact will still remain that the Danish, however poor and lowly it may be, is better suited to Denmark than the Latin or French or German or any other great thing in the outside world that you may name. But although this admission might have been wrung from him, the very next day he would have been seized anew by his visions, and must sing again, must con-tinue to prophesy Denmark's happiness, even in the middle of the hardest winter. And so it continued to be with him even into extreme old age. His love only deepened with the years; and in this connection let me quote just one more poem, where he celebrates Denmark under the image of a mermaid:

> Beautiful mermaid
> From Oresund's deep,
> Dancing on a hillock
> And reaching for the sky,
> What oft I have sworn to,
> Now I have seen,
> I praised you far too little.

> You met in the field
> A gray-haired skald,
> And him, for his song,
> You kissed straight on the mouth,
> Caused roses red
> On his cheeks to glow
> And kindled anew his lightning-glance.

You have brought back the blue
To the graying sky,
You have far surpassed
Your praise and your fame,
So an age or two longer
I now must sing
To rightly praise you wholly.

Deathless you swim
Among the islands,
While love still surges,
The heart cannot die,
And you keep ever young
The bird that sings,
By Oresund's shore, love's praises.

The bird was himself, kept ever young by singing Denmark's praises until as a nonogenarian he took leave of his earthly fatherland.

VIII
The School

One of the fairest fruits of the Enlightenment had been its lively interest in schools and education. Here it left its enduring mark. Generation after generation built pedagogically upon the theories advanced by Rousseau and Pestalozzi. Nor did Romanticism here constitute a break. We need only recall Herder's humanism or Fichte's resolute demands for popular education. And as in outside Europe, so in Denmark. Grundtvig grew up at a time when the school question was constantly on the agenda. In the 1790's the first normal schools were established, and Copenhagen had its first vocational high schools. In 1809 came a statute designed to reform the whole grammar school system, and in 1814 followed the great Education Acts, which introduced universal compulsory education for children of from 7 to 14 years and transformed the whole common school system. And here Grundtvig was eminently a child of his time.

While still quite young we find him taking a lively interest in education. He tried hard to get a teacher for Eskildstrup, and he dreamed of someday himself "going all out for peasant education." Practical opportunities to thresh out educational problems came to him first as tutor on Langeland, where he settled to his task with real enthusiasm, and later as schoolmaster in Copenhagen. When he got the appointment at Præsto, the preparation of the young for confirmation was again one of the duties he took most seriously. Later on, when he had children of his own, such problems entered his life even more closely. Here, as elsewhere, his ideas clarified themselves through sharp opposition to existing conditions. As time went on, he became more and more convinced of the inadequacy of contemporary school-training, with its spiritless cramming and memorizing, with its faulty understanding of child nature.

It is obvious that he had picked up points from the new pedagogy, both from Rousseau and Pestalozzi and from many others, Fichte in particular. On the basis of his own childhood experiences he wished, like Rousseau, to make the home education's real hearth. From modern pedagogy he also picked up the demand that everything be allowed to follow "the order of nature," that teaching be adapted to the child's capacity. In consequence, he found the prevailing system of elementary education altogether ruinous; it made "the roses wither on a child's cheeks." "Spirit-destroying is any considerable brain-fag for the human being in childhood, before the brain with the rest of the body has attained proper development, and before life, inner as well as outer, has become so far familiar to us that we may recover it in the describing and feel a natural desire to be enlightened about its conditions. Therefore by seeking to implant the order and calm of age, its discretion and prudence, in children, we only innoculate them with the deadly infirmity of age in both soul and body; in many of them we destroy the life-force entirely, so that as half-grown boys they waste away like shadows, and in them all we are working to break down human nature by defying its laws." Childhood is "fantasy-time," and education should therefore not be aimed at reason and emotion, which are as yet undeveloped, but should through image, myth, and story make life graphic. Grundtvig is also at one with his time in his firm belief in "enlightenment," though he put a far deeper meaning into the word. The whole opposition to the "black school," to unpractical, dead learning, likewise belonged to the time, and no one had insisted more emphatically than Rousseau and Pestalozzi that the object of education was not communication of knowledge but the development of human nature: to make the young responsive to life and bring them into a concrete relationship with the practical phenomena of existence—all material which passed directly over into Grundtvig's educational theories. No doubt even his dream of large-scale popular education by way of an introduction to history likewise drew upon both Herder and Fichte.

But when all this has been said, one has still not reached the heart of the matter at all. In its essence, Grundtvig's educational view is something quite other than an echo of the period's many fruitful pedagogical ideas. It springs straight from his own hard-won view of human life and its conditions. This at once appears in his very use of the word "school." In his mouth its range is far wider than usual. It includes not only the elementary school, the high school and the university, but also poetry, art and science, everything that contributes toward throwing light upon human life. The school's task may be defined quite briefly, in a single word, namely enlightenment. Here Grundtvig has gone straight to the 18th century and has recaptured its optimism, its glad and happy confidence in earthly existence. In this there was no attempt to run away from life's naked reality and console oneself with a bloodless world of dreams. The enlightenment which was the task of the school was not an enlightenment of everything possible and anything whatsoever. It had little in common with what the 18th century called by the same name. It was an enlightenment of human life, and worked out quite differently according to whether one lived in the old-fashioned penetrable and wieldy world where all may be measured and computed, or whether one has had his spiritual eyes opened to see that man is a divine experiment, a union of spirit and clay. Enlightenment's object was not knowledge and dead learning, but an awakening. Its only aim was to place men face to face with that reality of life which is richer and more mysterious than all our ingenious speculations.

That the real enlightenment brought awakening and new vitality was Grundtvig's firm conviction: "What sunshine is to the black mould, true enlightenment is to the mould's kinsman." As the sunshine calls the green shoots out of the earth, so did true enlightenment have power to awaken man to a realization of himself, his circumstances and his destiny. This enlightenment had nothing of the pretentious and academic about it; it did away with the gap between lay and learned, since it went straight to the center of everyday life:

> Is light for the learned only
> To spell out, right or wrong?
> Nay, heaven is good to more,

And light is heaven's gift,
And the sun with the farmer rises,
Not with the learned at all,
Best lights from top to toe,
Him who is most on the move.

Enlightenment shall be our joy,
If by rush-light only,
But first and last by the people's voice
Enlightenment of life;
This springs from a nation's deeds
And grows as it is cradled,
Shine it shall in our folk-wit
Till the evening star be quenched.

The school's task was the same with respect to all men: to give enlightenment as to the human, that is to say, make them realize man's nature as spirit and clay, and not in the form of a dogma which all can parrot, since life itself is not captured in dead formulas, but so that the spark is kindled. This was not done by means of dead books, but only through the living word. The essence of schooling was therefore not book-learning but free talk. Grundtvig had learned what the living word meant from Steffens, the man who could "teach school" like no one else in the North, a school for life.

Lightning's son, who before my eyes,
In the early morning dawn,
Like an angel from on high
Rolled away the stone anew!

says the memorial ode on Steffens's death (1845), and then goes on to describe Steffens's deeds in words that just fit Grundtvig himself and what was to him the school's business:

Yes, the free, the powerful talk
About what the hand cannot grasp,
But which yet can make its way
From valleys deep to the stars,
[*The word* which is by the spirit spoken,
  Which makes lightning whence a voice is heard,
Awakened, Steffens, here with thee.

Be it known that you have lived
As few upon this earth,
Lived most where least is written,
Lived *royally* in the North;
Said a word which shall not be forgotten,
Waked a spirit whose power will be felt
While we have a mother-tongue.

As is readily seen, this whole theory of enlightenment and of the word as its medium had the closest consistency with Grundtvig's whole view of human life, and this is a point of such importance that it hardly seems beyond reason to quote one more passage which likewise has reference to Steffens's work:

Now imagine, if you can, suddenly without call or notice Steffens turning up in the middle of the capital and taking the chair like fire and flame, a German philosopher and æsthete of the newest school, far more poetical than any poet one knew, playing with lightning like a youthful Zeus, and by some strange providence a thousand times mightier with our mother tongue than those who had never crossed the Elbe . . . that there really exists something that must be called enthusiasm, not facetiously but in all seriousness, yes, that in the human breast there may slumber a higher vitality which, when it bursts forth in a word-stream to correspond, and we do not obstinately stop our ears, carries us with it until it stops—of this I am livingly convinced; and . . . this winged word. . . . I learned to know and admire, to love and to wish for, and by it I was converted to belief in the life-power in the invisible, in spirit and the world of spirit as something absolutely real, and as a far higher and more powerful reality than what our eyes behold. . . . Its effect resides not in the immediate approval that a train of thought calls forth, but in the depth and firmness of the faith it always wakens in the world of spirit. . . . There you have the key to the man-riddle in every nation and every age, in the whole race as in the individual: a spiritually living, spoken word in the mother-tongue, that is the secret revealed through world-history, the secret which every man must believe if life is to be intelligible to him, which every nation must believe if it is to be powerful and happy, and which the race must continue to believe if it is ever to attain its goal and see its career glorified.

The school's weapons were not Latin or foreign languages, not books and pen and ink, but only the winged word, which is capable of awakening a man as well as a nation from torpor. So had Grundtvig himself taught school at Borch's Collegium in 1838, and so did he wish to have the word spoken in the high school he was striving to create. This of course did not mean that books should wholly be banned. For in books may be hidden magnificent vestiges of spiritual life, and books may contain valuable information, but awaken can they never, since they themselves are dead: "Consequently when I speak of the spirit's work and transmission what I mean by spirit is: the manifestation of power from a higher level in life, the temporal and tangible, and I therefore make sharp distinction between vestige of spirit or sign thereof and its living expression when I assert of the latter that the only way under the sun in which this higher view of the world and life can livingly express, transmit, and communicate itself is the spoken word as heard."

But what then was the substance of the enlightenment which the school was to give? Here Grundtvig is plainly a realist and empiricist. No more of life is grasped than has been experienced, and this applies to the individual as to the race. Therefore enlightenment must come "in the order of nature," must be adapted to each age, but it also follows that history, mankind's great experience and adventure, is the pillar of all enlightenment: "Understanding comes but gradually, from experience, and therefore only by observing the human race's career and one's own may one gain understanding of human life, so that the speculation which refuses to be life's son and pupil is obviously but a changeling." "Only in history do we find man complete as he has so far been revealed; only in history does man manifest his actuality and true form, which there will not let itself be hidden from posterity." In history one encounters existence both in its marvellous sublimity and in its limitless debasement, and it is with this existence that the school, if it achieved its object at all, would place men face to face.

The school must therefore be "historico-poetic." This "historico-poetic" is fundamental, but it is a term which has all too often been misunderstood. It has little connection with what in

everyday speech we call "poetic." The Heimdal myth is for
Grundtvig the symbol of historico-poetic speech. Of Heimdal it
is narrated that "he fixed his dwelling as high as possible on Sky-
mountain, and was so far-sighted (poetic) that he could see a
hundred miles ahead of him, and so sharp-eared (historic) that
he could 'hear the grass grow,' and so strong-voiced as well
that through his Gjallerhorn or speaking-trumpet (platform
eloquence) he could be heard for a distance of a hundred miles."
Opposed to this was the prevailing view of history, for which
history remains an accumulation of facts and figures, trends and
movements, merely a sort of harder arithmetic, and which entirely fails to grasp that history is human life's revelation. To
understand, one must oneself be spiritual, must have the ability
to see far and to listen to history's speech. In the "school for life"
the road leads to all in past or present who have spoken truly and
genuinely of man and his real nature, whether they be poets or
philosophers, religious prophets or social reformers. The road
leads to all who with poetic clarity have seen visions and who
with historical acumen have been able to interpret them and thus
throw light on human life. Primarily, however, for Grundtvig
himself and for the first brood of high school people, the road
came to lead to the myths, the Scandinavian myths, which reveal
what the Northern folk-spirit and its power are.

The school's task was awakening, to awaken to an understanding that man is spirit and belongs to a people, to place him
face to face with reality—nothing more. The school must not
declare any particular view, must not preach, must not even
preach Christianity. Its task is not to make Christians of the
young. It could not. Only the Holy Spirit in the church can do
that, and the school should not be a church any more than the
church should be a school. No, its task was to make them men.
There must therefore be freedom in the school, freedom for all
persons and for all views. This does not mean, however, that
Grundtvig's educational view was what modern terminology calls
neutral, without postulates. Nothing lay farther from him than the
modern tolerance which is rooted in a fear of special prejudices.
No, his view of the school was closely tied in with the view he
had adopted as to human life. But he had the courage to let it

stand alone, on its own legs, without props or protection. If his view was true, it would prove itself so by being victorious, by winning all who had truth in them—and others did not interest him.

Grundtvig's own understanding of human life was as "creation, the fall, and salvation"; that this was the truth about man, he never doubted, but for precisely that reason, because his view had sprung from reality itself, the problem was only to place men face to face with reality, with life in all its exciting abundance and its dire calamity, in its marvellous sublimity and its terrifying horror, and then let them live life for themselves. If men understood something of this, they would also understand the talk about man as a divine experiment; yes, and not that alone; they could not escape the realization that there was something called a Fall. Thus far did the human bring us. Grundtvig could therefore even teach school in company with the Romanticists and Schelling. Though not with that dead worship of reason which shut itself off from actual life. The Naturalists knew something about man being spiritual; they knew also that there had early befallen him "a great misfortune which had put the earthly in him out of joint with the heavenly, time out of harmony with eternity." Though the Naturalists would hardly use the expression Fall of Man, we could term it "an error" ourselves; this would not affect matters greatly.

The disagreement between Grundtvig and Naturalism only assumed serious proportions when it came to the question of how to repair the damage. For here all Romanticists believed that the life-urge when awakened was itself capable of reaching out through strife and deed toward wholeness, happiness, and fulness. "Christians, on the contrary, believe that human nature has through the Fall become so depraved that all cure is fundamentally impossible, but they deem baptism a bath of regeneration, wherein the believer is spiritually transformed and reborn to a life with Christ." But this is no school-matter. It belongs to the church, and in the church the Naturalists and the Christians have no community. School on the other hand they might well teach together, since they are agreed as to the problem being to awaken man to a realization of his own spiritual nature. Grundtvig was therefore quite right in saying that Steffens was father to the school for life he wished to create.

The school should not be a church, but on the other hand Grundtvig never doubted that a living school would act as a preparation for Christianity, as a church porch. This is what was expressed in the famous and disputed thesis: "Man first, then Christian." The school should awaken a man to the understanding of life, but if it succeeded in this, then he would some day also realize that life was not sufficient unto itself, he would learn that only Christ could save life from sin and death. That was how it had gone with Grundtvig himself. Through his encounter with Constance Leth and Romanticism he had been humanly awakened, but what happened then had had its sequel in 1810-1811: Man first, then Christian. Once the school had led to a recognition of life's conditions, then God's grace would not be far to seek:

> Let each upon this earth then strive
> True man to be,
> Open his ear to the word of truth
> And render God his glory!
> If Christianity be truth's way,
> And he is not a Christian today,
> He will be by tomorrow.

The school and human enlightenment were not of themselves enough. They opened upwards. Here lay a vital difference between Naturalism's school and Grundtvig's. With the former, all strands led mainly inward, to man's own soul and its powers. When Grundtvig taught school, they led outward and upward to Christ as savior and redeemer.

The school must be like a John the Baptist who prepares God's people: "If we consider the Hebraic and Israelitish nationality . . . we readily see that everything in Judea was so ordered as to maintain and strengthen nationality, and that when, notwithstanding, this had sunk into deadly torpor, it was miraculously re-awakened by John the Baptist before Christ's coming: for he turned 'the children's hearts unto the fathers, and the parents' hearts unto the children' to prepare the way of the Lord

and to give him a people made ready." But the school must do
no more than prepare the people. This idea is summarized by
Grundtvig in an article, *Nationality and Christianity:* "Now just
as it is only in the mother-tongue that word as to the unseen has
life and power for us, so does our living relation to the past and
future as a whole rest on the sense of our intimate connection
with our parents and with our descendants, so that it is as necessary in Denmark and everywhere else as in Judea that God's
word shall find a prepared people, that a national word in the
mother-tongue shall have first turned the children's hearts to
the fathers and the parents' to the children, so they feel that
death in all its forms is man's hereditary foe, and that He is the
only true savior who can and will give us the gift of eternal life."

Anyone will readily see that this whole educational view
turned not on child education but upon a school for adults. Mention has already been made of schooling for the youngest age-
group. Regarding "boys' schools" (for 12 to 18 year olds) Grundtvig never reached any settled position. The prevailing vocational
and Latin schools he considered thoroughly mistaken, in that
they aimed to give instruction about life to children who did not
as yet know what life was. "The only good boys'-school for civic
life I can conceive of is the house of a capable and enterprising
citizen, where boys may acquire both a liking for occupations
they will later pursue and a grasp of them, whereas all confine-
ment in scholastic houses of correction is simply their ruin for
active civic life: innoculation with effeminacy, sloth, shiftlessness,
bookworm habits, and all civic vices." This is, however, hardly
a developable practical directive. But Grundtvig's whole interest
centered around something else: a school for Danish civic and
national life. It was directed toward the real years of youth, after
eighteen, the time when men awaken as conscious independent
individuals and must find their place in life and in the community. It turned not upon technical training of one sort or
another—for that the means could always be found when need
arose—but upon an all-round "national knowledge and folk-
culture and folk-enlightenment," which was the "necessary giant-
stride that must be taken without delay, if disintegration is to be

forestalled, the national folk-life preserved, and if science and learning are to prosper." This would lead to a free and easy development of our powers, and at the present time when the people were again bestirring themselves and when there was talk of popular councils and popular rule, it was an absolute necessity. "So far as I can see, revolutions like death-agonies will convulse the new people's-world and dissolve both learned and lay society, unless they are forestalled by reforming the school-grave into a nursery-garden for life, so that it may have both leave to develop and light to see what will truly make for its temporal peace and comfort." The need of such a national school had long been felt, "for surely it was a sense of the unnaturalness and deadliness of prevailing Latin scholarship, inimical to everything practical and living, which, in its enthusiasm for the fads of Rousseau and Basedow, had, in the past century, produced this whole ferment in pedagogy," but this had so far led to no useful result, and unless such was reached the whole must end in barbarism. The mid-point of this national culture must be mother-tongue and native-land, but with a view to actual life and the demands of the moment.

It was with such thoughts in mind that Grundtvig cast his eye upon the baronial academy at Sorö, which seemed to him the ideal spot for founding a school for civic life, integrated about "the national character, the constitution and our native land." In this "School at Soer" (Sorö) his prime concern was with the liveliest and the most quick-witted, with those who would have seats in the popular council, attend the assembly as delegates, serve the state as officials. But although he was thinking only of a school for a quite small section of the people, his view at the same time extended to the whole population: "But now if a Danish high-school, as royal, free and national as possible, is necessary for the training of officials, why should it be any less so for the great share of the people, who do not wish to, or cannot possibly, become officials, but who must feed both themselves and them? That this nation's root and trunk, the tenants and free-holders both great and small, artisans of all kinds, seamen and traders, require no enlightenment and culture other than what they get behind the plough, in the work-shop, at the mast-head and in the goods shop, barbarians and tyrants may think, but neither with kings or people was this ever the Scandinavian way of thinking, and it could never become so, since it is true here as nowhere else that we are all of 'one blood,' so that the same aptitude for culture is found in huts and in high-ceiled halls. This indigenous quality, now properly found only in the Scandinavian kingdoms, where no invader has pushed in and made slaves of the old inhabitants, is something we cannot value enough since it is capable of giving our love of country a different depth and our national culture a different truth than would otherwise be possible. And had our on the whole deplorable educational history no other bright spot, one such spot it would still undeniably have in the fact that education from the time of the Reformation, and especially since 1660, has emancipated and so to say ennobled the boy from the humblest cottage so that he might share in the highest development and rise to the highest dignities."

Here emerges for the first time the idea of an actual high-school for the whole people, a school for practical life, built on experience. The school at Sorö never materialized, and perhaps this was just as well. Instead there grew up under other leadership a Danish folk-high-school inspired by Grundtvig's educational view, but for the rest without any fixed program. It was to adapt itself in each place to local conditions and specific needs. Just so long as it was everywhere a living school whose aim was not dead communication of knowledge but awakening and an increased zest for life. These schools must neither convey any set view of life nor give instruction in skills directly intended for use in practical life. To this end, cotters'-schools and trade-schools, agricultural schools and Latin schools might be established. But such schools could never replace the true high-school, no matter how much you tricked them out with liberal ideas and a dash of the national. The high-school assumes that the youths and girls who come there already have their occupation in life, and it only works toward enabling each one, in whatever field, to go back to the job with heightened zest, with a clearer view of human and civic relationships, especially in his own country, and with a livelier appreciation of that national fellowship which makes him a sharer in everything great and good that has so far been accomplished by the nation or that shall be hereafter.

Alongside the high-school for national and civic life, which has a mission for all, since we must all be enlightened, useful Danish citizens, there must, however, be other schools as well. Grundtvig himself mentioned the "church-school" and the grammar school. The former, whose purpose was to give enlightenment regarding the Christian life, will be discussed in a later connection. The necessity of the grammar school it never occurred to Grundtvig to deny. But he was very critical of our universities here in the North, which to him were merely poor imitations of the University of Paris. In their place he could imagine one great Scandinavian university—here emerges the idea of the school at Göteborg—"instead of the four Latin ones with which we are now afflicted." The point was that he did not regard a university as at all a suitable place to train pastors, jurists, and other functionaries, since it would have difficulty imparting "the patriotic education that should be every nation's own and as far as possible common to all, both learned and lay." No, even functionaries should have their training in the national high-school, supplemented by attendance at a special seminary where they would get the necessary technical training.

This training with a view to the practical life would naturally not give a complete grounding in the learned sciences. Nor should it. Yet both mathematics and the natural sciences, and, above all, the historical sciences are of such great importance to human life and to the civic community that it is extremely important to find out how a thorough and comprehensive scholarship may best be furthered. To Grundtvig it was axiomatic that the object of science was the enlightenment and explanation of human life on the basis of the accumulated experience of the human race. This effort at explanation was, however, certain to take a different turn with different peoples due to their special characteristics and conditions: "Just as every leading people on the whole expresses a leading tendency of human nature, so will each of them in process of time develop a set of scholars to correspond, men specifically distinguished for illuminating that side of human life of which their people had been the most vigorous expression." So too with the Scandinavian peoples, the triple race. "Nowhere has there existed a naturally deeper sense of the marvellous kinship between heaven and earth or a more heartfelt desire to see the whole great marvellous life of man gradually develop and explain itself." A Scandinavian Christian scholarship flits before Grundtvig's eyes, and to this end he wants the three Scandinavian countries to pool their powers. This could best be done through founding a scholars' high-school for the whole North, located at Göteborg. Here at least 300 Scandinavian scholars would live wholly for the cultivation of knowledge, exempt from the whole odious examination system, and, in living interaction far more than through book writing, advance the sciences, to the glory and benefit and joy of the whole human race.

This plan for a Scandinavian high-school at Göteborg—which Grundtvig well knew would be regarded as a pure air-castle—first presupposed that each of the Scandinavian countries had its separate high-school and its own seminaries for the training of functionaries. It thus rested on a realistic recognition of the three nations' differences in speech and natural conditions. These national peculiarities of theirs they should never give up. But it rested also on the presupposition that through all their differences they had something in common, namely the Northern spirit, which had lived and moved in the North from time immemorial and which made the Scandinavians jointly one of world-history's leading peoples. Such a university would be a marvellous means toward uniting the Scandinavian peoples and breaking down all prejudices.

Had he been asked what these 300 learned men were to do with their time when they had no examinations and no daily lectures and could certainly not write books for 24 hours a day, Grundtvig would have answered that in his youth at Valkendorf's College in a common life with other men like Hersleb and Sibbern, and later while in residence at Trinity College, Cambridge, he had seen for himself what a matchless feast could so be spread by a free high-school. And it would work out the same way with a Scandinavian high-school, "where neither old nor young were in compulsory residence or coupled off, but where everything highly attractive or stimulating to the spirit was in constant interaction, where lectures and disputations . . . had been superseded by decorous scholarly conversations mutually profitable to the younger and to those among the older who had ears to hear." The research, the life and conversations shared by older and younger persons at the high-school would produce a marvellous symposium. "If we now imagine the Latin schools out of the way, imagine all boys growing up as far as possible on their native soil and in God's free nature, in living interaction with the people, trained to some useful everyday occupation or other, so that even those who from childhood have seemed best fitted for brain work will also have learned to use their hands, and so that few or none would think of attending the scholars' high-school unless they had made their mark in the folk high-school, then we readily see that the professors—whom for brevity's sake we shall call residents of the high-school—will find that they themselves, spiritually speaking, get as much as they give by having the young people there."

Grundtvig's educational view was a closely integrated whole, intimately tied in with his views of human life and of the Christian life. Realization this view has never attained to. Perhaps too little thought had been given to its practical working out for that. But even as to detail very little has been accomplished. The free-school and the folk high-school have even in Denmark remained schools for only one section of the population, elementary and boys' schools have lived on in their old forms. The school at Sorö has never been created any more than the scholars' high-school at Göteborg. This is sad to be compelled to admit, but such is the actual state of affairs—whether one chooses to deplore it, or to think that it is all for the best. That Grundtvig's thoughts and words should in manifold ways have influenced practically every educator and type of school in the country is another matter. Each has taken what he could grasp and has sewed it like a new patch on the old garment. And it is not to be denied that by this method rich fruits have been produced—even though one may still have a feeling that these fruits are but a poor substitute for what might have been achieved.

Let me close these remarks on "the school" with a few lines from the rhymed epistle Grundtvig wrote in 1839, no doubt on the occasion of his two sons' confirmation:

A plain and cheerful, active life on earth
Like that, I would not for a king's exchange,
A clear-cut course in noble fathers' footsteps,
With equal dignity in cot and castle,
With eyes, as first created, heavenward turned,
Alert to beauty and greatness here below,
But with those deeper longings well acquainted
Which only eternity's splendor can satisfy;
Such a life as this have I wished for all my race,
And diligently pondered to prepare,
And when my soul was wearied by its musing,
It rested itself by praying our Lord's prayer.
Then did I feel the solace of truth's spirit,
Like happiness hovering over the planted garden,
When the dust lay there in its creator's hand
And everything was awaited in nature's order:
Only the fresh green shoots in early spring,
And wealth of blossoms in the summer warm;
Then ripeness would come to the plants
And gladden with its fruit when autumn came!

IX
Man First, Then Christian

If empty to us are the words and sound
Of "own people" and "land of our fathers,"
If we know not what more they mean
Than soil, seacoast, and population,
Then vain is every word we say
About God's kingdom's hills and dales,
God's people and congregation.

If we do not feel in our hearts,
We are sprung of heaven's race,
If we cannot feel with sorrow,
That we have become debased,
Then we only make mock of the word
That God will redeem us and give
Rebirth as his own children.

Thus boldly could Grundtvig speak of the sublimity and nobility of human life, thus forcibly could he emphasize the importance of the Danish and the national. "Man first, then Christian—this alone is life's order," and to respect this order is a "capital point." So strongly too could he express his confidence in enlightenment and the school that one might often be tempted to believe him some 18th century worthy arisen from the grave. Nor is it any wonder that quite a few people had their Christian doubts about this talk of the human and the national. Was not this pure humanism, where Christianity could at best only serve to give a higher luster to the whole? Did not this talk imply that human life of itself held eternal values? Comprehensible as such anxiety may be, it was however quite unfounded.

On this point there was no call to have any doubts in Grundtvig's case. Through his youthful crisis of 1810-11, he had learned, so that he never forgot it, that a cleft exists between life and death, between good and evil, between God and the devil, and that man, with all that is his, has irremediably got on the wrong side of it. Those were not empty words that he sang about there being only one to whom "it was given from death unto life on his own wings to fly." He had learned from experience that human life without Christ is "to worse than the grave cast out:"

> In and of itself, the soul
> Severed from life's spring,
> Like a river cut off from its source,
> Sooner or later runs dry.

And separated from life's spring man had become. Only in Christ did the spring gush forth anew, in Christ as he was found in the living word in the congregation. The many who even today reject Grundtvig's "Man first," and accuse him of an un-Christian humanism, may well be reminded that this very man who stands accused of idolizing the human and the Danish taught his children and his friends to sum up all life in the prayer beginning with the words: "hallowed be *thy name, thy kingdom come, thy will* be done."

It is true that after the English journeys Grundtvig attained a far clearer insight into both human and national life, but this did not render the break with rationalism and naturalism any less definitive. All his life long, any talk of man's self-sufficiency remained an abomination to him. That man was a sinner in need of salvation remained his immovable conviction:

> The soul in its herdsman's hut
> By the great meadow gate
> Dreams sweetly, to falsehood's profit alone,
> Of its own self-sufficiency,
> Wins of itself only woe,
> Unless to the spirit of truth
> It surrenders its cherished self.

> Every soul which does not bow
> Low before God's only son,
> But pridefully exalts himself above

Him who in light or secret still is God,
Has suckled at the breast of falsehood's nurse,
And whispers ever the selfsame thing,
The boast of the anti-Christ.

In this connection let me quote also one of the shortest
hymns in the *Hymns*:

Whimper and complain,
By night and by day,
Must he who wakens on the chasm's edge;
Thou hearest the law
Thundered from above:
Die or do what thou, sinner, canst not do.

Sing and chant,
Weep for joy,
Must he who rests in the Savior's arms,
Finds himself comforted,
Feels in his breast
Grace upon grace and cure for all regret.

To endure with a smile
Affliction and trouble,
Rejoicing bear your cross in the Savior's footsteps:
That by degrees
The spirit will teach us,
Teach us the taste of heaven on earth.

And should any be in doubt as to the factors that govern human
life in this respect, there stands death as the indisputable evidence
and the great unconquerable foe. Grundtvig never reached the
point of reconciling himself to death, the great ravager of life.

But what has this to do with the human and the Christian? Of man's being a sinner who must be saved there can exist
not the shadow of a doubt. But although this is explanation
enough of his misery and may well cause him to whimper and
complain night and day, at the same time it is also an indication
of his sublimity and nobility. Animals and plants are not sinners,
only men are that; men are not mere flesh and blood, urges and
instincts, but are also spirit, created in God's image. That is why

man can be saved. Not that he is in himself capable of doing
the slightest thing toward it. In the old theological dispute as to
whether man himself can help, or whether he is only saved by
grace, Grundtvig sides altogether with Luther:

> Grace, she is of royal blood,
> Will not change place with queens,
> Yet does not hold herself too good
> For the most ramshackle hut;
> Wherever seated, she holds sway,
> Charming she is in any garb,
> Lovely as pearls of dew.

> Christianity is God's grace's word,
> Gives us light and life,
> Grace still only in grace believes
> Which has our sins forgiven;
> A graceless heart is sundered from God,
> For it belief is by law imposed,
> Grace a word it does not know.

But it is man who is saved, and salvation does not mean something wholly new being created, a new life, as one can see from
the Bible. No, salvation is rebirth of a human life already created.
Life's drama has as its rubrics: creation, the fall, and salvation,
but creation comes first. A somewhat extended quotation from
The Christian Catechism will elucidate this point:

> So long as an ape needs only to sit on its hind legs, be clothed,
> and mimic our eating passably and our tailoring a little, to become
> in our eyes as assuredly a human being as other simple folk, so
> long will it avail nothing to talk to us or write *about real human
> life, either that with which we are born from our mother's womb,
> or that to which we are born in the Lord's baptism from water
> and the spirit.* And not only that, but even when we have come
> to realize that it is mouth and voice, *word and talk* that truly
> separate us humans from all "dumb creatures," human life will
> for us still remain in total darkness so long as the word is to us
> mere breath with a characteristic sound, for any essential distinc-
> tion has still not been made between the human word and bellow-
> ing or barking, to say nothing of the mimicry to which starlings
> and magpies, and particularly parrots, can be trained. Only when

it dawns on us that in the human voice and human talk on our tongue and lips there can and must be *something wonderful, and something matchless,* which neither bird nor animal can be trained to mimic, in short, something *creative and divine,* which we must so call because, as experience has taught us, we have it in common only with one another and consequently with our common, unseen God and creator, only then are we qualified to think about human life. . . .

We now without difficulty discover that the human word and human discourse can and must have a three-fold nature . . . three so called properties which plainly distinguish them from all that is mere prattle or repetition. For although there both can be and is a great difference in the degree of *power,* of *truth* and of *love* that is livingly expressed in human speech, still something of each must be found in all human speech worthy of the name, so that when we find not the slightest power, pith, or force in so-called speech, we call it dead and empty, and when we find not a grain of truth in it, we call it false and spurious, and when we find absolutely no love in it, we call it inhuman and heartless. It thus being irrefutably established that *human life has in human speech its one powerful expression, sure measure and clear mirror of a higher, unseen power, of inner truth and unfeigned love,* we now have a vantage point from which it can and must be seen, can and must be ever more clearly comprehended, that *although born and re-born human life are worlds apart* as to the quality, extent, and degree of the higher power, of veracity and truth and of love and goodness, with which human life expresses itself in human speech, *yet on the other hand it is always with the selfsame human life that we are dealing, with the same laws and the same primary properties, the same vital powers and distinguishing marks, so that human life in its very darkest, poorest and most impure forms is still fundamentally of the same nature as human life in its very richest, purest and brightest forms, so that, in a word, the same human life was shared by the thief on the cross and God's only begotten son, our Lord Jesus Christ.*

If that were not so, God's only begotten son could no more have become man, than a man of woman born could become a son of God, born of water and spirit.

This line of reasoning caused Grundtvig to denounce with the utmost violence not only those who would deny the creation of man, but the Lutheran theologians who so over-emphasized the Fall as to make man beast or devil:

"This is also responsible for the fact that all scripturists who cling to the principle that through the Fall man became as alien to God and everything divine as if he had never been created in God's image—that man is therefore either a mere beast or a monster—also insist quite logically that all sinful men are the devil's children, who yet, through belief in Him who came to undo the devil's work, shall, in a manner not only incomprehensible to us, but essentially impossible to the true God and the eternal word of truth, be transformed into God's children." God's word comes to its own, and though man has fallen into sin and death, he has still not become stick or stone. Even the lowest, like the thief on the cross, is still of "divine origin." To this the whole Bible story bears witness. In it God, despite the Fall, speaks his word to patriarchs and prophets, yes, Abraham is even called "God's friend."

The above constitutes the background for the poem which has given rise to so much misunderstanding, and the first line of which has been made the heading for this chapter:

> Man first, then Christian,
> This alone is life's order;
> We may be called sheep, but do not think
> Of animals to be herded!
> And devilry to Christianity
> God himself cannot transform;
> Cast not your pearls before swine!
>
> Adam was still a heathen man,
> Heathen was Enoch no less,
> Yet both were in God's good graces,
> This we can't hope to prevent;
> Perfect Noah in his time
> Was still, beyond doubt or dispute,
> Neither Christian nor Jew.
>
> Abraham was God's good friend,
> But Christian he was not,
> David and many true God's-men

Could not have been so either;
Had Christians been before Christ came,
Falsehood and farce would Christianity be,
This is not hard to see.

Man first, then Christian,
That is the capital point,
Christianity costs us nothing,
Is a pure stroke of luck,
But luck which can only happen
To one at bottom God's friend,
One of truth's noble race.

Let each upon this earth then strive
True man to be,
Open his ear to the word of truth
And render God his glory!
If Christianity be truth's way
And he is not a Christian today,
He will be by tomorrow.

That Christianity is "pure luck" seems to Grundtvig certain
enough. It is not something that man can acquire or deserve. It is
wholly and entirely God's gift, brought to earth by our Lord
Jesus. But Jesus came to his own, and the gift was given only
to man, hence: "Man first, then Christian." This is the only right
relation between the human and the Christian. It in no way
implies that the human is self-sufficient or includes within itself
eternal life. Man is a sinner and in need of salvation. This statement is not affected in the least. Still less does "Man first, then
Christian" mean that acceptance of the gospel must be preceded
by a certain cultural and social development, that man before
becoming Christian must have attained a certain material and
spiritual well-being. No, it states only one thing: that a man must
be living, must have the life-instinct in him before it can do any
good to tell him about eternal life. It means that Grundtvig has
taken the creation idea seriously: man is not merely an intelligent
ape or a higher machine, he is a divine experiment that unites
spirit and matter, and as such must become conscious of himself;
he shall and must comprehend something both of life's mysterious

richness and of life's desolation. In this the purpose of education
also consists. Education is for Grundtvig not a cultural matter or
a scholarly concern; it is possible to be highly "educated" without having any knowledge worth mentioning. No, education
must awaken to life through contact with reality, and this is the
making ready which must precede any talk of the eternal life.
That is why Jesus did not talk "to the dead young man on the
bier about the road to eternal life," but with heart-felt pity for
her bereavement said to the widow: "Weep not!" and to the
young man: "Arise!", "for where temporal life is either lacking
or well night crushed under heartbreak, talk of the eternal life,
if not a mockery, is still inevitably useless."

Christianity is pure luck, God's undeserved gift, but the seed
was sown only in the earth, not among stones or in water:

> The mould, at heart,
> Looks upward with joy:
> There the sunbeams may dwell,
> There heaven's barley may grow;
> He who hears the mould as it sighs
> Bedews it with sparkling tears . . .

Men must be living before they can become Christians:
"Whoso prefers to talk to and with the dead, him I in no wise
envy either the pleasure he gets from it or the honor he gains
thereby, but I repeat what I have said before, that of the two I
myself would rather talk with a living thief than with a dead
saint, since the former can still repent and reform but the latter
can do nothing at all." Human life is sinful but it is still of divine
lineage and can therefore through Jesus Christ be reborn to eternal
life. Christ did not come to earth with a whole new life and a
whole new language, but became a man and entered human life,
to which he thereby gave rebirth into the life the creator had
willed from the beginning. Salvation is not the genesis of something wholly new and unknown, but is a *re*-birth of the created
life, and salvation presupposes creation.

> It is therefore God's own brood
> That gives itself into God's hands,
> For he cries not for gold,

Who gold has not known;
Where nothing of God's is,
Heaven's torch never lights;
Where truth is not welcome
Ill is Christianity lodged.

Yet none is good
Of himself here below,
But only through the Lord's flesh and blood
In the congregation;
Naught goes anything but well,
God with us, Immanuel,
When we as members of Jesus Christ
Forget ourselves in him.

And as with the human, so with the national. In nature's order the national comes before the Christian. To this even history bears witness. The new and vital thing in the saga-song *Christianity's Pleiads* was that Grundtvig had got light on the relation between the Christian and the national. In antiquity three distinct national churches appear: the Hebrew, the Greek, and the Latin. To these were added in the Middle Ages three new ones, corresponding to three new language-communities, England, Germany, and the North. This development Grundtvig saw prophesied in the Book of Revelation's epistle to the churches, so that the only thing still left unexplained was where the seventh church was to be. But whether one endorsed this use of Saint John's "Lord's Day vision" was immaterial. The vital thing was that people were being taught to regard the Christian life throughout as a spiritual folk-life, in living interaction with a leading people's specific development and mother tongue. Thus an explanation is given of the various church aggregates and of the wide divergence each from each of their views of Christianity, though all remain one in their profession of the crucified but risen Savior at baptism and at communion. This also goes to show that there must be a close inner connection between a people's national and its Christian life.

It then naturally follows that the Christian confession, preaching, and songs of praise, which are the Christian people's only plain life-tokens, can neither be purer, warmer, nor clearer than the people's mother-tongue, with the result that the people's mother-tongue, like the evangel, which brings nothing with it except "the Lord in the spirit," affects life-expression and enlightenment through the years. Now history teaches us that every people's mother-tongue corresponds to its national horizon and stage of development. Thus, in terms of a time and place, living Christianity must always be national and can only be comprehended in the degree to which the people and the mother-tongue are Christianized. . . . That it is only speech in the mother-tongue which spiritually touches our hearts, that, therefore, the tongues of the spirit spoke the mother-tongues of all listeners on the great day of Pentecost, and that, therefore, living Christianity has never brought its own language with it, but borrows the mother-tongue of each people that it visits, is a fact that has thus far scarcely been noticed in church history, which has by this oversight been unintelligible.

This does not imply any such absurd confounding of the national and the Christian as Grundtvig has often been accused of. On the contrary, he took great pains to keep the Danish and the Christian separate, not as being two irreconcilables but as being utterly distinct.

In the first place, Danishness certainly existed before Christianity came to the country. Secondly, the Danish had to do with temporal welfare only, whereas Christianity pointed toward salvation and the eternal life. It is, furthermore, indisputable that Danishness has validity only in one little corner of the North, Christianity throughout the world, Danishness only for a time, Christianity both for time and eternity. But Christianity does not float unattached in the air and it does not talk a heavenly, nonhuman language—one of the very things that alienated Grundtvig from the pietists was that their Christian life struck him as a sham life and their discourse as Canaan speech. Living Christianity brings nothing with it but the Lord himself in the spirit, and as guest takes up its abode among a people and borrows its mother-tongue. Thus, the church, though foreign by origin, had been able to become Danish in thought and speech, had for centuries been the hearthfire of national life:

> In the North now we understand better
> Than a song handed down from our fathers
> The high symbolic language of the East.
> Our mother-tongue bows low,
> Nimbly and gracefully follows
> The line of thought of the Lord.

And of how this came to pass, there exists an explanation that leaves no room for doubt:

> The word of the Lord and Pentecost—
> Which alone explain the matter—
> Gave you all the spirit of tongues:
> The spirit which can do all,
> Which in Christ Jesus' church
> Loosens all bonds on the tongue.

Christianity, the heavenly guest that comes to a people, does not fashion its own abode but finds one ready prepared; and the sort of abode is no mere matter of indifference; God had through a long history been preparing the Jewish nation before he sent his son to earth as a man among his own people. "If we thus consider first the Hebraic and Israelitish nationality . . . we can readily see that everything in Judaea was adapted to maintaining and strengthening nationality, and that when, notwithstanding, this had sunk into deadly torpor, it was miraculously reawakened by John the Baptist before Christ's coming: for he turned 'the children's hearts unto the fathers, and the parents' hearts unto the children' to prepare the way of the Lord and to give him a people made ready."

Nor is it otherwise with other peoples. If we reflect how Christianity came to Denmark, we surely see that it was not as a bully whose threats placed the folk he visited under the yoke; no, it came as a gentle, defenseless friar asking permission of the king of Denmark to proclaim the glad tidings of the Savior who was born in Bethlehem. And Christianity's influence in Denmark rested exclusively upon such influence as it could itself obtain among the Danish people. Yet no more was it a case of Christianity stealing in among the people, obtaining a multitude of adherents, and then seeking to bring king and people under the

yoke. This would have been treachery as mean as that of the dog
in the fable who begged a kennel in which to put her puppies,
and when they got big bade the owner defiance and said: "Take
the kennel from me and my pups if you can!"

No, violence and duplicity are never in keeping with Christianity's spirit and by way of them nothing Christian can ever be
attained. Love and truth, on the other hand, are in Christianity's
spirit, and consequently, it can never will the use of cunning or
force to obliterate or crush any nationality. The great mistake
of the medieval hierarchy and papacy was the introduction of
spiritual coercion and legal constraint as instruments in the
service of Christianity. Thereby Christianity became non-popular,
hierarchical. One of the Reformation's great giant-strides forward was the introduction of the mother-tongue as church language. Thereby it again became possible for the national to get
its rights and for adherence to Christianity to be a voluntary
matter. Properly understood, an awakening nationality will also
find in Christianity an ally against all alien rule.

If we consider Danish nationality, which, nebulous though
it may be to most, is, Grundtvig says, the one that we know best,
since by nature we have it in us, we find that the explanation of
the prevailing indifference to spiritual things, the blindness to the
world of the spirit, bewailed alike by zealous clergymen and all
thinking persons, resides in a lack of living nationality so utter
that whatever of Danishness yet remains alive resembles to a hair
the disconsolate widow at Nain's gate as she followed her only
son's body to the grave. Under such conditions, to talk of living
Christianity is of course quite useless. The people's spiritual deadness must be remedied through a resuscitation of nationality
before it will be anything but breath wasted to talk to or with
the people about living Christianity.

> The reason why a people must be vitally conscious of itself
> before there is any use mentioning to it any spirit other than its
> own is, for the rest, the same as the reason why a man must be
> conscious of himself before there is any use talking to him about
> what he as a man has or has not, what risks he runs, or what
> safety measures exist. For, as we all know, what naturally lifts
> human life above animal life is the word. This opens the world

of the spirit to us and makes of the present only a corridor stretching from before the beginning of time to beyond the end of the ages, thus placing us in the midst of an enveloping and therefore to us necessarily incomprehensible eternity. Just as it is only in our mother tongue that word about the unseen has life and power for us, so our living relation to past and future depends as a whole on our sense of an intimate connection with our parents and our descendants, with the result that, of necessity, in Denmark and everywhere else, just as in Judæa, if God's word is to find a prepared people, then a national word in the mother-tongue must first have turned the children's hearts to the fathers and the parents' to the children, so that they feel that death in all its forms is their, and mankind's, hereditary foe, and that He is the one true Savior who can and will give us eternal life.

The national is the prerequisite of the Christian, but can never replace it. It is here on earth, on this side of the chasm between life and death. Nothing could be farther from a deification of the national. It cannot save mankind. Talk of the national, as of the school, opens upward:

> Much as I love the beechwood
> And the forget-me-nots in its lee,
> Danish land, Danish daring,
> Seeland's king, church, town,
> O, yet would the Danish bulwark
> Seem but vanity, if Christ's church
> Crowned not the whole with its spire.

But the spire is set upon the Danish bulwark, and Danishness and nationality are therefore no casual matter. And to the same purpose Grundtvig ends the chapter of *The Christian Catechism* on the born and the re-born human life with a strong statement about the national:

> Senseless and perverse as it would be to wish to ban and as far as possible eradicate the old, primeval human life in order to give the new Christian human life room and scope, equally senseless and perverse is it to ban and as far as possible eradicate the national life in order to put the Christian life in its place. For if one says to the folk-spirit: "Depart, thou unclean spirit and make room for the Holy Spirit!" though one may thereby get rid of

the folk-spirit, one will still be so far from getting the Holy Spirit in its place, as actually to be closing oneself and the people, as far as possible, to all spirits, to all spiritual influence and inspiration, all spiritual and emotional understanding and enlightenment.

Finally, there is just one more poem of Grundtvig's that should be mentioned in this connection. This is the poem "To Self-Examination," dating from the year 1848. He here mentions the things which the heart clings to and which may therefore obstruct the road to heaven. In his youth, books had been his heart's delight, but he discovered that the written was dead, and miraculously burst the chains which bound him to learning. When he later thought of forsaking and sacrificing all for heaven's sake, he was confronted by his children; but he had learned to bid farewell to them also. No, the real difficulty is to learn to renounce oneself:

> Yes, to renounce oneself, that is the thing
> That reaches bottom, separates soul from mind;
> This we all should do, yet no one can
>
> Who has not hidden in the Savior's hand.
> See, that is love's sacred riddle!
> See, that is godhead's grace before grace!

To this poem he some days later made an addition, however, in which he says that books and children and what wealth he possessed he might well risk when the fate of the nation was at stake—his two sons were that moment at the front:

> But—would not God have our hearts entire,
> Despite mother and father and wife!
> Should I not willingly sacrifice what is Danish
> To perfect a Christian life!
> Could I and would I to the Savior's glory
> Danishness on earth willingly forego?
>
> No, not willingly, that must I confess,
> Even though I believe to me Jesus is all;
> Nowhere on earth could I turn me,
> If all the days of Danishness were done;
> My only hope, with God in heaven still,
> Cleansed, transfigured, the eternal to find.

There is something impressive about this poem. Should God desire of him also the Danish and the national as a sacrifice, yes, then must he confess that this sacrifice he does not make willingly, for then there would be no life on earth left to him. If he is to live on earth, he must live as a Dane. If this be taken from him, there is only one thing for him to do: await the eternal life and hope that he shall then once more experience what it means to live. But here on earth he can only live as a Dane.

X

The Church

The Human and the National; the School; Man first, then
Christian—these headings bear witness to the new light Grundtvig had obtained upon human life and its conditions. The prelim-
inaries to the clarity thus won had been manifold: his early
youth's commonplace education, his Langeland period's romanticism and enthusiasm for Northern myths, his many years of pre-
occupation with Denmark's history and language, and last but
not least those English journeys which had sharpened his sense
of reality and fortified his belief in freedom. But the vital element in all this was still only one thing, namely, the ecclesiastico-
historical view which he had adopted in 1825. Through this, he
had first arrived at the interpretation which all his life long was
to remain for him the most trustworthy comment on human
existence.

From human's life's rebirth in the congregation by means of
the living word, light had been reflected upon everything that
bears the name of human, and whatever Grundtvig later thought
and said, humanly and nationally, all pointed toward this reborn
life, the Christian life, or, rather, the Christ-life, as it can only
be lived in the congregation, where Christ himself is a living
presence. The ecclesiastico-historical view also brought with it,
however, a whole new understanding of the church and the
churchly life. First this no doubt dawned gradually on Grundtvig himself, then, after 1825, several years were to pass before he
drew his full conclusions, and it was longer still before there was
any talk of putting into practice the new demands made upon
the church. Indeed in large part these were never carried out.
This does not, however, affect the existence of clear and easily
traceable strands leading from 1825 to the congregational life

which later grew up about Vartov, and which from there spread practically all over Denmark.

Wherein the "matchless discovery" consisted, might perhaps be epitomized in Grundtvig's own statement that he had learned not to seek the living among the dead, not to seek Christ among the dead pages of the Bible, but as the living and present Lord in the congregation. He saw the church not as a reading-circle, but as a society of believers, and the congregation, not the Bible, as Christ's body. Christ was therefore only to be found in his congregation, not in the book. Most bitterly did he denounce what he regarded as the great error of the Lutheran church in wishing to make the Bible the church's foundation. This was an enormity, if only on the ground that the church is obviously older than the Bible inasmuch as the Bible is the work of the church, not the other way round. The orthodox Lutheran church believed in building the altar upon the book instead of laying the book open upon the altar. This was due to a total confusion of life and learning, church and school. To be sure, Luther himself had made two giant strides forward: he had introduced the mother tongue as church language, and he had known enough to distinguish between the essential, namely the church's immovable foundation, God's word, and all the rest, the nonessential, which can differ at different times and in different churches without disrupting the fellowship. But Luther's church had not succeeded in holding to this distinction. It had therefore irremediably come under a papacy of theologians and exegetes, where changing currents of fashion made themselves master in the church. People had failed to understand that scripture and theology belong in the church school, where one seeks light on the Christian life, and that they have nothing to do with the church's foundation, which is the Lord himself alone, in his word as spoken to the individual at baptism and at communion. From then on, and until his death, Grundtvig waged war against such "script-theologians" as still failed to grasp the distinction between the dead book and the living word.

This view of church and scripture in nowise implied that Grundtvig undervalued the Scriptures. Though they formed no part of his concept of the church, they were still the indispensable basis for doctrine, and doctrine was neither more nor less than light on the Christian life:

"The Bible can not speak for itself, for it is neither a god, a man, nor a spirit, but only a book, therefore a dead thing, of itself unable to speak, and both spiritually and physically subject to such treatment as men choose to give it, so that when we discuss the Bible as if it could think and talk and work miracles, this is simply a remnant of medieval superstititon. If it is less obviously ludicrous than the old priests' and monks' babble about their talking and weeping and saving Mary-images, and about all the miracles performed by material relics of the Lord and the Apostles, it is still, at bottom, neither more Christian nor wiser, but precisely the same thing. If, on the other hand, we confine our praise of the Bible to what may properly be said of the greatest book in the world, a book which has never met its match or anything in its class that will bear the slightest comparison, then we can never go wrong in lauding to the skies a book which, as surely as Christ sits at God's right hand, is filled with heavenly wisdom, yes, is the inexhaustible store-house whence the holy spirit that animates the congregation dispenses to all what they need, and of which it teaches the New Testament's devoted servants, as scripturists trained for God's kingdom, to use both new and old for the church's enlightenment and edification."

Scripture is neither the source of life nor the foundation of the church but it is a unique and unblemished source of enlightenment upon apostolic Christianity, and therefore for all times a matchless textbook in matters pertaining to God's kingdom. Here Grundtvig spoke out of his own experience. For him, Scripture was always a unique source of Christian enlightenment and edification. To this both his sermons and his hymns bear witness, permeated as they are with Biblical thought and language. In the Bible's "Mosaic-Christian" view he found also the clearest account of human life and its conditions: creation, the fall, and salvation.

> So hast thou us given
> In Scripture so proud
> A day-book for life
> On earth, in God,

And of God's kingdom
A map, moreover,
That is never in error.

Only thine is the exploit,
With living voice,
But thine too is Scripture
For doctrine and solace;
Where this is not valued,
Thou art absent as surely,
As where it is everything.

And one more stanza:

And witness to bear,
To give true and clear knowledge.
Of our Lord's life and teaching
And of the apostolate,
To which end, papal bulls
Are all manifest nullities
Beside apostles' letters and books.

When Grundtvig thus won clarity as to the Scripture's place, he simultaneously found the means to free the church from the guardianship of theologians and exegetes. Theologians must not be lords in the church, but teachers in the church-school. There they would have full freedom for research and teaching, and there the fact that they differed would not matter, quite the contrary, they would have leave to differ. Thus all cause for anxiety about historical criticism also vanishes. The foundation of the church it cannot shake, since that consists only in the attendant congregation and its Lord. And on the other hand it can be of use: it can show that the Protestant theologians' doctrines of the inspiration of Scripture from end to end are both unhistorical and untenable. The main thing is simply to make precise distinction between Christianity and theology, between church and school. This principle Grundtvig honorably endeavored to carry out even as to his own theology. To him it seemed quite clear that the congregation and what it said and did at baptism and communion were one thing, and that the ecclesiastical "elucidations" whereby he himself thought he could throw light on the

congregation's life were another. To be sure, this distinction between the Christian view and the specifically "Grundtvigian"
theology never got much farther. This is particularly apparent in
the strictures he passed upon the reformed churches, or upon the
Russian and the Swedish churches, both of which he regarded
as having altered the baptismal covenant. But in principle it was
nonetheless established that school was one thing, and church
another. Thus Grundtvig would have denied neither to the
Roman Catholic nor to other confessions in general the name of
Christian. They merely had another "school," another theology.

Grundtvig himself belonged to the Lutheran school. From
childhood, he had accepted Martin Luther with the greatest enthusiasm. On the vital questions of the word and faith, of grace
and of the universal priesthood, he was also fundamentally with
Luther. But at the same time he went beyond Luther, and notably
beyond the Lutheran church, and on the two points which had
always been the Achilles-heel of Protestantism, namely the concept of the church, and the scripture-principle. Ever since Melanc-
thon's day there had been in the Lutheran church a strong disposition to turn the church into a school and to make the reading
and interpretation of scripture the pillar of divine service. This
to Grundtvig meant nothing else, however, than putting man's
word in the place of God's word and thereby opening the door
to everything arbitrary and individualistic, as the history of the
Protestant churches in fact testified by their pendulum swing
through orthodoxy, pietism and rationalism. Such a concept of
the church made theologians and interpreters lords in the church
and guardians over the belief of laymen. Nor could the latter
ever attain certainty, since the learned theologians were always
in disagreement, and one must always wait to see which of the
conflicting opinions would prove to be correct. In view of this
whole scripture-theology chaos within the church Grundtvig
turned his attention to the congregation gathered about God's
own word at baptism and communion, not about man's word.
Here was one word which the theologians must let alone, the
Lord's own word of covenant to the individual whereby he was
received into the congregation, and the word at the Lord's Supper
whereby his Christian life was replenished. And in view of this

ecclesiastical chaos he at the same time dismissed the Scripture as
church foundation, a capacity in which it had proved quite useless, and assigned it to the school which was to serve the church.

In place of Scripture, Grundtvig designated the oral tradition
at baptism and communion, as it had been heard in the church
ever since the Lord's own institution of the sacraments; this was
the tradition whereby the word of the risen life had from generation to generation been livingly present. His contemporaries were
already accusing him of catholicizing tendencies—understandably
enough. Was he not putting tradition in the place of scripture?
Yes, but a tradition which had very little to do with what went
by that name in the Roman church. Grundtvig had at one time
interested himself in the apostolic succession and had been inclined to ascribe a special significance to the office. At that time,
in the 1820's, catholicizing tendencies might perhaps have been
argued, but gradually, as he saw more and more clearly the consequences of the ecclesiastico-historical view, he became more and
more unsympathetic toward the Roman church. Its tradition was
false, its doctrine wrong, and above all it wished to make of the
church a material power, a kingdom of this world. It was a church
of the papacy and hierarchy; in it there was no room for freedom
and the universal priesthood. Thus the very concept "Rome"
became a sort of common term for practically everything that
should be avoided in the church, yes, scripture-theology itself is
called "the anti-Pope":

> Long did the dispute over thralldom's yoke
> For God's son's freeborn faith—
> It was wry and it was crooked—
> Go on betwixt popes twain:
> The hardest to beat was the anti-Pope,
> When the word was replaced by the letter,
> By the schoolmaster's rod the spirit.

In a long "Roman-Ballad" from the year 1837, Grundtvig
enumerates all Rome's sins and for good measure includes the
Latin yoke in the school and the whole un-Danish spirit which
rules there, each verse being followed by the refrain:

So must we with our fathers
Pray: God help us,
God free us from Rome!

No, between the Grundtvigian and the Catholic no reconciliation was possible. Grundtvig was Luther's disciple, had
merely drawn his conclusions far more sharply than Luther himself from the understanding of Christ as the living word and
from the idea of the universal priesthood. Thus, though his view
has correctly been called "churchly," "church" here has nothing
to do with the Catholic Pope-church, resting on the hierarchy.
Having once attained clarity as to the churchly-historical view,
one had still to discover that it demanded absolute freedom
within the church, since spirit and spiritual life thrive only in
freedom. Where spirit is concerned, nothing is ever gained by
use of might and force.

But there was a second thing that conclusively aligned
Grundtvig with Luther against Catholicism. The Catholic doctrine of salvation always concerned itself more or less explicitly
with the concepts of nature and grace, grace coming as a supple-
ment, a perfecting of human nature which took place through
the sacrament, whose power thus consisted in "infused grace."
Grace was construed as a sort of new substance which was infused
into the soul's metaphysical being. Thus the Catholic church is
also in essence a sacramental church. But when Grundtvig perceived a way wholly new to the Lutheran church of gathering
the life of the church about baptismal font and altar, his understanding of the sacrament itself remained wholly the Lutheran
one, and wholly un-Catholic. In the sacrament the fundamental
and creative element is the word, not the physical action. Salvation lies entirely in what a modern theologian has called "the
dimension of the word," not in "the dimension of nature," and
the opposition here, as with Luther, is between sin and grace,
not between nature and grace.

Several years were to pass, however, after 1825, before the
consequences of the ecclesiastico-historical view with respect to
the arrangement of church affairs became clear to Grundtvig
himself. In *The Church's Answer* his object was, quite un-

equivocally, to prove that Professor Clausen and the rationalists had no right to be in the church, and he hoped thereby to get the state church on his side and force his opponents to withdraw. It was in reality the old Lutheran orthodoxy's stalwart mode of action all over again. Such being the background, one also sees how tremendous a disappointment it must have been to Grundtvig when the total result of his action was a libel suit whereby he himself was fined and turned over to the censor. The actual outcome of the affair naturally helped to turn Grundtvig's thoughts toward the question of religious freedom, and on this subject he wrote three articles for the *Theological Monthly,* the last of which was, however, banned by the censor. These tell an entirely different story from *The Answer,* namely that under any circumstances it is wrong to employ coercion in matters of faith. Nowadays, he says, coercion is used even against staunch supporters of the state religion (the conventicle folk with their old-style beliefs), yet it ought not to be directed against the rationalists either. Religious questions should under no circumstances encroach upon men's civil rights. And if at the moment there is a split within the church, this can only be reconciled when people cease trying to force the contending parties to remain together. Religious freedom is the solution for it: let those who do not wish to be Christians have leave to withdraw outright from any religious community, and let old-style believers who cannot reconcile themselves to the state church be allowed to form congregations of their own. What he wrote was apparently quite innocent, but in its intention it was a radical attack on the existing order, that of a state-guaranteed church which in return guaranteed and backed up the state. As yet, Grundtvig did not think it possible to find an ecclesiastical arrangement whereby the conflicting parties could remain together.

In the tract *Religious Freedom,* however, another solution was already dimly discernible, and a few years later, in a little tract *On the Baptismal Covenant,* it attained open definition as the prime and principal requisite of the church. The tract had been provoked by the changes that diocesan-dean Clausen and other rationalistic clergymen had arbitrarily and high-handedly made in the church rituals, even in that of baptism, about which

Grundtvigians were especially sensitive. Grundtvig admits that
church usages may often be altered—they do not partake of the
immutable—but the baptismal covenant must not be tampered
with. And if the rationalists cannot be forced to keep the ritual,
since that would be applying coercion to their conscience, then
at least as much respect must be shown for the old believers'
conscience, and the only means to this end is a loosening of the
parish bond. Once this childishly simple change is effected,
Grundtvig will give the modern theologians all the freedom they
wish. Wherein, then, did the dissolution of the parish bond con-
sist? Simply in providing that no man should be bound to his
parish priest with reference to confirmation and the administra-
tion of the sacraments, but all have free access to whatever priest
they wished. On these terms, both parties could remain in the
state church. Here the basis is already laid for the later Grundtvigian theory of the state church as a civil institution.

This theory attained its first formulation a few years later
in the little tract *The Danish State Church Impartially Viewed,*
where Grundtvig establishes the principle that Christianity is an
unalterable fact from past times, whereas the state church is an
"establishment" which the government has license to turn and
twist at will, provided it does not make the slightest encroach-
ment upon freedom of conscience, which is both the supreme
principle of all religion and every good citizen's inalienable right.
He then goes on to make precise distinction between the state
church and the true church of Jesus Christ. The former is only
"a civil institution," but in it Christ's church may abide as guest.

All that may reasonably be demanded of the state church is
that it provide good living conditions for the true church. But
for this, dissolution of the parish bond is required, and full freedom for the clergy as well. It is not enough that the congregation
be free to choose what priest they will hear and be served by.
The priest must also be free both in his preaching and in the
matter of ritual. There must be no compulsory ritual. From the
priests nothing more must be demanded than that they teach to
the best of their conviction in accordance with the Holy Scripture,
and that they administer the sacraments in accord with their
conviction as to the Lord's ordinance. As early as 1831 the specific

demand for priestly freedom emerged in the following form: since one is constrained to admit that the Augsburg confession, despite its excellence, is man's work, "and since one must also foresee that a certain number of priests, from weakness or for secular reasons will have remained where they do not properly belong, it would surely be most useful to the state church, if, instead of affronting the old-fashioned Christians, their priests were granted a greater doctrinal freedom than the law now allows them." For this, the only thing requisite would be a loosening of the parish bond. At one time it seemed to him that the dissolution should mean doctrinal freedom but liturgical constraint. Grundtvig soon realized, however, that this would be only a half dissolution, since "any honest man can neither grant nor accept freedom to openly contradict himself, nor can I think of anything more shocking to a pious mind than to hear a priest conduct the baptismal or the communion service in words which are plainly contrary to the doctrine he expounds in the pulpit, to his confirmation candidates, and for his catechumens." And he felt that "the farther priestly freedom extends, provided it goes hand in hand with the listeners' freedom, the better able will Christian priests be to get along and do good in the national church, so that in terms of this mutual freedom, but of course only in these terms, an enlightened servant of Christ must yet a while prefer priestly office in the national church to secession from it."

On the whole, thoughts of withdrawing from the church and forming free congregations were again very present to Grundtvig in his latter days. Only, he pointed out, one must of course realize that a free congregation gives no better guarantee than the state church that it is actually God's congregation there assembled. The free congregation can no more be identified with the true congregation out of hand than any other. The latter is neither palpable nor demonstrable, but is recognized through its signs of life, which are confession, songs of praise, and preaching. And these life functions require freedom and good conditions. If such do not exist, one must resort to free congregations, in the hope that these will offer the true congregation better lodging.

These radical Grundtvigian demands for freedom have been

only to a limited extent realized. Religious freedom came with the constitution of 1849. Not until 1855, after many years of struggle, was a law dissolving the parish bond put through much as Grundtvig wished it. Later came legislation covering the right to form free congregations and the right of parishioners to summon outside priests and be served by them in the parish church. Priestly freedom, however, has never been established by law, even though in practice it has been partly realized in the endeavor to maintain a so-called tolerant national church, meaning that the priestly vow is not enforced in the case of heterodox priests and that a certain freedom is also allowed with respect to ritual—an arrangement which in its vagueness and irregularity must surely be termed typically Danish.

To one last question that might be asked, namely, what lay back of the Grundtvigian demand for freedom? the answer is simple. Grundtvig's interest was to secure the spirit and the word freedom to work within the church and also to free the laity of all guardianship by priests and theologians. This could only be done by centering everything about the divine word itself, which makes all equal and levels out all differences.

XI
The Skald

The reader will perhaps wonder at this book's not getting around to mentioning Grundtvig as poet until the last chapter, and even then at no great length. After all, is it not first and foremost the poems and hymns that keep his name alive today. Nonetheless there is good reason for this. Whatever his poetical achievement, Grundtvig was not primarily a poet. He was a prophetic revealer and preacher, he was the seer who saw mighty visions and read life's riddle, he was the popular awakener and educator, and all this found expression through his powerful and sonorous poetry. But this poetry never became for him an end in itself. It was only a weapon in the war he fought, though to be sure the most distinguished weapon. For, as a modern poem, but quite in Grundtvig's spirit, puts it: "The heart's language is verse and song"; song strangely and marvellously succeeds in expressing what man's eye has not seen and man's ear has not heard. Grundtvig never wrote his verses merely for writing's sake, or for beauty's, and only rarely did his rhymes spring from an urge to give poetic expression to personal moods and feelings. No, he wrote because he had seen into the spiritual world, and because there was something he desired. Song and poetry were for him a means to this. Therefore he wrote without regard for poetics or aesthetics. He did not court the poets' wreath or feel himself to be of the guild. Quite honestly he awarded Oehlenschlaeger the laurel wreath as skald of the North, while of himself he wrote:

> I am no skald, not whole, not half,
> That will I loudly declare;
> I plough with the old ones' calf,
> All my honor lies there.

177

My lay is only an echo
Of our fathers' hero-ballads,
And my song therefore only extends
To giving the fathers praise.

Now there is no doubt that Grundtvig both here and elsewhere quite misjudges his own skaldic art. How often does he
sing both Oehlenschlaeger and all the rest to bits! And although
he may have learned from the ancients, there is hardly anyone
who has a note so truly his own as Grundtvig. But it was still a
fact that he himself attached no importance to form and showed
a sovereign contempt for poetico-aesthetic rules. This is why literary judgment of his works has always been so uncertain and
changeable, yes, still is even today, for it is almost inseparable
from the practical question of whether one has ears to hear the
message conveyed. Form and content are inextricably one, or
rather, form has no independent existence, is merely a means of
expression for something that shall and must out. And "shall and
must," be it noted, here has no subjective, personal character, does
not mean that there are certain feelings and an inner urge on the
part of the poet which shall and must find an outlet. No, it means
that there are truths in the spiritual world whose nature shall be
proclaimed, that life's conditions must be understood. Small wonder that this man became the hymn-writer without a peer. About
all his poems there is this quality of revelation, coupled with that
rapturous praise of the Creator and his work which comes out
so strongly in the hymns and which is instrumental in giving
them their particular stamp.

Contemporary literary criticism faltered when confronted by
this singular skald who had raised his thunderous voice amid the
poets of the Golden Age, and more often than not judged him
harshly, yes, the real literary experts would have preferred to
deny him the name of poet altogether. In 1824, when he was
visiting in Copenhagen and finally paid a long awaited call on
Grundtvig, Steffens, under the influence of the town's literary
arbiters, condemned his literary work utterly, and urged him to
simply put his pen on the shelf. According to Steffens, his literary
efforts, whether theological, historical or poetical were thoroughly

mistaken, had a mawkish patriotic flavor and a reprehensibly egoistic tendency, were a crime against nature, against historical thoroughness, against both poetical and scholarly form. Unless he could mend his ways, he had better be silent. Plainly audible behind these words of Steffens was the Oehlenschlaeger-Oersted-Mynster circle, which thought it held a patent on everything that passed for poetry, scholarship or culture, and which completely condemned Grundtvig and his work. Not for nothing had he in his youth fallen foul of the three great ones of the circle, Oehlenschlaeger, H. C. Oersted and J. P. Mynster. But even when this is taken into account, one still wonders at such lack of discernment in such clever and gifted men, undeniably a fable for literary criticism for all time.

The man who in the autumn of 1824 was, through Steffens, exhorted to lay down the pen, was the same who in the summer of 1824 had written and published *New Year's Morning*—in my opinion perhaps the most powerful and most moving thing ever written in Danish. Aptly has Roenning said that while reading it one feels "close to the source of all life's riddles." At the time, however, it created no stir; literary criticism simply passed it over in silence; and even today there are some who actually think that, poetically, *New Year's Morning,* if not worthless is at least essentially unsuccessful. And in 1837 when Grundtvig published the first volume of the *Hymns*, so shrewd an aesthete as P. Hjort admitted, to be sure, that there was something "ingenious" and poetical about the book, written as it was in a pithy Danish, but his main verdict was almost entirely negative. He balked at bombast and wordiness, national coquetry and much else before winding up with the assertion that there were very few "psalms" but more lyric poems, that "Grundtvig is not humble enough to write real hymns." Grundtvig was not of the guild. Both his behavior and his poetry were clumsy and shocking. Obscure, too, was most of what he wrote, and the cultivated world simply did not understand it. But the remarkable thing was that this odd poet whom critics and aesthetes failed to understand and would have silenced altogether, found readers among the plain people, and on their lips his obscure poems, both hymns and popular songs, began to come to life.

Nowadays, though nobody will deny that Grundtvig's poems and hymns are among the most beautiful and most powerful in our literature, even so, people are still far from having reached even a passably unanimious valuation of them from the aesthetic viewpoint. Nor will such unanimity ever be reached, since judgment will here always reside, more positively than with any other author, in whether one understands what rings through the verses, in whether through reading and singing them one feels something of life's mysterious nearness oneself. Nor shall any attempt at an artistic evaluation be made here. Instead, Grundtvig's poetry shall be discussed from the viewpoints that were his own, namely that poem and song are weapons of the spirit, and that, such being their purpose, they do not depend on "nicety" and clarity but on the truth and power of the content.

In his early youth Grundtvig had, to be sure, been animated by literary ambition in the usual sense of the term, and the "rhyme-devil" had ridden him hard, but the specimens preserved to us from those early years did not promise well for the future.

> O! never, no never, am I allowed to forget
> Thy charm, which ever increases my anguish.
> Still sounds thy lovely harmonious voice
> Like an echo in a mountain-wreathed valley.

Thus did he celebrate in song one of the parson's pretty daughters at Gunslev, and despite repeated attempts there was no great improvement at the first. Neither the mighty events of 1801, with the battle of King's Deep, nor Steffens's lectures, worked any change for the better. The change first came when he himself awakened and found new content in existence. It was the Langeland experience that made him a poet. First it was Constance Leth and love that he sang in somewhat thin, yet living verse. Soon, however, it was Northern antiquity and his country's destiny that filled his mind.

"I now come to the point," says the day-book, "where my new life began, where my eyes were opened to love's sanctity, and thereby were made keen to view poesy's wonders, and antiquity their prototype in time. But long did I drudge in the

temple fore-court without once venturing a look at the shining
cherubim, for the very thought of them represented to me only
the heavenly beauty I was condemned never to enjoy. . . . I had
a sense for poesy; but the unhappy tie that bound me to the
poetic material of actuality, did not permit me to enjoy in a
higher state of being what I must nonetheless always lack here.
Oehlenschlaeger wrote Vaulundur's Saga, and it made a deep
impression on me; but the same faint-heartedness, the same fixa-
tion on one subject still hindered my inner nature's assuming an
active form, and the constant alternation of momentary intoxication and months of despair made me quite unfit to walk alone
in the world of ideas."

Thus his mind was awakened and ready. When 1807 brought
deep humiliation to the fatherland, Grundtvig's mind was brim-
ming with the Northern spirit and love of country, and skaldic
notes were thereby born on his lips:

> Only when flames from Akselstad leapt
> High in the sky,
> Under clamor of arms, did life
> Come to my song.
> Yes, by Denmark's affliction
> Wounded, my heart first opened,
> There I saw Dannebrog float
> Homeless upon the loved waters,
> There I saw enemy barks
> Advance in boastful ranks:
> The fathers' dishonored name
> Back of the ravished prows
> Heard the ships'-guns of the British
> Thunder across the Belts' billows—
> Then smote I the skaldic harp,
> With strings of steel,
> With notes as sharp,
> Crash!, yes, a crash is thy language!

Thus did Grundtvig himself describe, in 1813, in the poem *Peace,*
his poetic awakening—not to a worship of beauty or to an
amusing diversion, but to strife and sacrifice in the spirit's service:

Fatherland! Yes, I have played and sung,
As sword might clash upon shield,
And through the din a voice has rung,
Like a voice from thy heathen years.
Always I sang what I had in mind,
War was my song, for war I intended:
Fight we must in this current time,
Life here below is strife!
Strive must the spirit, and sorely, down here.

Long in warfare our tongue must wag
To be worthy to sing of peace;
Never is heart to love melted,
Until the blood has boiled;
Who knows peace and has not striven?
Where is the saved who has suffered no ill?

It was the North's hero-spirit that had seized Grundtvig and
made him a poet. One first suspects this in the *Masked-Ball's*
shocked indignation at the apathy of the day. But as yet he was
unsure. In a poem of 1808 to Molbech he describes himself as
viewing the future with anxious forebodings; then his gaze drops
to the past, and he asks if this is to be Denmark's grave:

O, if you believe the power can awaken
And proudly renew the olden days,
That the sun still has for Denmark's land
One remaining ray in reserve—
Then share with me thy sweet faith!
And comfort and hope and blessed repose
Shall banish fear from my breast.

And before the year was out, the poems in *Northern Mythology,*
the Willemoes elegy and the *Gunderslev Wood* poem, had shown
that his inner life was now ready to assume "an active form,"
that he was fit to "walk alone in the world of ideas." The
Mythology verses in particular plainly stem from a poet who has
"deep in the North his home."

The harvest of the next few years included the great poems on the *Decline of the Heroic Age* and the *War of the Norns and the Asas*. Dramatically, to be sure, these "scenes" have very substantial defects. Any real characterization of individual figures the author is unable to give, and the action lacks true dramatic suspense. Monologue and dialogue are produced, not drama. The verses are monotonous, often actually clumsy; for rhythmic grace, as Grundtvig himself was quick to sense, they did not measure up to Oehlenschlaeger's *Hakon Jarl* and *Palnatoke*. But, granted all this, the fact still remains that Grundtvig has here made the Northern spirit his own and grasped its opposition to Christianity in a way that the renowned poet of *Hakon Jarl* has not. The Scandinavian period of break-up and its problems have become flesh of his flesh and blood of his blood, and even if the *Scenes* do for the most part remain long speeches and conversations instead of becoming drama, they still have an inner power which must transport any reader who has ears to hear at all. Here, in Grundtvig's first real literary work, one is already confronted by what is so typical of his whole output, namely, that it is only too easy to find fault on the basis of aesthetics and general literary standards or even to prove the whole attempt a failure, but regardless of all defects and artistic ineptitudes, his verse, as is often true of his prose as well, exerts a peculiarly compelling power, the nature of which may perhaps best be expressed by the obscure statement that here it is a matter of the spirit speaking; here one comes to grips with life itself, and the rules of grammar, poesy, and rhetoric must get on as best they may. For the rest, *Scenes from the Decline of the Heroic Epoch* was favorably received by contemporary criticism and gave its author an undisputed place in the literary world.

During these years, it was the Northern myths and the ancestral sagas that drove Grundtvig as poet, and his predominant note was therefore one of seriousness and austerity. Often the verses stand as if carved in stone. Perhaps the most striking example of this quality is the splendid inscription on the memorial at Seeland Point, one of the strongest and most monumental pieces in our literature:

The barks met at eve on the sea,
And the air began to glow.
They played all over the open grave,
And red the billows flowed.

Here am I set as a runic stone,
To bear witness to men of the North
That they were Danes, whose mouldering bones
Beneath me crumble to earth.
Danish of tongue, of race, and of mind,
Meet to be called in this current time
Their forefathers' worthy sons.

Here we encounter one of the keynotes of the skald's poetry:
love of country. Soon, however, another element was to enter in.
his thoughts turned from antiquity to the Christian middle ages,
and, gripped by the crusading zeal, he wrote his powerful and
stirring ballads, *The Pilgrims, Peter the Hermit,* and *Today's
Crusade.* His Scandinavian zeal took toll from the Old Testament, and the prophets' judgment pealed like rolling thunder.
The war had become a war against contemporary unbelief. At
this point he was checked by the "hammer-blow" of the crisis,
which silenced both Northern skald-notes and prophetic severity.
His new experiences were instead embodied in a series of rather
halting verses, mostly unfinished religious poems and hymns.
For a time it even looked as though his religious awakening were
literally going to make him count poetry as "dross" that he might
"win Christ." However, this did not prove to be the case. Before
long we get: "The harp which I had hung above God's altar,
he himself returned to me, when he had blessed it to his use,"
and from the next few years date a long series of grandiose
poems, among them *The Dune of Egelykke,* with the celebrated
strophes:

> May God in his grace have pity
> On me who am wretched and poor . . .

> My spirit opened its eyes,
> Scanned the precipice rim,
> Looked hard and closely around

For a rescuer, and found,
Found, wherever it glanced,
God everywhere:
Found him in the poets' song,
Found him in the sage's word,
Found him in myths of the North,
Found him in time's passing;
Yet most visibly and surely
Found him in the Book of books.
Ever it sighs and longs
And with all creation yearns
After that glorious time
When its daughters and its sons
The Lord shall with freedom reward.

The Christian and the Danish—these have now become the strings of his lyre, as they remain the power of his prose. Not without reason did he use the following verse as title-leaf motto for *Danne-Virke:*

The bell in the Danish church
Is the clanging shield of the sagas,
To build the Danish bulwark
It summons each intrepid Dane!
Yet rings it true in the field
Only in chorus with churchly song
Led by Thyra Danebod!

To awaken the people as Christians and nationally was the goal he fought for, and through this task he became conscious of his calling as poet. Both in prose and verse he explored the question of the poet's mission, but most explicitly in the introduction to *Roskilde-Saga:*

Tempests howl and billows foam,
Distressful sits our mother of the North,
Must not the harp be dumb,
In crape be wrapped?
Who dares rashly force
Its strings to sound?
Must it not jar and crack
Under any sudden strain?

So queries the skald in the first strophe, and recalls how he has
often touched the harp but always with the same purpose:

> Only about God's and the Skjoldungs' kingdom
> Did the strings sound.

He has seen visions and must cut runes despite the hatred and
scorn with which the world would smother his song:

> Yet the harp dare I, while the hours advance,
> Tune to a sound,
> Not to a dolorous sound, as when bells
> Toll for the dead,
> No, to a sound as when folk flock
> Where the bells ring out for a feast and Thee.

His poetry shall be as a hymn that proclaims spring and Pentecost
to the Danish church, to king and people, and his songs shall be
as a wreath of roses to deck the house. By way of this introductory
poem Grundtvig passes however to a consideration of the poet's
calling itself and his election, and on this subject he writes in
the "Preface-rhyme" words which had lifelong validity as applied
to himself and to his concept of what he as poet should do for
his people.

First he expostulates with contemporary poets, "poets in
these wretched days," who believe that they have license to sing
fast and loose, true or false, provided it sounds well in the world's
ear, and can touch the heart. As poets they are equally good whatever way hearts are turned and whatever the fire that is kindled.
To these poets Grundtvig sends his letter of challenge, since they
confuse people's minds and seduce their hearts, and in this letter
of challenge he proposes to speak up about "Minstrelsy":

> Skalds, skalds! Remember
> Your high calling and election!
> The Lord in his own garden
> Set you among the flowers
> To see in them with eyes made clear
> The splendor from on high,
> To see how they marshal themselves
> Toward a mystic name, to His
> At whose "Be thou" they became,
> Toward a sacred aureole.

Yes, this is our sweet election:
Here, as in an early spring,
Wreaths we can imagine,
With vision's inner sense can see
Ourselves in the fount of life
Clarified in heavenly splendor.
The garden that God gave us here below
Borders on the Lord's Eden,
In spirit to us wafted
Through the openings of the lattice;
And by surmise we catch
Perfume from what is therein.
Rejoice thee tremblingly, O skald!
As thy choice is and thy calling;
Through thee must be imaged
What thou sawest in life's spring.

And immediately after come the two lines which better than anything else express Grundtvig's view of the poet:

Thou art life's chosen reconnoiterer,
Thou art the Lord's collaborator.

The poet is the man who sees visions, gets out to life's borderland, where heaven and earth meet, where the boundary is set between truth and falsehood, where the great decisions are made. He can therefore speak truly and powerfully of life and its conditions. He is life's reconnoiterer, who may perhaps not have seen into everything, but who has nonetheless in visions and dreams approached the innermost secrets, and he is the Lord's collaborator, since as skald he can interpret the visions and convey what he has beheld. One must therefore not demand clarity of the skald, in any event not as the first and most important thing. Clarity is not the starting-point but the goal that beckons onward, and the poet has himself not reached the goal, he has only seen the visions; often these have not been at all clear to him, and they become even darker when he seeks to translate them into earthly speech. So it was with Grundtvig himself, and he had felt it. "The poet when inspired is not inactive or inanimate but is actually in a state where he feels life in fuller power and warmth than usual. He views what is set before his eyes, and sings what he beholds, but as every poet knows, should he seek to sharpen the images by taking thought, they vanish or become mere shadows; should he seek by reflection to find the proper words, then must he be silent or cease to speak from inspiration. . . . In this corporeal world there exists no higher symbol than the tuned string's being stirred to sound by a puff of wind."

It is thus part and parcel of the prodigious conditions of the poet-life to be at the mercy of inspirational power:

> It is strange to be a skald!
> The voices from above we hear
> In that secret accent;
> What we say, ourselves we know not;
> But woe unto the bard who questions!
> God must know what God has said,
> He created what the skald's eye saw.

And for Grundtvig the whole thing hinges on whether the poet has really seen visions. Accordingly it is by the truth of the visions that he must be judged. Form is scarcely taken into consideration. "Whether Oeh's [Oehlenschlaeger's] later works are more rugged in style and versification than his earlier, truth to tell, I am unaware, for although I cannot call the curved rectilinear, the crooked straight, or the rugged level, still a good poem goes down smoothly with me despite all knots, and the bad slips no better at all for being smooth." He is of the belief that whatever is worth anything always comes in the right vessel, and that the vessel of itself in no way elucidates: "I am therefore heterodox enough to believe that it is only the historically consummated art which can produce a form which can with unblemished beauty encase the highest visions; thus it is much better that the form crack than that the vision be broken." What he inquires into is "the beholding," whether it has "truth, life and power." That is the requirement he sets for his own poetry, but by the same token it is evident to him that poet in the usual sense he is not. He clearly sees his shortcomings with respect to mastery of form. "The contemplation of Oehlenschlaeger taught me that I am no poet." He was, so he said, half bard, half book-worm.

Poetry was for him not a self-valid calling. He was life's chosen reconnoiterer, who was to bring awakening and gradually contribute to a clarification of life's riddle. But for this very reason obscurity must be the preliminary form, clarity the goal that lay ahead.

With reference to *New Year's Morning* and its obscurity, and with reference to the lack of appreciation on the part of his contemporaries, which, in spite of everything, pained Grundtvig, he wrote Ingemann in 1824:

Whether I might be qualified to produce in any one spiritual direction anything worth preserving I do not know and almost doubt, since I am obviously a mixture, a ferment, which clears up only at the expense of its life; but to do that I know is not my mission. My vocation is to give expression to the ferment, as livingly and yet at bottom as lovingly as possible, to express it for what it is: the working of the little leaven, to which God's kingdom is likened, upon the whole dough of which man is fashioned. God gave me a poetico-historical eye, with which I, in His light, scan the vast chaos which our more or less misguided human efforts have produced. I can see a marvellous coherence in the whole, yet for the most part glimpse it but darkly, and my readers often glimpse but darkly what is plain to me, and see sheer blackness where I glimpse darkly. It is unreasonable of my readers to demand that I express anything more clearly than I see it, or that I be silent about what I see of the great and wonderful because it is, as it must necessarily be, dark. Clear it will never become unless it is first brought out of the murk in its necessarily dark state. . . . You think that I still might sing clearly, and you find this sufficiently proved by the fact that I actually have so sung. What this amounts to is that I can with tolerable ease appropriate to my uses a raft of historical song-forms and in them speak my mind, my thoughts, but then I am not inspired. As soon as that happens, all the forms I have at my command burst, and I catch at fragments of all of them and thus denote hieroglyphically what I cannot possibly by means of them express. . . . My poetic language I must then either scrupulously forget or in it speak as darkly and ruggedly and often jarringly as is now the case, and since the former at least to myself would be a loss like that of life itself, there is nothing for it but for me to be patient. . . . You may rest assured that I often fight with myself for a clear and pleasing form. For who does not wish that his song may please and be understood? But the only choice I ever have is between life and death. . . . So is it also with Axel's epic and with a rhyme to Count Danneskjold's memory with which I have long been occupied. If I let it go in its own clothes and at its own gait, up and down, from rock to rock like a chamois and straight over the sea like Sleipner, it goes so that my heart leaps in my breast, and I think: No, this is altogether too mad, there must be some moderation, whereupon it stops and gives me all kinds of leisure to figure out where I would go if I could get going again.

Seldom is a poet heard to speak with so clear a critical sense about himself and his production. If you read all of Grundtvig's many verses through, you will see the correctness of the judgment, even though it is perhaps more severe than is fair. A more uneven output can hardly be imagined. You may get page after page of heavy verse without flight and without beauty, and right in the midst of all this there may come three or four or perhaps ten strophes which will never be forgotten as long as Danish speech is heard. One verse may have the flattest of imagery, yes, actual puns, and in the next the loftiest intensity will be encountered, and an ability to find striking images that is unequalled. But his output is likewise uneven in another sense, that of having marked variations. Grundtvig knows how to tune many strings. His first string is the Danish, his second, the Christian, his third the home, but these are accompanied by a multitude of secondary and intermediate tones that is often amazing. Now his poetry is like rolling thunder or prophetic judgment, now it is suggestive of Baggesen's loquacity and delight in argument. At times his style attains the highest intensity, at other times—and here Grundtvig is a pioneer—it is in the best sense simple and popular. Mention was made earlier of his faculty for fashioning short, concise sentences, capable of living on the people's lips almost like adages. At the same time he can strike the most tender and delicate notes, as in the poem to the mother tongue or in the poems to his own mother, but most beautifully and most affectingly perhaps in the farewell poem he wrote to his daughter Meta upon her marriage—which took place some years after his serious mental illness in the early 1840's, at which time his daughter had been the only one who could calm his mind and nurse him:

> Little one, dear one! When my mind was sick,
> My head was confused, but my heart was meek,
>> When madness threatened
>> And friends were in dread,
> You looked at me smiling through tears,
>> My only daughter,
> As I now look at you on this summer's eve
>> And whisper farewell.
>
> Little one, dear one, may God repay you,
> Wherever you go under heaven, or come!
>> You soothed the smart,
>> You warmed my heart,
> You cooled my brow, you eased my pain
>> With your kisses;
> And so, with my blessing, this summer's eve
>> A kiss for farewell!

In eight stanzas, each more ecstatic than the last, he builds up his farewell, then ends with a reminder of the eternal abodes where once again they shall meet:

> Yes, there shall we meet and smile at sorrow
>> Some summer's morning,
> And so, with a smile through tears, farewell
>> Of a summer's eve.

From comment and explanation I shall refrain, and merely ask the reader to take out the book himself and read the whole poem, and at the same time "the spiritual cradle song," "Sleep sweetly, little babe," which dates from about the same time. These are in my opinion two of the most affecting poems Grundtvig ever wrote, and I have yet to see anyone who can read them "with dry eyes."

From childhood Grundtvig had been accustomed to sing in church from the Evangelical-Christian Hymnbook, but before many years it became a constant torment to him. Above all else he felt how inadequate this product of the Enlightenment was as a medium for congregational hymn-singing and for proclaiming the gospel tidings. Later times have unconditionally justified Grundtvig's verdict, even if repudiation has sometimes been carried too far. It is thus quite gratuitous to assert that this hymnbook was actually neither evangelical nor Christian. It was a child of its time, and as such had its relative merit, something which Grundtvig, moreover, recognized. But it undeniably marks a definite break in the hymnological tradition. Preaching and praise have been superseded by the question of the individual, by exhortations to warm, noble sentiments; man himself has become the hymns' central point instead of God and his revelation. Thus the hymns dogmatic content breaks down completely and gives place to emotional emphases. To all this add, finally, the fact that the Evangelical-Christian hymnbook had come into being at a time when there was much interest in aesthetic rules but little understanding of poetry and verse. Measured by a purely poetical yardstick, particularly when compared with its predecessors, the collection is simply pitiable.

The idea of creating a new hymnody and a new hymn book to go with it appears to have emerged early with Grundtvig, but many years were to pass before he himself hit upon the right note. Attempts from the years 1810-1812 to rewrite old hymns were only partly successful and his own poems from that time have no hymn value, except for the remarkably perfect Bible-history poem about the three holy kings. In the next few years he made several new attempts, but not until he had arrived at the "historico-ecclesiastical view" did the fountain burst forth which was later to stream out over the field of the Danish church for far more than a generation.

All in all Grundtvig wrote about 1500 hymns, a great share of them translations, however. He translated, or rather adapted, hymns from the Hebrew, Greek, Latin, German, and English, and at the same time paraphrased a long series of Biblical narratives in his Bible-history songs, which, by virtue of a sure-fire narrative art and a peculiarly childlike piety, have survived for several generations on Danish school-children's lips. Though Grundtvig reached his height in the original hymns, there are several of the adaptations from foreign languages which are not only far superior to their models, but which actually approach perfection. There is perhaps particular cause to mention in this connection the translations from Old Anglo-Saxon song, pearl among which is: "By night there was a knocking at the gate of hell." Only at one point was Grundtvig almost always unsuccessful. Namely, when he sought to rewrite or adapt older Danish hymns; several of Kingo's and Brorson's he simply murdered. It was as though such a task constricted him too much, gave his own creative power no chance to unfold.

Any examination or characterization of the whole bounteous treasure with which Grundtvigian hymn poetry has enriched the congregation shall not be attempted here. This has on several previous occasions been undertaken by men far more expert in these matters and better qualified than myself. Furthermore, to yield dividends it would have to be accompanied by so copious a reprinting of individual stanzas and whole hymns as to exceed the limits of this little book. I shall therefore confine myself to a few brief, and perhaps somewhat rambling, observations.

First, a little about language and style. In these respects, Grundtvig's hymns are completely individual. Almost never is there any possibility of mistaking them. And yet Grundtvig's poetry here represents a return to the old church hymnody, antedating both the Enlightenment and Pietism. In content and use of imagery his hymns are typically Biblical. Inquiry into the matter immediately shows that almost verse for verse they are directly inspired by the Bible, and chiefly by the Old Testament. In style they are absolutely dissociated from their day and age; they have something of the past's power and intensity about them. Here is no pandering to what the age demands or fashion prescribes. In a supremely characteristic manner Grundtvig has however succeeded in so employing the biblical and antiquated churchly idiom that despite all allegiance to the old it is completely emancipated from the conventionally devotional. Often this emancipation is associated with an actual "Danicizing" of the biblical world. It is Danish nature and the Danish mind that we find mirrored in the biblical figures and tales. And Grundtvig's own hymns exemplify to a rare degree what he himself once expressed thus:

In the North, we now understand better
Than a song handed down from our fathers
The high symbolic language of the East.
Our mother-tongue bows low,
Nimbly and gracefully follows
The line of thought of the Lord.

Or—as he also expressed it—the Danish language borrows fire and powers from the epic of Zion.

New and surprising words and images here crop up in the churchly idiom. Let there be only hissing in "Serpent-gaard" is said of the realm of the dead. Christ is called by the old word for king, "drot," and also the "head-king." Pentecost is like "a morning in May when the green appears." God's kingdom blooms like a rose-garden, and in its woods nightingales warble their trills. So might one multiply examples. The new and surprising goes farther, however, than choice of terms and images. There is in many of Grundtvig's hymns a conscious approach to the folk-ballad note, most pronounced in the historical hymns and in the bible-history songs. Here artless simplicity and natural charm are coupled with biblical intensity in a wholly new and original manner.

A glance at the content of Grundtvig's hymn poetry leaves no room for doubt that it was the historico-ecclesiastical view which made him a psalmist. This does not mean, however, that the "theory" of the "little word from our Lord's own mouth" stands out with any particular prominence, but that his whole poetry is born of the assurance that a living congregation exists, and that in it, through his word, our Lord Jesus is present, bestows forgiveness of sins, and promises eternal life. Therefore the hymns become in a marked sense churchly or congregational hymns, not "I-hymns" but "we-hymns."

There are few of the hymns which do not clearly bear their maker's mark. But of the "personal," in the usual sense of the term, namely as giving expression to purely personal experiences and thus drawing the poet's own thoughts and feelings into the foreground, there is next to nothing. Grundtvig himself in a letter points out that a "principal fault of our fathers which we as their children must strive to correct, was their desire to negotiate with the Savior each for himself and possess him, something which will never do, as, among other things, 'our Father' should have taught them." It is of God's act of creation, of the large facts of salvation, Jesus' life, death and resurrection, it is above all of the Holy Spirit and its work in the congregation, of baptism and communion, of the living and creative word, of the church, that Grundtvig sings. In a letter of 1843 he mentions planning a hymn-pamphlet for the use of the Vartov congregation, and says that the farther into the work he gets the clearer it becomes to him that, owing to the modest proportions the pamphlet is to have, there will be little room for what is customarily called the devotional, "namely that which each of us oftenest hums to himself and prefers to sing with a few good friends. For the main thing here is first the church, baptism and communion, and secondly our church festivals and church gatherings as a whole."

There is something of the organ's roll and the chapel festival about Grundtvig's hymns. It is no accident that at the great calendar feasts of the church they are used more than almost any others. So much so that at times one may well feel the lack of some touch of the Brorson note of personalized revival with its Christ-love and its emotional intimacy. But, although no one could claim that we ought to be content with Grundtvig's hymns alone, all will surely agree that it is these that most enrich our hymnal, not alone numerically, which is obvious, but also in terms of what they mean to the life of the congregation.

In the matter of content, exactly the same thing has happened with Grundtvig's hymn poetry as in the matter of style. He has reached beyond the Enlightenment and Pietism to the old reformation, and in part pre-reformation, hymn poetry. Just as with Luther, the aim here is not to express personal feelings, but to spread the gospel and sing Christ's praise. Of Luther's hymns, a wise man once said: "The decisive factor is the content. Luther's hymns lack any lyric form, that is to say, any underscoring of the emotional aspects of the subject. The speaker here neither indulges in all sorts of accusatory, encouraging, instructive and admonitory acclamations, nor does he press others by exhortation or suggestion to take this or that to heart. What these songs do contain is worship, and objective statement, confession of faith, admission of sins, revelation. One would surely have to read in a curious manner not to hear line by line the Christly mind and its manifestations, or rather, quite irrespective of whether the hymn's subject is an 'I' or a 'we,' to hear the congregation of God's children speaking. In its name and for its use did Luther compose his hymns. But neither God's child nor his congregation do we find in these hymns concerned about self, preoccupied with self, but on the contrary find them with the utmost possible concentration solely preoccupied with the second article of faith, understood in biblical simplicity, as for the purpose of attaining to a knowledge of God and of praising him. Precisely thus do life, love, experience, the reality of personal revelation here find expression."

These words fit Grundtvig's hymns exactly, except that his orchestra is far richer than the Reformer's. In his prose writings, Grundtvig very often denounced the Enlightenment's Reason-Christianity and the sentimental Pietism of the Awakened, and it was through this polemic, so to say, that he first arrived at his own idea of Christianity's actual content. Not so in the hymns. There everything polemical is eliminated. There it is as if the understanding of Christianity, of the word, of the congregation, gushed straight up from the earth. And the verses adapt themselves in the most marvellous manner to be bearers of this life message.   Possibly there is one thing in the above quotation about Luther which some may regard as not exactly applying to Grundtvig, namely the statement about his hymns centering around the second article of faith. In Grundtvig's case, most people would be more likely to put "third article." It is customary to designate Brorson the singer of Christmas, Kingo of Easter, and Grundtvig of Pentecost. Nor can it be denied that a great many of Grundtvig's finest hymns, especially among his original ones, are Holy Spirit hymns. Purely historically it is also an accurate observation that the Enlightenment did not get much farther than the first article, and that the pietist awakened held chiefly to the article about Jesus' suffering and death, whereas in the Grundtvigian church-concept a belief in the spirit, the word, and the church revived.

But the characteristic thing about Grundtvig is this: that through his belief in the spirit and its work in the congregation he got back to both the second article of faith and the first. Not for nothing had the turning point in his life been the experience of 1810-1811, when Jesus had become present to him as expiator and as assuming power over his believers. Nor did 1824 change this. On the contrary! Yet he understood that our Lord Jesus had not made a special covenant with each individual human being, but had called them jointly and planted them in his kingdom, where he rules by the spirit and the word. But from this concept, and, as before mentioned, this is the notable thing about him, Grundtvig also got back to the first article, belief in God as lord and creator. That is, the Enlightenment's belief in providence and its glad optimism together with its lauding of this world as "the best of all possible worlds" have been recaptured entire by Grundtvig, but given a wholly new perspective. Thus a wholly different force is also given to his talk of God as creator and providence, and this talk merges in a notable manner with the talk of Jesus as lord and savior. This is plainly brought out in the peculiarly rough-hewn poem "They praise the Lord, my mouth and my heart."

With all that there is to be said regarding Grundtvig's partiality for, and particular knack at, writing Holy Spirit hymns, I still believe that his hymnody's true greatness lies in this unique combining of all three articles of faith so that each is made chief in turn, but always in such a way that the two others are present as background and accompaniment. That is why these hymns are better able than any others to sum up the gospel and the Christian life, and why they have in a unique sense become the backbone of the Danish congregation's hymn-singing.

Tempting as it might be to present many extended excerpts in illustration of what has just been said, space does not permit. I shall conclude with a single hymn, given not because it is the most beautiful or from a Christian viewpoint the most valuable— who could make choice among such riches?—but since it may possibly give an occasional reader as yet unfamiliar with Grundtvig's hymns an inclination to read more.

Thou who proceedest from the living God,
Spirit of spirits there on high!
A race of liars that wearies their advocate
Stands stubborn before thine eye;
But by God's grace, O stay thou here!
The night is gloomy, and it is near.

Tongues of fire but also preaching mild
Give unto them thou dost anoint and send!
Let salvation's word in the apostles' wake
Travel to earth's farthest end,
Until there be no place man's foot has trod
In which its voice has not been heard.

May joy and light go with them to the towns,
And make the earth to blossom where they tread!
May strength and courage make the weak to stand,
All those who weep be comforted!
At the gospel's gentle voice
May mercy wake in every breast.

Shine on the field, like a morning of song,
A morning in May when the green appears!
Let the power of delight charm sloth awake,
As there by God's grace perceived!
Let the deepened tones at dawn and eve
Touch even the heart that is hard as rock!

Let Pentecost's baptism to hope of God's glory
Give all the tribes rebirth!
May the telling and text of our savior's achievement
Bloom like the roses red!
May life's tree shoot from the Cross's root!
Let all taste that our king is good!

Let salvation's joy, through the Savior's virtue
Be the lot of all mankind!
May the Father's word and the Spirit's deed
In the Savior coincide!
So that out of the whole which God has made
The race of perdition alone is lost.

Both in form and substance his hymns were the high-water
mark of Grundtvig's output. But upon Danish poetry he exerted
at least as much of a creative influence through his patriotic songs
and national poems. With these as with the hymns, his first
attempts go far back in point of time. The note had been struck
with the memorial ode to Willemoes. The historical ballad attained its first and almost classic form in the *Roskilderime,*
through the two poems "Bishop Wilhelm and King Svend" and
"Master Ole Vind." The most popular, perhaps, of all Grundtvig's patriotic songs, "Far Loftier Mountains," dates from 1820,
and during these years a number of scattered, one is tempted to
say occasional, poems likewise appeared. But just as it was the
ecclesiastical view which first gave body to his hymn-writing,
and just as it was the concrete demand of congregational life
which led him to a purposive hymnody, so with his national
poetry it was in part the historical-churchly view, though his
English experiences far more, that awakened him to an understanding of nationality and freedom such as to give content to
his poetry, and it was contact with that national life and that
folk-life's new demands which gave impetus to that poetry.

The first time national song, so to say, burst forth spon-
taneously was at Grundtvig's lecture at Borch's Collegium, on
the evening when he had spoken of Willemoes, and when Frederik Barfod struck up Grundtvig's song about the hero of King's
Deep and Seeland Point. The year after, in the spring of 1839,
Grundtvig and his friends founded the Danish Society, whose
object was the use of the mother-tongue for living discussion of
the circumstances of Danish national life. In this Society Grundtvig was a frequent chairman, and here popular song burst forth
in earnest. Most of the songs which had previously been used at
social gatherings of this type had come down from the 18th century clubs. A large part of them were merely drinking songs,
others had a more general secular content. But it was something
entirely new for people's heads to be full of songs about fatherland and mother-tongue, about history and its heroes.

Various people wrote songs for these gatherings, but none
could measure up to Grundtvig, who was here faced with a
demand which seemed to release his latent abilities. P. O. Boisen

collected the Society's poems into a Song-book—the first popular
song-book our country had ever possessed. This gained wide circulation in the many "Danish Societies" which were founded
throughout the country, and was likewise used in the first popular
schools. It was thus a forerunner of the far later *High-school
Song-book,* which even today is of all books the one that means
most to Danish national and popular life. If you look in the
High-school Song-book, you will soon discover that nearly a third
is from Grundtvig's hand, and if you have any acquaintance with
the book's use, you will know that here, as with the hymn book,
it is this Grundtvigian third which is most frequently sung.

Grundtvig's democratic national sentiments have been discussed in another connection. I shall not repeat what was said
there, but shall merely recall that it was this national democracy
which set its impress on his patriotic songs and differentiates
them from those of most other writers. There is, as one feels more
strongly every time one sings them, a bottom to them. They are
not merely strong emotions versified; they have their myth, their
metaphysic, if you will. You here encounter a man who knows
what he is talking about, and who also knows precisely what he
intends by his song. He does not intend to awaken to nationalism
but to national democracy, he has no desire to set bounds or to
find points of separation from others. No, his ideas are born
of a universal-historical and common-humanitarian study. This
actually even applies to the purely national poems notwithstanding their frequent appearance of being barbed against other
peoples, first and foremost against the Germans. The national
here never becomes a sort of inflated common egotism of the
whole people. It expresses the form life has for Danish human
beings, the conditions under which they have received the gift
of life, and under which they alone can guard it.

But at the bottom of all this lies respect for life itself as
something that is greater than man, a divine gift which, in the
last analysis, is common to all. Therefore the national always ends
in the inter-popular—not in the international. Internationalism
is unrealism, an attempt to evade life's actual conditions. You are,
once and for all, not a human being in a general way, but belong
to some one people, be it Danish, German, or English, and this

fact shall and must be taken seriously. But sooner or later you get in touch with the others, be they Germans, Jews, or Poles, because you understand that they in their way must live the same life and be subject to the same conditions. Therefore history too is something other than images of the past for national self-glorification; its goal is to throw light upon actual, national human life. And like all life, this holds an element of the mysterious; it is not something which is ours to command as a matter of course, which we can completely explain and shape as we will. Man is, once and for all, not the lord with sovereign right to take life into his own service. That is why it is the poet's vocation, he being life's chosen reconnoiterer, to throw light upon national life, and that is why the latter finds better expression in song than anywhere else.

This is the national view which lives in Grundtvig's songs, and which, down through the years, has in schools and high-schools been sung into Danish youth. Nobody who has seen and experienced something of what this can mean can help hoping that there may come a time when, in its Grundtvigian sense, national song will be the whole country's common possession. In poetic power and beauty only a few of the national songs—"Fatherland," "Mother's Name," and certain others—rank with the hymns, but in return Grundtvig has in this field gained a number of disciples—Hostrup, Mads Hansen, Jakob Knudsen—who have managed to take over the inheritance and augment its yield. It was the first Grundtvigian generation, the free schools, the high-schools, and the youth associations that brought song to life on the people's lips, and song has perhaps in larger measure than anything else been the channel through which Grundtvig has succeeded in enlightening his people as to the conditions of human life, just as it was through the hymns that he succeeded in speaking to them of the Christian life.

> The mother-tongue is the power's word,
> Which lives in the people's mouth,
> Which is loved in North and South,
> Is sung there so sweet in the groves,
>   Sweet in joy and sweet in need,
>   Sweet in life and sweet in death,
>   Sweet in after-fame.

Translator's Notes

CHAPTER I: CHILDHOOD AND YOUTH

PAGE 3. *Steffens, Henrik,* 1773–1845, son of Susanna Kristine, younger sister of Grundtvig's mother. This 10-years older cousin, a fervent disciple of Schelling from his student days at Jena, returned to Copenhagen during Grundtvig's undergraduate years and delivered a series of lectures which, in a sense, gave Denmark both Oehlenschlaeger and Grundtvig himself. He later became professor at Halle and at Breslau, was a friend of Goethe and Schiller, and a leader in the German as well as in the Danish Romantic movement.

Mynster, Jacob Peter, 1775–1854, stepson of F. L. Bang, brother of Grundtvig's mother. His first charge, to Spjellerup and Smerup on Seeland in 1801, was followed by the curacy of Our Lady's Church in Copenhagen, 1811, appointment as court preacher in 1826, and as royal confessor and priest for the court and palace in 1828. In 1834 he was consecrated Bishop of Seeland and for 20 years remained primate of Denmark. Thus, eight years older than Grundtvig, he was always in a position to say No to Grundtvig and almost always did so. Their differences in opinion appear to have been largely fortified by temperamental antipathy.

Four sons: Otto Grundtvig, 1772–1833, entered the University of Copenhagen in 1789 from Herlufsholm boarding-school in South Seeland, was clergyman on Falster and later near Copenhagen; Jacob Ulrich Hansen Grundtvig, 1775–1800, entered the University from Viborg Grammar School in 1795, died as clergyman in the Danish colony on the Guinea coast; Niels Christian Bang Grundtvig, 1777–1803, entered from Viborg in 1796 and also died as clergyman on the Guinea coast.

PAGE 5. *Berlings-Avisen,* ancestor of *Berlingske Tidende,* one of Denmark's oldest newspapers, and descendent of the *Extraordinaire Relationer,* founded in 1721 and acquired by Ernest Heinrich Berling in 1748. At first largely a court circular, the Berling sheet has throughout its career been an organ of conservative interests with a semi-official status, i.e. a sort of Danish analogue to the *London Times.*

PAGE 6. *Huitfeldt, Arnild,* 1546–1609, prolific Danish historian who used sources which have since been lost.

Suhm, Frederik, 1728–98, author of a *History of Denmark* from the earliest times.

Heiberg, P. A., 1758–1841, one of the principal political prose writers of the period, and author of *The Adventures of a Banknote* (1793), a daring treatment of important public questions, and of a satirical dictionary of current usage (1798) which led to his exile in Paris, where he died.

Rahbek, Knud Lyhne, 1760–1830, dramatist, director of the Royal Theatre of Copenhagen, editor of *The Danish Spectator,* and author of *Letters of an Old Actor to His Son* (1782), a theoretical treatise on dramatic art. His villa outside Copenhagen was a haunt of the celebrities of the time.

Bruun, Malthe Conrad, 1775–1826, an early liberal, banished along with Heiberg to Paris, where he died. In France he became a noted geographer.

Horrebow, Otto, 1769–1823, disciple of Voltaire and editor, 1797–1801, of *Jesus and Reason.* His view that the New Testament had falsified the message of Jesus was stoutly combatted by Bishop Balle and successfully controverted by A. S. Oersted.

Balle, Nicolai Edinger, 1744–1816, bishop of Seeland, was a brother-in-law of Johan Grundtvig, in other words Grundtvig's uncle-by-marriage.

Kingo, Thomas Hansen, 1634–1703, bishop of Funen, first of Denmark's three great hymn-writers, and also the principal secular poet of his period. J. C. Aaberg's *Hymns and Hymn-Writers of Denmark* (Des Moines, 1945) gives a comprehensive view of his life, and translations of a considerable number of his hymns. Magnus Stevns, in *Grundtvig-Studier* 1949 (English summary given), offers a detailed study of Kingo as Grundtvig's model, and at the same time his counterpart. Grundtvig had always loved Kingo's Hymn-Book (1699), but in adapting Kingo's hymns found much that he wished to alter in both doctrine and emphasis. Son of an indigent weaver of Scotch descent, Kingo early impressed teachers and others by his gifts, his ability to work, his nice personality, and his vigorously religious attitudes, qualities which always made friends for him in the years when he needed them, and which were indispensable to him as Bishop of Funen, a job which combined the travel problems of a pioneer circuit rider with those of ecclesiatical executive. To the arid post-Reformation period, with practically nothing to sing, Kingo's hymns brought the vigor of early Lutheranism together with the old church fathers' sense for nature.

Aarhus Latin School. In *Grundtvig-Studier,* 1951, F. Paludan-Müller asks why Grundtvig had not gone from Lauritz Feld's to Viborg Grammar School as the two middle brothers had done, and discovers that their record at Viborg had been somewhat inglorious.

PAGE 12. *Maundy Thursday*—In the battle of the Baltic, or the Battle of Copenhagen, April 2, 1801, the British seized or destroyed the ships of the Danish fleet to prevent their falling into Napoleon's hands.

PAGE 15. *Wessel, Johan Herman,* 1742–85, a Norwegian emigrant, author of *Love without Stockings* (1772), a parody on imitation French tragedies and Italian melodramas, and of verse tales in a fine comic vein.

CHAPTER II: LOVE AND ROMANTICISM

PAGE 23. *Staffeldt, Schack,* 1769–1826, sometimes linked with Henrik Steffens as one of the two mouthpieces of Danish romanticism.

Palnatoke, a celebrated bowman in the army of Harald Bluetooth who was also the original of William Tell, it being told of him that when he boasted of being able to pierce an apple set on top of a pole, King Harald ordered him to shoot one from the head of his son. Later, Palnatoke incited Harald's son Svend Tveskaeg to rebel against him, and himself killed King Harald in battle.

PAGE 24. *The actual falling in love at Egelykke.* Gustav Albeck, in reviewing a number of essays and books on Grundtvig, *Grundtvig-Studier,* 1949, remarks that Grundtvig destroyed those parts of his diary which described his arrival and first summer at Egelykke, 91 pages in all, thus rendering the problem of the nature of the episode insoluble. He states, however, on the basis of other documents, that Grundtvig appears to have been very susceptible at the time, and may have "read a good deal more into Fru Constance's smiles and handclasps than he had any right to do."

Bjornson, Bjornstjerne Martinius, 1832–1910, Norwegian novelist, dramatist and poet, revolutionary thinker and social reformer, an intense nationalist whose literary influence was world-wide.

PAGE 25. *Marheinecke, Philip Konrad,* 1780–1846, German protestant theologian, and an outstanding representative of the "speculative theology."

PAGE 31. *Oersted, Hans Christian,* 1777–1851, son of an apothecary, was the discoverer of electro-magnetism (1822–1823) and of the metal aluminum (1824). He was strongly influenced by Fichte and Hegel. His collected philosophical writings were published in 1850 under the title *The Spirit in Nature.*

PAGE 32. *Oehlenschlager, Adam Gotlob,* 1779–1850, the most eminent Danish poet of his day, inspired by Steffens's interpretation of German romanticism, but chiefly noted as poet and dramatist of old Northern hero material. His plays drove French-style classical drama from the Danish theatre. The tragedy *Hakon Jarl* (1807) was written at Halle. *Vaulundur's Saga* is an amplification of the *Wayland the Smith* legend: for a translation of the Norse version of this legend see *A Pageant of Old Scandinavia,* ed. Henry Goddard Leach (New York, 1946). For a consecutive treatment of Oehlenschlaeger's life and work see *The History of the Scandinavian Literatures,* ed. F. Blankner (New York, 1938), which also lists works that exist in English translation.

The Eddas. "Edda" in Icelandic originally signified "ancestress," and by extension "mother earth." The *Prose Edda* is a treatise by Snorri Sturleson written about 1220 upon the art of poetry, conceived in historical and philosophical terms and interspersed with extracts from pre-Christian Icelandic poetry. The *Poetic Edda* is the general title of a collection of Northern poems made near the end of the 13th century in Iceland and sometimes designated the *Elder Edda* in consequence of a now disproved theory that it was an older work of which Snorri's *Prose Edda* is an abridgement. For translated excerpts, see *Pageant.*

Masquerade Ball in Denmark. A series of poems put in the mouths of mythical or historical characters and choruses, with prose "stage directions." Though first published as a self-contained work, it occupies only 8 octavo pages in the latest collected edition of Grundtvig's writings. When included in a collection of his verse, Grundtvig appended a note to the line "Both sons of the All-Father," stating that he had not meant to imply that Christ was such a figment as Odin, and that, feeling the impropriety of the line he had never sent a copy of the book to his late father. No notice was taken of the work in the Copenhagen press except by Povel Dons, whose mention of it led to his friendship with Grundtvig.

PAGE 33. *Valkendorf's College,* formerly a Carmelite cloister, provided free living quarters for 16 poor students. After 1820, the number was increased to 20.

Schouboe Institute, a boys' school founded in 1794 by Frederik Christian Schouboe, with two divisions, classical and modern. In the latter, not only were modern languages taught, but bookkeeping, gymnastics, dancing and painting. As history teacher here, Grundtvig read many of his historical poems publicly for the first time. In spite of its great popularity, this school was closed by the founder in 1814.

PAGE 34. *Voluspa,* the first and most impressive poem in the *Poetic Edda,* is a sibyl's recitation, at Odin's bidding, of the history of the universe, from the days of the giants to its destruction and the foreseen creation of a better one. The title Voluspa is equivalent to Valans Spadom, or the prophecy of the sibyl, its narrator. Translated pp. 22-28 of *Pageant.*

Sayings of Odin, the proverbial wisdom of Norse antiquity, translated pp. 28-37 of *Pageant.*

PAGE 35. *Molbech, Christian,* 1783–1857, historian, linguist, and an instructor at Soro Academy. His son, Christian Frederik (1821–1888), poet and critic, edited the voluminous correspondence with Grundtvig.

PAGE 36. *Poppo,* the Christian priest who heard King Harald Bluetooth (c.940–c.985) and his courtiers discussing the relative strength of Christ and Odin and Thor and offered to carry red-hot iron in his hands. The challenge was accepted, and the miracle of his performing the feat without harm is said to have caused Harald to accept the new religion.

Odinkar, Hvide, d.1045, and Odinkar the Younger were bishops in the primitive Danish church.

CHAPTER III: THE YEAR OF CRISIS

PAGE 39. *Dons, Povel,* 1783–1843. After a legal education, Dons turned to belles lettres and poetry, and formed friendships with most of the great writers of his time.

Sibbern, Frederik Christian, 1785–1872, a philosopher with a strong interest in natural science, and friend of the Oersted brothers. He accompanied Steffens to Berlin after a visit of the latter to Denmark, studied there 1811–12, met Goethe and Schelling, later became rector of the University of Copenhagen, where he taught logic and psychology.

CHAPTER IV: LUTHERAN CHRISTIANITY

PAGE 61. *From Udby to Spjellerup:* A Danish mile is equal to 7,532 meters, or about 4½ English miles.

PAGE 63. *Christ the Focal Point of the Ages:* Steffens's view had been that after the fall, man continued to sink until the time of Nero, and that since then, with Christ as the living center, man had been slowly on the upgrade.

PAGE 64. *Zinzendorf, N. L., Count,* 1700-1760, was born in Dresden, lost his father early, and under the tutelage of mother and aunts became strongly and mystically religious, founded free congregations, though a Catholic, and made many contributions to Catholic hymnody.

Herrnhut, the town in Saxony where Zinzendorf is buried, organizational headquarters of the Herrnhuttians or Brotherly Congregations, a sect of pietist Christians, largely Bohemian and Moravian, drawn together in part by Count Zinzendorf.

PAGE 65. *Hornemann, Claus Frees,* 1751–1830, professor of theology in the University of Copenhagen, and among those attacked in Grundtvig's 1812 *World History.*

Oersted, Anders Sandoe, 1778–1830, the philosopher and jurist who laid the foundations for modern Danish and Norwegian jurisprudence; brother of H. C. Oersted.

PAGE 71. *Roskilde-Rim.* The first reading of an early draft of this tremendous poem was given in 1812 before a semi-annual rural meeting of clergy held in Roskilde. Grundtvig was then still curate at Udby. Two descriptions of the reading exist, one of them Grundtvig's own:

"Hearts were moved beneath the priestly gowns and tears ran down priestly cheeks, because over the church there still gleamed a light from the knights' hall, as an omen that Rosenkild's spring had never run dry but only withheld its waters because so long as the ice rules and defends itself against the sun no rose can grow, and that it will again in God's good time stream over the Danish land, bearing refreshment and growth."

The other is by Grundtvig's host on this occasion, Adjunct (later Dean) Daniel Smith:

"The other essays were over, and the good deans had had a good meal and a pipe with their coffee; but alas! there was no siesta. They had to go up to the county hall again, and at nine o'clock our poet and curate began. He sat beside the good District-dean Boegh, our mutual patron, who, with the patience of an angel, relit the candles every time Grundtvig's enthusiasm drowned them out. Münter was less patient, he rose and walked around to the bookshelves and looked through the books. But with the other district deans nature overcame duty: they slept and, among others, Dean Hammond snored disgustingly. But Grundtvig unleashed his voice of thunder when he came, on his poetic odyssey, to the Kirkesvalen section where he sees the light, takes courage, steps in and to his astonishment beholds the knightly cross upon the priestly robes and all the bishops' portraits on the walls. He then shouted loudly:

> Sit you well, you bishops all
> From Palladius to Balle!

and addressed the Bishop as 'old Baltzer's son.'

"The Bishop dropped the book from his hand, the deans awakened, and if Hammond had had any hair it would have stood straight up with fright over his staring eyes. This ended the evening, and it was nearly midnight when Grundtvig stuffed his manuscript into his pocket, and we had to skirt in semi-darkness the turns of the winding stair before we could reach the church, where the images in the moonlight moved as if they had been awakened by wizard Grundtvig. The extraordinary haste with which the deans pushed by one another really augured some quickening of heartbeats. I noticed that Grundtvig came last of all, and I could not refrain from whispering to him, 'You have scared the good prelates, and they think: whoever is last will be caught in the devil's black pot'."

Grundtvig also read the poem to his father shortly before the latter's death on January 5, 1813.

The two famous ballads would be familiar to the Danish reader. Here are translations:

BISHOP WILHELM AND KING SVEND

That near to church stands castle
Can very easily be,
But bishop and king hand in hand
Is something you seldom see;
Yet Denmark saw, as friend with
      friend,
Bishop Vilhelmus and King Svend.
These friends we only liken can
To David and his Jonathan.

All that the world saw in these friends
Was how curiously they behaved,
What the world never can understand
Is pious people's ways:
They chasten most whom they hold
      dear,
This the world calls folly;
They follow each other to death and
      the grave,
This the world calls madness.

It was one holy Christmastide
And the king was giving a feast,
Well-born was every Christmas guest,
But many of them died badly,
Each guest was hot with mead and
      wine,
Dear this cost many a noble fine.

Of wine and wrath beware ye,
Every Christian king on earth!

Bells rang as holy custom is,
This was a New Year's morning,
And into the church the bishop went,
He went therein with mourning;
Alas! How evil a tiding
Early morning to him had brought.
And Villum loved King Svend,
As Jonathan his heart's own friend.

A stain there was on the chancel floor,
How red of hue that smirch,
It came when Knud had Ulv mur-
      dered
There in the very church;
Now round about it had been made
By Ulv's son a ring as red,
Well might he sorrow, the king's good
      friend,
For Ulv's son he was King Svend.

King Svend he donned his fur mantle,
He had his sword girt on,
He meant to enter the church
With his knights and with his men;

From inside resounded a New Year's
song,
But hollow and weak from the choir
it came.
Round the gloomy bishop and the red
flood
The black-robed clergy pallid stood.

The king had no mind to tarry,
He wished to enter forthwith,
But there the bishop stood with his
staff
In his vestments long,
He raised his staff and thrust the spike
Against the king's breast full boldly.
Pious men's love is surely queer,
They chasten most whom they hold
dear.

What wilt thou, wolf, in the sheep
flock?
So spake the shepherd of Christ,
Hast thou not yet enough of blood,
Hast thou still a lust to murder?
Nay, get thee hence, thou impious
man;
And know thou art under the church's
ban!
But Villum yet did love King Svend
As Jonathan his heart's own friend.

The king's men closed in on the
bishop
All with swords unsheathed,
But the priest of the Lord budged not
one step,
He was not to be dismayed,
God's angels stood by him, stood close,
And blunted those keen swords,
He was thinking only of God and
Svend,
His dear, his fallen, heart's own friend.

Stiff and cold as a pillar,
And pale as corpse in earth,
So stood for a moment the monarch
bold,

And after that found speech:
O touch him not, he stands in God,
He is keeping guard over Christ's own
bride.
So must needs the liege-lord bold
Leave the church before mass was told.

Bishop Villum before the communion
table
His *Kyrie Eleison* chants,
King Svend he kisses black earth
In the garb of penitence,
There lies he, bare of foot,
For his pillow a flood of tears,
But which of them suffered most
God in heaven only knows.

His *Kyrie Eleison* was sung
By the bishop with tears and anguish:
Be thou merciful, Lord, and forgive,
Touch thy servant's heart!
With Amen the choir resounded:
King Svend the black earth kisses!
Up from the altar the bishop got
With tear on cheek and joy in glance.

Before the church door Bishop Villum
stood
In his vestments long,
And the king lay in a flood of tears,
Penitent and fearful;
He quaked before God, who avenges
blood,
He confessed before the Lord so good,
And when such confession is made
down here,
Then joy there is in the angel choir.

Thou the tears of remorse hast shed,
So did the bishop say,
From the church's ban thou art
released,
And may God give thee grace!
So he took the king in his embrace,
Blessed him in Jesus' name,
And Villum was beloved by Svend,
As David by his heart's own friend.

King Svend he stood in gold and steel
With melancholy mien,
So made he his confession
Before both lay and learned,
He gave the church so rich a fee
That tears there were in every eye,
But at that confession in the North
God's angels chorused songs of joy.

Now Svend from the depths of his
    heart did fear
His God and walked with care,
And when the day came and the hour
For him this earth to leave,
A sign was shown folk by these friends
Which the world never can under-
    stand:
To go together to death and the grave
Is something the world calls mad.

Bishop Villum stood in the chancel!
Now dig ye well, ye men!
And dig ye wide, for soon in earth
Shall be lowered coffins twain,
And I shall then be with King Svend
Even in the grave, as friend with
    friend.
These friends we only liken can
To David and his Jonathan.

In the chancel how hollow echoed
Out of that stall deep down:
"A house we build for dead men
With mattock and with spade!
If you up there are dead, be still!
But if you are alive, then wait!"
They knew not that one can
Love like Villum and like Jonathan.

Vilhelmus brandished his bishop's staff
So that those men did tremble;
"Dig ye in haste a grave
With room for coffins twain!
Perchance the worms have taught you
That all which you deem odd is vain;
My coffin in the earth shall be
When they carry Svend to the grave.

And there were the realm's good men,
Coming with the dead,
The bishop rode forth with clerk and
    groom
The corpse of the king to meet;
Strange indeed was what happened
    there,
For he did meet his liege-lord dear,
Even as in God one can
Think that David met Jonathan.

The bishop rode forth to the burying
With learned men and clerks,
That the corpse of the king was hard
    by
He himself could remark:
"Now stand thee still, thou groom!
On foot I shall meet my friend."
They met even as one can
Know that David met Jonathan.

His garment he spread out
And knelt him there in sorrow,
Toward heaven lifted he his hand,
To heaven's God his heart;
He prayed so fervently and still
That angels joyed his prayer to hear,
They bore his soul full softly hence;
In God it found its heart's own friend!

He gently rests and sweetly sleeps,
So did the clergy whisper,
That his body was cold and dead
At last they realized,
And with his cloak and with his stave
His body preceded the king's to the
    grave.
Those friends we only liken can
To David and his Jonathan.

That near to church stands castle
Can very easily be,
But bishop and king hand in hand
Is something you seldom see.
Yet Denmark saw as friend with
    friend
Bishop Vilhelmus and King Svend;
It has also seen one other pair
In Absalon and Valdemar!

MASTER OLE VIND

Where walls now stand in ruins
In Axelstad so low,
There once stood Our Lady's house,
Above the bishop's tombs,
There sounded many a holy word,
There in the choir were orders con-
ferred
On many of God's chosen.

And Master Ole Vind it was
Who with his sharp tongue,
With the spirit's sword, thrust deep
Into both old and young;
It pierced to marrow and bone,
And when it hit a heart of stone
Then ears were sure to ring.

The courtiers strode mocking in,
Up to those high seats,
And with doubled ardor of purpose
Then did Herr Ole preach,
He preached of those soft skins
That fools go swaddled in,
Of men in royal castles.

"Ay, there," so fell his piercing words,
"There you will *Christians* find!
Yes, Christian folk at the drinking
board
With mug and jug and womankind,
And God's word left on a corner shelf,
Where, fettered in a clasped book by
itself
It lies like a prisoner.

Although Saint Paul was to Felix
brought
Many times, when he spake
Of righteousness, temperance, judg-
ment to come,
It made our Felix quake
And say: for the present you may go,
I am busy, but will let you know
At some more convenient season.

Just so, God's word shall be notified,
If it will be polite,
And strike the seventh commandment
out,
Which is so hard to get right:
Yes, that is what made Herodias wroth
At the Baptist; to be *polite*
God's word can never learn.

And a summons came from the castle.
(Now what does that mean, Herr Ole!
Fine thanks for your pains you yet
may get
From those sitters in high seats)
And when he came before the king
The talk went: Master Ole Vind!
What is this you are preaching about?

"About what it says in my Bible,
About what goes on upon earth."
What preached you yesterday?
You struck like a thunderbolt.
"About what it says in my Bible
About sinners in the king's house."
That sermon we fain would hear.

Herr Ole gave his sermon again
In a spirit equally ardent,
And just as he reached the Amen
Made a sign with his hands for silence:
"These, by God's death, were the very
words
About lying, flattery, drinking, adul-
tery,
That I spoke in Our Lady's church."
,
And a summons came from the castle.
(Now what does that mean, Herr Ole!
Fine thanks for your pains you may
get
From those sitters in high seats.)
And when he came before the king:
Good day, *our* priest! Now, Master
Vind!
You shall preach God's word at court.

"Nay, thanks just the same, O high-
    born King!
That would not work at all,
I speak the truth, and have a calotte,
But the courtly note I have not got;
What does our local proverb say
About a sparrow at a crane-dance
And an owl among crows?"

But that was King Christian the
    Fourth,
And now he had his say:
You are a priest of worth
And preached just as you ought,
At those courtly notes we laugh,
Take three calottes if you will,
And let us hear the truth.

Norway. In spite of Grundtvig's feelings for Norway and his long-held hope to end his days there as a teacher or pastor, he visited Norway only once, in 1851, when he was 67 years old. The occasion was an annual meeting of university students from Norway, Sweden and Denmark, held in Kristiania (Oslo). To get there from Copenhagen, Grundtvig left on a mail-steamer at 1 p.m., and slept on the boat, which lay to near the coast for the night and was in motion again by dawn. Meanwhile a letter of welcome had been forwarded from the shore. When the boat reached Kristiania, at 11 a.m., Grundtvig was given a most enthusiastic reception by students and townspeople, and spent Whitsuntide week seeing as much of Norway as could be reached by carriage drives. One of his speeches was to a mass-meeting of peasants held in a neighborhood rich in historical associations, one of which led Grundtvig to remark that just as King Olav Harald-soen's goal had been achieved by reducing all the small kings to peasants, so should the Northern spirit now dwelling in Norway achieve its goal by making all the peasants into kings. As Grundtvig left this meeting, the peasants cheered him so loudly that his carriage-horses took fright and stampeded. On the Friday, Grundtvig preached at Our Savior's Church, and the Storting, then in session, adjourned to go and hear him. After the service, Grundtvig visited the Storting, and heard the end of the debate which led to legislation giving Jews all the civil rights and privileges enjoyed by their fellow Norwegians. (These details come from the account of this visit by Folk-Highschool Principal Salomon Nielsen of Stoevring, in the Danish-American weekly *Dannevirke* (Cedar Falls, Iowa), issues of July 18 and July 25, 1951.)

A spiritual Dannevirke. The original Dannevirke was the great wall built along the southern boundary of Jutland by order of Queen Tyra, wife of Gorm (d.950) to stop the invading Germans who had attacked Jutland while Gorm was fighting off the Swedes. For this exploit Tyra was called Tyra Dannebod, the "curer" or savior of Denmark. Dannevirke also figured as an actual line of defence in the wars of Grundtvig's day.

Page 72. *Song of Beowulf.* The American scholar Professor Kemp Malone of Johns Hopkins in his article on *Grundtvig as Beowulf Critic (The Review of English Studies,* Vol. XVII, 1941) credits Grundtvig with being "the first and greatest of Beowulf scholars," and to his existing reputation for identifications and as textual critic adds praise of him as a literary critic of *Beowulf.*

Page 74. *Ingemann, Bernard S.,* 1789–1862, entered the University of Copenhagen in 1806, three years after Grundtvig's graduation, aided as student volunteer in defending the city against English attack in 1807, after graduation was a resident of Valkendorf's college, where he produced work which established his reputation as a lyric poet, then had two years of foreign travel under government subsidy, and upon his return in 1822 became lector at Soro Academy, and remained there. The historical novels of his middle period, dealing with the 13th and 14th centuries, did much toward rousing the Danes to pride in their national past.

CHAPTER V: THE HISTORICO-ECCLESIASTICAL VIEW

PAGE 80. *Praesto,* a small city a few miles from Udby. Grundtvig's mother had been living there since Johan Grundtvig's death.

PAGE 81. *The Seven Sleepers.* Legend has it that seven Christians of Ephesus hid in a cave during the persecutions under Decius, were discovered and walled in. Two hundred years later a herdsman of Ephesus saw the masonry work, pulled it down, and discovered them. They awakened to find Theodosius on the throne and Christianity no longer proscribed. Their appearance was a sensation, and a bishop who had denied the Resurrection was converted. The seven very soon returned to their cave and died there.

The 1820's. The unhappiness of the period was largely in consequence of the forced cession of Norway to Sweden by the Treaty of Kiel, 1814, with resulting loss to the Danish exchequer, and of the great depression that engulfed Denmark following a fall in corn prices that effected all Europe.

PAGE 83. *King Valdemar and His Men.* The publication of this historical epic in 1824 gave the romantic poet Ingemann a new status as patriotic poet. The work deals with the career of Emperor Valdemar (1131–1182) who, aided by Absolon, elected Bishop of Roskilde in 1158, routed the Wendish pirates, extended and solidified the Danish empire, and was in 1182 acknowledged as an equal by Frederick Barbarossa, two of whose sons married two of Valdemar's daughters.

PAGE 85. *Dannebrog.* The Danish flag in its present form consists of a white cross whose arms divide a red field into rectangles. Legend has it that in this form it came from heaven when Archbishop Suneson, in the field with Valdemar the Victorious in Estland in 1219, prayed for divine help as defeat seemed imminent. In some early types of the flag the white squares were filled with the coats of arms of the constituent kingdoms, and Biblical pictures were sometimes incorporated in it—which explains the Grundtvig poem's reference to the flowering rod of Aaron. "Broge" is Old Danish for a piece of colored cloth. The Danish national flag is the oldest possessed by any nation today. (Dannebrog is also the name of a Danish order of knighthood.)

PAGE 86. *The Land of the Living.* In an article on *Grundtvig and Kingo's Hymns,* in *Grundtvig-Studier* 1949, Magnus Stevns points out that this poem was later rewritten as the hymn "O Christian Faith," and also that it uses the meter of Kingo's great hymn "Farewell to the World," but that for Kingo's renunciation of the life of the world Grundtvig substitutes his positive confession of faith in God's kingdom of love.

PAGE 88. *Udgaard-Loki's.* In Snorri Sturleson's Edda, Midgaard was the giant's world and Udgaard the outer world ruled by Loki, a figure having many features in common with Satan, being at once under restriction and yet so powerful a wizard that Thor himself was unable to cope with him. He lived in an immense hall surrounded by all sorts of terror-inspiring objects.

Rudelbech, Andreas S., 1792–1862; a strong upholder of Lutheran orthodoxy who collaborated with Grundtvig in editing the *Theological Monthly,* gradually became more orthodox in his Lutheranism than Grundtvig, and dissociated himself from Grundtvig's idea of the Apostles' Creed, when recited, being "the word of God's mouth." For a time he represented Danish Lutheranism in church discussions in Saxony but proved so stubborn in his ecclesiastical toryism that he was recalled, and, following rebuffs by university authorities, ended his days as a parish priest.

Lindberg, Jacob Christian, 1797–1857, a theologian and a very industrious and distinguished authority on oriental languages, epigraphy, and numismatics. He joined Grundtvig and Rudelbach in the conduct of the *Theological Monthly* and, like Grundtvig, attacked Clausen, his brochure being entitled: *Is Dr. Prof. H. N. Clausen an Honorable Teacher in the Christian Church* (1829). He was not, like Grundtvig, sued by Clausen, but he was put under censorship. Lindberg's whole life, however, seems like an abridgement of Grundtvig's, or a mirror-image of it, for he too began as a believer in absolute monarchy and gradually moved toward the left, to ideas of freedom and equality. In later years, he became a parish priest, devoting his leisure to a new translation of the Bible, and went into politics. He was a member of the Folketing until 1855 and of the Rigsraad from 1855 until his death.

The Theological Monthly, published 1825–26.

The Conventicle Act of 1741 was a reinstatement of earlier prohibitions against religious meetings in private homes and other places not under clerical supervision. At the time referred to in the text, the "congregations of the godly" had increased as a protest against the growing rationalism of the established church, and as a "layman's movement," that is, a protest against the sole right of the clergy to conduct religious services. One of its important centers was Kaerteminde. The leader here, a small tenant, Kr. Madson, was apprehended under the Conventicle Act, but the Governor of Funen, Prince Christian, intervened in his behalf.

The Apostles' Creed. The idea that the Apostles' Creed was something communicated to the Apostles by Christ himself has no critical justification. The earliest historical traces of it are to be found in Tertullian, second century, although it is quite likely that the apostles did make and require a simple confession of Jesus as Lord, that is, of Jesus as being Savior (a trinitarian idea) rather than as teaching ways to salvation (a unitarian idea). Meanwhile in the Danish church today the Apostles Creed is always used, and the Nicene and Athanasian creeds are never used.

Clausen, Henrik N., 1793–1877, son of H. G. Clausen, studied in Berlin under Schleiermacher and in Rome. In his writings he emphasized the common elements in all forms of Protestantism as against Catholic doctrine. He considered rationalism and the Bible as the two sources of a right theology. His social ideals were largely those of Grundtvig: Danishness, Scandinavianism, a free constitution. He was a member of the Landsting 1855–1868 and an honorary member of the Students' Union, under whose auspices he again met Grundtvig.

Clausen, Henrik George, 1759–1840, was opposed in theology both to Mynster and to Grundtvig and was one of the six clergymen who led the protest against Grundtvig's initiatory sermon. He stood for freedom in the baptismal rite, and when that policy was not adopted he ceased to perform the rite and in 1838 resigned his office.

Schleiermacher, Friedrich Ernest Daniel, 1768–1834, German theologian and philosopher, was given his early education under Herrnhut teachers, was influenced by Kant, Jacobi, Fichte and Schelling and became a close friend of Friedrich Schlegel, who introduced him into the Romantics' circle.

PAGE 93. *Irenaeus,* Bishop of Lyons at the end of the second century, was born not long after 130 A.D., had in childhood heard the preaching of Polycarp, and had met Christian presbyters who had known John the disciple of Jesus. He devoted his writings to the reconciling of the various sects which threatened to destroy the church by splitting it into fragments and his chief work *Against the Heresies* is the first systematic treatise on Catholic belief.

PAGE 94. *Kierkegaard, Peter Christian,* 1805–88, brother of Soeren Kierkegaard and like him a gifted philosopher; studied theology in Berlin; came under the influence now of the Grundtvigians, now of the followers of Mynster. His wavering course as a theologian appears to have been determined in part by the fact that he was a lifelong invalid, in part by his early home background.

CHAPTER VI: THE YEARS THAT FOLLOWED

PAGE 100. *Ansgar,* 801–865, "the Apostle of the North," was a Frenchman of Picardy, a Benedictine monk in the cloister of Corbie, who, with Ebbo of Rheims, undertook a missionary journey to Denmark and Sweden at a moment when King Harald Bluetooth was predisposed to listen to the urgings of Kaiser Ludvig—to whom he had appealed for help against the French—that he permit himself to be baptised. Ansgar was afterwards made archbishop of Hamburg.

PAGE 101. *Rigsbankdaler.* The rigsbankdaler was legislated into existence in January 1813 and, at a certain devaluation, took the place of the "courantdaler" as a standard silver coin exchangeable against notes. The dalers which Grundtvig was assessed would be a little less than 50 cents each in present-day American money.

PAGE 105. *Siemonsen, Lorentz,* 1800–1872, born in Flensborg, was a clergyman who criticized the state church and became progressively attracted to the free church movement. He accepted a pastorate, but, having taken the wrong side in the Schlesvig-Holstein controversy, was in 1850 forced to flee from pursuing Danish troops, and was deprived of his office. After the treaty of Vienna, 1864, he returned to his birthplace, where he died a discouraged man.

Müller, Peter Erasmus, 1776–1834, pastor, historian, philologist, and noted writer on Christian apologetics. Through his books and periodical writings an evolution is observable from the current rationalism of his younger years to a deeper type of Christian life, but in the 20's Grundtvig's followers regarded him as the embodiment of Rationalism. He was made bishop of Seeland in 1831 rather against his will, as he was a quiet man who hated strife.

PAGE 108. *Gunni Busck,* 1798–1869, was a Copenhagener by birth whose father wished him to study law. Converted through the influence of a country ale-wife, he finished his law course, then immediately turned to theology, was ordained, and became an adherent of Grundtvig at the time of the controversy with Clausen. He made every effort to heal the breach between Grundtvig and Mynster. A small inherited fortune enabled him to subsidize Grundtvig's first hymn collection.

PAGE 109. *Brorson, Hans Adolph,* 1694–1764, second of Denmark's three great hymn writers, and sometimes called "the sweet singer of Pietism," was born at Randrup in the border province of Schlesvig, the bridge over which the German Pietist movement entered Denmark, sweeping everything before it, making a convert even of the future King, Christian VI. The three Brorson brothers, who had attended the University of Copenhagen during the period of stiffest Lutheran orthodoxy, became pioneers of Danish Pietism and were affectionately known as "the rare three-leaf clover from Randrup." With the coming of a Pietist king to the throne in 1739, all three were invited to preach at court. The two elder brothers were later made pastor of Nicolai church in Copenhagen and Bishop of Aalborg respectively. Hans Adolph became Bishop of Ribe. For his private life, that of a sensitive man who suffered many afflictions, and for translations of a considerable number of his hymns see *Hymns and Hymnwriters of Denmark.*

Borch, Oluf (Ole), 1626–1690, a practicing physician who made a fortune and devoted part of it to founding Borch's Collegium, with free maintenance for 16 poor students. To this institution he bequeathed his own book collection, together with 24,000 rigsdalers for a library building, both collection and building being later destroyed by fire.

PAGE 110. *Wieselgren, Peter Jonassen,* 1800–1877, studied at Lund, entered the church, and in 1857 became Dean of Goteborg. He was a philosopher and historian but also took an active part in public affairs, church reform, and the temperance movement.

The Danish Quatrefoil (Danish Four-Leaf Clover), is a short study of the process of government in Denmark, the title symbolizing its four "factors," namely king, people, fatherland, and mother tongue. In February, 1838, the princess Karoline Amalie wrote a friend the following impression of Grundtvig and of this and the two related pamphlets: "I have had another visit from Grundtvig during which I felt myself far more at ease than on the former occasion, and I believe too that he was more pleased with our second conversation than with our first. The first time (I now know) he had been so absorbed in the object of his discussion with the Prince, namely the excommunication of Latin, that he had no room for any idea other than that. What an interesting man! How pleasant to be able to talk thus without beating about the bush, to be able to sympathize with the mistakes and weaknesses of our dear fellow-countrymen which everyone would wish to do his share toward eradicating. Just out is a brochure of his, related to the *Four-Leaf Clover,* and entitled *The School for Life and the Academy at Soro.* The foreword is especially liberal, and the first part, *The School for Life,* much clearer than his customary writings, and full of observations of genius."

PAGE 111. *Of what do you twitter.* The account of a conversation with Grundtvig written by his daughter-in-law Mina on April 8, 1856 from notes made a month earlier, and published with commentary by Steen Johansen in *Grundtvig-Studier* 1948, gives fresh details upon certain incidents, among them the interview with Bishop Mynster on New Year's Eve 1838. To Grundtvig's request for permission to confirm his sons Mynster replied: "Do you think we can give every giddy curate leave to confirm?" and we are told of Grundtvig's depression as he returend through the King's Garden in the clear starlight.

PAGE 113. *He therefore entered politics.* In an article on *Grundtvig and the Constituent Assembly, 1848–49,* in *Grundtvig Studier,* 1949, Kaj Thaning remarks that through Grundtvig's contribution to politics we get the most living close-up protrait of him which survives, that the 4,000 columns of stenographers' reports in the Parliamentary Gazette for 1848–49 give a vivid impression of "the dialogue carried on between Grundtvig and his period."

PAGE 114. *The defeat of 1864* was inflicted by Germany upon a Denmark fighting without allies, resulted in the loss of the duchies of Schlesvig and Holstein, and had such other unhappy consequences as a partial abrogation of the Constitution of 1849, with the return of certain privileges to the aristocracy in the matter of representation in the upper house. It was not until 1915 that popular government, in effect since 1901, was written into a new revision of the Constitution which, along with reaffirming the provisions of the 1849 Constitution, added a provision for woman suffrage.

Tscherning, Anthon Frederik, 1790–1874, was soldier, politician, and in his later years minister of war. Early in the reign of Kristian VIII, he became a leader of the opposition to autocracy and was made head of the "Friends of the Peasants" party.

PAGE 115. *Only his purely personal affairs.* Grundtvig's first wife was Elisabeth (Lise) Christina Margaretha Blicher (1787–1851), who became the mother of Johan Diderik Nicolai Blicher Grundtvig (1822–1907), archivist and historian, of Svend (1824–1883), notable collector of folk-songs and first editor of his father's collected poems, and of his daughter Meta, mentioned in a later chapter. His second wife was Anne Marie Elise Carlson Toft, widow of H. P. N. Toft of Ronnebaeksholm, who became the mother of Frederik Lange Grundtvig (1854–1903). Against his father's wishes, Frederik Lange turned from theology to the natural sciences, and after his marriage came to America and first settled near Shiocton, Wisconsin, in a small house in the forest, with the avowed purpose "of becoming clear about myself and my way." He spent his time in reading, hunting, and the study of natural history, in 1883 contributed to Vol. VIII of the *Bulletin of the Nuttall Ornithological Club* a paper on "The Vernal Migration of Warblers," and in 1888 wrote in Danish a paper on the birds of Shiocton, an English version of which appeared in 1894. He had at length determined to become "a Danish priest in America," was ordained at Chicago in 1883—the year of his father's centenary celebration in Denmark—and given a pastorate in Clinton, Iowa, whence he looked out for the interests of his Danish co-religionists all over the country. He wrote a number of songs for Danish song collections, and published one collection himself, *Sangbog for det Danske Folk i Amerika,* 1889, fourth edition, 1916. Disappointed about plans for founding a Danish theological school in Des Moines, Iowa, he returned to Denmark in 1900. Grundtvig's third wife was Komtesse Asta Tugendreigh Adelheid Krag-Juel-Vind-Friss, widow of H. C. Reedtz, who came of a Pomeranian family of nobles who had settled in Denmark in 1851. A poem written in 1867 for the seventh birthday of his daughter Asta Marie Elisabet Grundtvig appears in *Grundtvig-Studier,* 1951. It was during this third marriage that recognition in the formal sense chiefly came to Grundtvig. The celebration of his fiftieth anniversary as pastor, in 1861, was made an impressive occasion, and it was then that the king conferred upon him the title of bishop. His eightieth birthday, the following year, was signalized by a Meeting of Friends, which thereafter became annual, and was attended by people from all parts of Scandinavia. For a summary of Grundtvig's personal life and his contribution to Danish hymnology and for rhymed translations of all or part of four of the hymns from which Professor Koch gives excerpts as well as a number of others, see *Hymns and Hymnwriters.*

Page 116. *Ronnebaeksholm,* the estate in Hammer left to Anne M. C. Toft by her husband, dates from 1321. The beautiful pavilion in the garden was used as a summer study by Grundtvig following his marriage to the owner.

Page 117. *Heimdal,* the Northern god who guarded the gods' abode by standing on the bridge Asabro, which from the earthly side appears as a rainbow. He needed practically no sleep, his glances encircled the compass, and he could see a hundred miles by day or by night. His ears were so sharp that he could hear the grass growing. Heimdal owned the gjallarhorn, hidden somewhere under the tree Ygdrasil. When he recovers it, he will blow upon it to summon the heroes to the last great fight, Ragnarok, which will bring about the end of the world.

VII: THE HUMAN AND THE NATIONAL

Page 119. *South Jutland.* The Schlesvig-Holstein question dates back to the 10th century, when Schlesvig, which had been from time immemorial a Danish fief, was annexed to Germany. Knut obtained it from Emperor Conrad II in 1027, but after long being administered separately by the Danish crown it passed in 1375 to the counts of Holstein, which had been immemorially a part of the German-Roman empire. Schlesvig, however, never became completely Germanized, and Danish place names have always been found far south in Schlesvig. From 1839–48 there was a separatist Schlesvig-Holstein movement, countered however by an equally strong "Denmark to the Eider" movement, the Eider being the frontier river towards Holstein. In North Schlesvig nearly everyone was Danish-minded, while the peasantry from Flensborg to Dannevirke were Schlesvig-Holstein sympathizers. They had mostly talked Danish in 1800, but German church services and school over a period of years caused them to regard Danish as an inferior language. South of the Dannevirke, the population was entirely German. Early in the reign of Christian VIII two great popular meetings were held where thousands of Danes from the kingdom and from North Schlesvig pledged themselves to fight for Danish South Jutland's rights. To prepare their young people to take part in the writing and speaking necessary to carry on this fight, the North Schlesvigians established through voluntary contributions the first folk high school, in Rödding. There was heroic fighting in South Jutland in 1848, but the Danish troops were deprived of the fruits of victory over the Schlesvig-Holsteiners by the intervention of Prussia. After a year's truce, Prussia concluded peace with Denmark, promising not to help the rebels and in 1850 the Danish army again advanced in Jutland, was victorious, and took its stand on the Dannevirke, but it all ended with Schlesvig neither being united with Holstein nor incorporated in the Danish kingdom, and with the Danish language merely having equal rights with German in South Jutland.

In 1864, further difficulties about the duchies drove Denmark into war with Prussia and Austria, and Schlesvig came under the German rule with German as the official language. Danish culture, however, continued to be propagated through private channels, and in a plebiscite after World War One, three-quarters of the inhabitants of North Schlesvig voted for reunion with Denmark.

PAGE 125. *Aladdin's palace. Aladdin, or the wonderful lamp,* included in Oehlenschlaeger's 1805 poem collection, was a dramatic romance symbolizing the romantic idea that only the poet can penetrate into the spiritual realm of reality. It is regarded as his masterpiece and as having created an epoch in Danish literature. *The Scandinavian Literatures* lists a translation by Theodore Martin, London 1863.

PAGE 130. *Bragi,* god of poetry, a late-born son of Odin.

PAGE 133. *Oresund,* the narrow body of water separating the eastern side of Seeland from Sweden. The narrowest point is between Elsinore and Halsingborg. Farther south, Copenhagen almost faces the Swedish city of Malmo, and there is continuous ferry service between the two cities.

CHAPTER VIII: THE SCHOOL

PAGE 135. *Rousseau, Jean Jacques,* 1712–78, a French-Swiss contemporary of Diderot and Voltaire whose preaching of an often perverse romanticism had an extraordinary influence on his contemporaries and on posterity. In education, his assertion that the life of the child epitomizes that of the race, with sensation preceding reflection, was a fruitful one.

Pestalozzi, Johan Heinrich (1746–1827), a German-Swiss, who was born in Zurich and spent his life there as a reformer of education. His pedagogy was based on a close study of the Swiss peasantry and their living conditions, and he wrote one work of fiction out of his close and loving observation, *Leonard and Gertrude,* which was an instant success and gave its author a secure place as an imaginative writer.

Herder, Johan Gottfried (1744–1803), the German critic, poet and philosopher who has been called "the gate-keeper of the 19th century," was at the same time, like Grundtvig, a revealer to his countrymen of their own treasures of early song and ballad. Goethe was in some respects his disciple, mediating much that Herder had first revealed to him.

PAGE 136. *The Black School* was, to begin with, a college of magical practises located in Wittenberg until the popular mind transferred it to the University of Paris and then to Salamanca. When the more academic schools of Denmark fell into disfavor, they were nicknamed black schools, and the phrase was used with great effect by Grundtvig in criticizing schools where Latin was employed in the class rooms.

PAGE 141. *Sky-Mountain* (Himmelbjerget), the hills in east N. Jutland between Skandeborg and Silkeborg which constitute Denmark's highest elevation. The steepest, Kollen, 147 metres, gives a remarkable view of the surrounding country and its sheer rise makes it seem the highest, though some of the gentler slopes overtop it by 10 metres. On its crest a number of memorials have been erected, including a tower for Frederik VII, and a memorial stone for S. S. Blicher the short story writer.

PAGE 145. *Basedow, Jean Bernard,* 1723–1790, a prolific popularizing writer on philosophy and an educational reformer who was for a few years a teacher of moral sciences at Soro Academy.

Soro Academy, at Soro in central Seeland, was founded in 1584 by Frederik II as a school for his sons and certain other young noblemen. After a few months it closed, but was reopened in 1586 as a school for 30 noblemen and 30 commoners. In 1623 Christian IV added a "knightly academy" which was run independently of the school and not only attracted nobles from various countries but had King Carl X Gustav of Sweden as a pupil. Later the fortunes of the school declined. Today it is a completely staffed public high school with an enrollment of over 300 students.

PAGE 146. *Under other leadership.* Grundtvig's nearest approach to a blue-print for a folk school was his proposed use of the old royal academy at Soro as a free folk high school, but this plan was never carried out. The first actual folk-school was established at Rodding in North Schlesvig in 1884, with the avowed aim of giving the Danish peasantry of North Schlesvig a cultural stronghold against the rising national spirit of the Germans. During the Dano-German war of 1848–50, the school was closed, and afterwards the proposal was made to turn the Rodding school into an agricultural college. The idea was successfully opposed and the educational activities of the Rodding school were transferred to the town of Askov on the Danish side of the new Dano-German boundary, with the courses so modified that the school became for the first time really representative of Grundtvig's ideas.

The pattern for other folk schools which now began to multiply was set by Christian Kold (1816–1870), a shoe-maker's son who had worked out his own ideas of oral teaching independently of Grundtvig and applied them to the teaching of younger children, a policy which he later abandoned as he found that Grundtvig's insistence on adult education was justified. Kold established and successfully taught in schools in many parts of Denmark. He was soon joined by five members of a theological study club, all familiar with Grundtvig's views, and all shocked by the tragic war of 1864 into giving up their careers to devote themselves to folk high school teaching. In the 70's and 80's others followed their example. A training school for folk school teachers was later established at Askov. The success of the folk schools led to the establishing of agricultural schools run along similar lines, but with technical training as their chief activity. The first typical one was founded in 1867, others were formed by converting original folk schools into agricultural schools, and by 1938 about twenty were in operation.

The folk school idea was slow in being assimilated by town workers but after some experimentation and through the cooperation of trade unions and the political parties of the left, a Workers' Educational Association was founded on January 1, 1924, whose program appealed to industrial workers but was devoted to cultural ends. Recent extensions of such education include the found-in 1924 of the Krogerup "folk high school for citizenship" located between Copenhagen and Elsinore, and now (1951) headed by Dr. Hal Koch.

CHAPTER IX: MAN FIRST, THEN CHRISTIAN

PAGE 151. *Man first.* In an article on Grundtvig and Holberg (*Vartovbogen* 1947) quoted in *Grundtvig-Studier* 1949, Henning Hoirup points out that Grundtvig admired the Danish dramatist Holberg and had apparently read his *Moral Thoughts,* in which this sentence occurs: "Children must be made human beings before they can become Christians."

CHAPTER X: THE CHURCH

PAGE 170. *Melanchthon* (1497–1560), Hellenized name used by Philip Schwartzerd, professor of Greek at Wittenberg, who became an ardent disciple of Luther, to whom his relationship is roughly comparable to that of Dr. Watson to Sherlock Holmes—a faithful friend who sometimes blundered. The popular idea of Lutheranism is, of course, that it is a "book religion," which merely replaced the authority of the Pope by that of the Bible. But Luther should not be blamed for this. Within his own life-time, Melanchthon's reinterpretations of some of Luther's doctrines had confused the issues originally raised by Luther, and after Luther's death there was a sharp division between those who regarded themselves as his followers, but who themselves often misread him, and the "Philipists" or followers of Melanchthon. The issues are minutely dissected in Prof. Ragnar Bring's *Forhallandet mellan Tro och Gärningar inom Luthersk Teologi* (The Relationship between Faith and Works in the Theology of Luther) published in the Acta Academiae Aboensis: Humaniora—IX (Abo, Finland, 1934) and not yet available in English.

CHAPTER XI: THE SKALD

PAGE 179. *Roenning, Frededik,* born 1851, was a Danish literary historian who wrote the most thorough work on the period of Rationalism in Denmark, and followed it by a life of Grundtvig in four substantial volumes.

Hjort, Peder, 1793–1871, son of a Bishop of Ribe who studied law at his father's suggestion, but finding neither law nor theology to his liking studied philosophy and aesthetics in Germany, returned to Denmark at the reopening of the Academy in Soro and taught philosophy there for some years. He took an ardently patriotic stand on the Schlesvig question.

PAGE 180. *King's Deep,* the name of the seaway or navigable passage in the Sound opposite Copenhagen.

PAGE 181. *Akselstad,* a poetic or rhetorical name given to Copenhagen, which conveys the idea, "the city of Absalon." As Bishop Absalon was never called Aksel, poetic license would here appear to have worked overtime.

The Belts, the Great and the Little, are the two sounds which connect the Kattegat and the Baltic, bordering Funen on the West and the East respectively.

PAGE 182. *Willemoes, Peter,* 1783–1808, was a naval lieutenant noted equally for competence and courage, whom, incidentally, Grundtvig had met on Langeland. During the Battle of King's Deep, in April, 1801, fought within sight of Copenhagen against Lord Nelson, Willemoes, then 17, and in command of a small vessel, steered straight under Nelson's own flag-ship, the *Elephant,* and hammered at it for several hours, until he had lost so many men and sustained such damage to his ship that he was forced to limp off. Later, Lord Nelson commenting to Crown Prince Frederik upon Willemoes' courage, said that he ought to be made admiral, to which the Crown Prince replied: "If I made admirals of all my brave officers, I would have none left for lieutenants and captains." In the spring of 1808 Willemoes was appointed adjutant to the commander of the fleet's only remaining ship of the line, the Prince Christian, which engaged five English vessels off Seeland Point, and in this fight he was killed by a bullet and buried with other Danish officers in a common grave in the churchyard of Odden Parish, which comprises the tip of Seeland. Grundtvig composed an elegy, and several other poems, from one of which the famed inscription on the memorial afterwards erected on the point was chosen.

PAGES 183-4. *Inscription on the Memorial at Seeland Point.* In *Grundtvig-Studier* 1948, Gustav Albeck of Aarhus University discusses this poem in the light of a rough manuscript version. The comparison shows Grundtvig as capable of being a careful and brilliant chiseler of form and editor of his own first inspirations, when, as here, he is writing as a classicist to whom the famous Thermopylae inscription was both familiar and dear. Mr. Albeck cites the Appendix to *Kvaedlinger* (1815) as evidence that Grundtvig was himself conscious of the artistic worth of the poem, its chief fault being "that it made no mention of God."

PAGE 186. *Skjoldungs* in the days of the antique heroes was the name of the royal line and before that had been applied to the military in general, the original meaning of the word being "shield bearers."

PAGE 190. *Sleipner,* Odin's horse, capable of traversing both sea and land, and, thanks to his eight legs, with unusual speed. He was a son of Loki, who had assumed the form of a mare and enticed from his work the horse Svadilfare belonging to the Giants' chief-builder. See *Pageant* pages 49-51.

Baggesen, Jens, 1764-1826, a Danish author of European fame, whose first book *Comic Tales,* 1785, was written under the influence of Voltaire, and his other works under Sturm und Drang impetus. His poem *Holger the Dane,* 1789, ridiculing his compatriots, resulted in his leaving Denmark, and travelling the length and breadth of Europe, meeting such outstanding personalities of the period as Klopstock, Schiller, Lavater and Reinhold. He created a poetic style, and freed Danish letters from French influence.

PAGE 193. *By Night there was a Knocking,* translated in *A Book of Danish Verse* as "The Harrowing of Hell."

PAGE 199. *Far Loftier Mountains,* translated in the above as "Denmark's Consolation."

Barfod, Poul Frederik, 1811-1896, author and politician, was a participant in the reform activities of his day and became a member of the Friends of the Peasants party and for a time edited their official paper. He helped to frame the constitution, gave allegiance to "Scandinavianism" and disliked German influences.

Boisen, Peter Outzen, 1762-1831, priest and educator, was called by Count Reventlow to the parish of Verterborg, which he served as pastor and school superintendent to the end of his life, having refused to relinquish either activity when called to the bishopric of Lolland-Falster in 1805. In theology he was a member of a sentimentally toned wing of the rationalist group and published a *Plan for the Betterment of Public Divine Service* which gained the approval of the ministry but offended both Grundtvig and his followers on the one hand and the severer rationalists like H. C. Clausen on the other. His theology, however, was so shallowly based that it did not affect the total situation.

Index

Grundtvig, Johan Diderik Nicolai Blicher, G.'s eldest son, born Praesto, 80; 116 n.

Grundtvig, Meta, G.'s elder daughter, 190; poem to her, quoted, 191.

Grundtvig, Niels Christian Bang, G.'s third brother, 3 n.

Grundtvig, N. S. F., and Kierkegaard, vii, viii; empiricism of thought processes but fidelity to main insights, ix, x; schooled in the Higher Criticism, x; as precursor of James and Dewey, xi; controversy with H. C. Oersted, xi-xii; urges dissolution of the parish bond, xiii; campaign for Praesto parliamentary seat, xiii-xiv; relations with kings Frederik and Kristian, xv; his letters to Queen Caroline Amalie from England, xvi-xviii; broader significance of his "Danishness," xviii, ix; birth, parentage, and childhood, 3, 4; the Jacobin schoolmaster, 5; at boarding school in Tyregod, 5,6; at Aarhus Latin School, 6, 7; child of the Enlightenment, 11, 12; student years: poverty, battle of Maundy Thursday, friendship with P. N. Skovgaard, 12, 13, readings in Northern history and for theology examinations, 13,14, reaction to the Steffens lectures and to Oehlenschlaeger's first poem collection, 14, 15, early attempts at verse, and his two plays, *The Schoolmaster* and *The Letter,* 15, 16, holidays at home and on Falster, Dean Blichers' daughters, 16, 17; literary efforts of first graduate year, 18; tutor at Egelykke on Langeland, and in love with Constance Leth, 18-20, first extant diary entry from Langeland period quoted, 20-21, this episode in the light of Romanticism, 20-24, G.'s Romanticism as contrasted with the flight-from-life type, 25, Romantic approach to poetry, 26-7, to life's problems, 27-9, impact of Fichte, 29, of Schelling as shown in *Religion and Liturgy* (quoted), 30, of the Schelling - Steffens attitude toward history, 31, as exemplified by Oehlenschlaeger, 32; abandons philosophical speculation for the *Eddas,* 32; *Masquerade Ball in Denmark,* 32-3; obtains graduate vacancy at Valkendorf's college in Copenhagen, and teaches history at Schouboe Institute, 33; *Northern Mythology* and *The Asa Doctrine* as a contribution to mythological research, 33-4, as prelude to popular awakening,

35, walking tour with Molbech, *Gunderslev Wood* (quoted), and *Invitation to Friends of the Ancient North,* 35, *Scenes from the Decline of the Heroic Epoch,* 36, *from the War of the Norns and Asas,* 37; a new chasm opens, 38; Valkendorf college friendships with Povel Dons, Molbech, Hersleb, Sverdrup, and Sibbern, 39; Schouboe Institute teaching leads him from Northern history to world history and reorientation toward Christianity, 40; the summons from his father, 40; storm aroused by his candidate sermon, 41; resumption of work: *Is Union of the North to be Desired?,* 42, *What were we of Yore, What are we Now?, The Pilgrims, Peter the Hermit,* 43, *Today's Crusade,* quoted, 43, 44, two poem collections: *Idunna,* 45, *New Year's Night* (*Three Holy Kings* quoted), 45-6; onset of the crisis, 46-7, the experience as later described in *New Year's Morning,* quoted, 48-9, Prof. Bang sent for, Sibbern accompanies G. to Udby to recuperate, and records tempestuous night at Vindbyholt Inn, 49-50, ordained his father's curate, 50; outcome as a Lutheran "experience of conversion," 50-53; attitude toward Scripture at this point, 53-4; the Christian myth replaces Romanticism's and G. becomes "the Bible's lone champion" against Rationalism and Romanticism in Denmark, 54-6; safe once more in Udby and in Lutheranism, his infatuation ends, and he becomes engaged, 57-8; *Biblical Sermons,* zeal for other pastoral duties, attempt to make contact with Oehlenschlaeger and Mynster, 59-62; *Short View of World History* and the furore it aroused, 63-66; not appointed to succeed his father, he moves to Copenhagen, 65-6; special nature of his Bible-Christianity, 66-8; *Saga,* 68; the essay *What is Poetry?,* and *New Year's Night,* 69; *Roskilde Rim* and *To the Fatherland,* 71; attempt to awaken the people through their past and their mother tongue: *Dannevirke,* translations of Saxo and Snorre, 72-4; controversies with H. C. Oersted and others, friendship with Ingemann, 74-5; marriage to Lise Blicher, called to Praesto and Skibbinge, 75; his "stroll in the grove of mankind":